Becoming Vajrasattva

BECOMING VAJRASATTVA

THE TANTRIC PATH OF PURIFICATION

Lama Thubten Yeshe

Foreword by Lama Thubten Zopa Rinpoche
Edited by Nicholas Ribush

Wisdom

Wisdom Publications
199 Elm Street
Somerville, MA 02144 USA
www.wisdompubs.org

Library of Congress Cataloging-in-Publication Data
Thubten Yeshe, 1935–1984
  Becoming Vajrasattva : the tantric path of purification / Lama Thubten Yeshe ; edited by Nicholas Ribush.
    p. cm.
  Includes bibliographical references.
  ISBN 0-86171-389-3 (pbk. : alk. paper)
  1. Spiritual life—Tantric Buddhism. 2. Heruka (Buddhist deity)—Cult. I. Ribush, Nicholas. II. Title.
  BQ8938.T45 2004
  294.3'444—dc21
                                                    2004000255

ISBN 978-0-86171-389-9   ebook ISBN 978-0-86171-902-0

22   21   20   19   18
8   7   6   5   4

Cover design by Philip Pascuzzo. Interior design by Gopa&Ted2, Inc. Set in Adobe Garamond 10.5/13.5

Wisdom Publications' books are printed on acid-free paper and meet the guidelines for permanence and durability of the Committee on Production Guidelines for Book Longevity of the Council on Library Resources.

♻ This book was produced with environmental mindfulness.
For more information, please visit wisdompubs.org/wisdom-environment.

Printed in the United States of America.

Please visit fscus.org

Contents

Foreword

One Solution to All of Life's Problems: *The Vajrasattva Purifying Meditation*

I WOULD LIKE TO EXPLAIN the great importance of the Vajrasattva meditation and recitation practice. Why, it is important even for people who believe merely in the existence of this life alone!

All life's success—including success in such ordinary things as family and friendship, business, health, wealth, and power—depends upon both purifying negative karmic obstacles and not creating more negative karma. How do we create negative karma? When we engage in the ten negativities out of selfishness and delusion. The deluded minds are those of ignorance, attachment, and anger; the ten negativities are the three of body—killing, stealing, and sexual misconduct—the four of speech—lying, slander, harsh speech, and gossip—and the three of mind—covetousness, ill will, and wrong views. According to the natural law of karma, if you hurt others, you hurt yourself.

It works the other way, too. If you want others to love you, you must first love others. If you help or benefit others, naturally they will help or benefit you. The cause and effect of karma is as simple as this. As for the Vajrasattva purification practice, which is more powerful than negative karma, it can prevent you from experiencing problems that negative karma would otherwise have brought. Thus the practice of purification is one of the most important solutions to problems, and is extremely necessary, even for people who believe there is only one life.

Unfortunately, such people's hearts are usually not open to learning new things about the reality of life or the nature of phenomena—new philosophies, new subjects. They won't even analyze new possibilities. All this prevents them from experiencing both temporal and ultimate happiness. If you don't want relationship problems, business failures, illness, notoriety, or the criticism of others, the practice of Vajrasattva is extremely important.

When it comes to spiritual growth, the Vajrasattva purification practice is even more important. As Mañjushri advised Lama Tsongkhapa, "The way to actualize the path to enlightenment quickly is to do three things: practice purification and the accumulation of merit, make single-pointed requests to the guru, and train the mind in the path to enlightenment." The practice of Vajrasattva is common to all four traditions of Tibetan Buddhism— Nyingma, Kagyu, Sakya, and Geluk—where it is used to purify obstacles, obscurations, negative karma, and illness. The root tantra *Dorje Gyän (Vajra Ornament)* states that if you are always unconscious and careless, even small negativities cause great damage to your body, speech, and mind, just as the venom of a poisonous snake will spread rapidly throughout your body, getting worse and worse every day, endangering your life.

The great enlightened being Pabongka Dechen Nyingpo said that if you have killed even a tiny insect and have not purified that negativity by the end of the day with a practice such as the Vajrasattva purification, the weight of that karma will have doubled by the next day. On the third day it will have doubled again, and by fifteen days will have become as heavy as the karma of killing a human being. By eighteen days it will have increased 131,072 times. So you can see, as the weeks and months and years go by, one tiny little negative karma will have multiplied over and over until it has become like a mountain the size of this earth. When death arrives, the karma will have become incredibly heavy.

Here I am talking about just one small negative karma, but every day we accumulate many, many negative karmas of body, speech, and mind. The weight of each tiny negative karma created each day multiplies over and over again, becoming unimaginably heavy. And there's no question that every day, besides those small negative karmas, we also create many gross negativities. Thus we have accumulated many heavy negative karmas in this life, and in all our beginningless previous lives as well. If you contemplate the continuous multiplication of all these karmas it is unimaginably unimaginable!

The *Dorje Gyän* states that if you recite the hundred-syllable Vajrasattva mantra twenty-one times every day, negative karmas are prevented from multiplying. The great, sublime realized beings also explain that this is the way to purify whatever downfalls and transgressions you have accumulated. Furthermore, His Holiness Trijang Rinpoche, who is actually Heruka himself, has explained that if recited twenty-eight times each day, the short Vajrasattva mantra (OM VAJRASATTVA HUM) has incredible purifying power. It not only has the power to prevent any negative karma created that day from multiplying, but it can also completely purify all negativities you have ever created—in that day, in that life, and even since your beginningless rebirths.

These are some of the incredible benefits of practicing the Vajrasattva recitation and meditation. Moreover, it is taught that if you recite the long Vajrasattva mantra one hundred thousand times you can purify even broken root vows of highest yoga tantra. Thus there's no question that you can purify broken root pratimoksha (individual liberation) and bodhisattva vows through this technique.

Experienced meditators have advised that, in general, it is more important to put your everyday life's effort into the practice of purification—this is the way to attain spiritual realizations. The Kadampa Geshe Dolpa said that if you practice purification and the accumulation of merit continuously and turn your mind to the path, lamrim realizations that you thought would take one hundred years to achieve will come to you in just seven. Such is the inspiring testimony of the highly experienced meditators who have attained the various levels of the path to enlightenment.

Lama Atisha used to say that there are an inconceivable number of doors to downfall for tantric practitioners who have taken highest yoga tantra initiations. For example, simply looking at an ordinary object such as a vase and seeing it as ordinary is a downfall. Just as a clean mandala left on the altar quickly gets covered in dust, so does your mental continuum collect piles of negativities in a very short time. However, don't conclude from hearing this that taking secret mantra initiations must make it impossible to reach enlightenment. Lama Atisha said that it is only people who don't know that secret mantra contains incredibly skillful means of purifying downfalls who think that way.

He said, "Just as one stone can scatter one hundred birds, there is the special skillful means called the practice of Vajrasattva." What Lama Atisha was saying was that on the one hand, in just one minute, it is so easy to accumulate a torrential downpour of downfalls and negativities—for example, looking at an object as ordinary—but on the other, there is the skillful means of tantra, the practice of Vajrasattva. This one practice will purify the countless negativities of broken root and branch vows, and in this way you can develop your mind in the path to enlightenment.

Therefore, the practice of Vajrasattva is extremely important—both for those who accept the existence of reincarnation and karma and for those who do not.

The Vajrasattva commentary in this book is an experiential instruction given by my guru, Lama Yeshe, who even to the ordinary view was a great yogi, and who took care of me like a father takes care of his only child. He gave me not only the necessities of life, such as food and clothing, but also guided me in the Dharma for more than thirty years.

Whoever studies this book and gets inspired to do the Vajrasattva practice and retreat is also being guided by Lama's compassion: he is liberating you from many eons of negative karma, many inconceivable eons of suffering—in the lower realms and in the human and deva realms as well—and leading you to liberation and full enlightenment.

May whoever sees, touches, remembers, or even thinks or talks about this book never be born in the lower realms, receive only perfect human rebirths, meet a perfectly qualified Mahayana virtuous friend, practice Vajrasattva purification every day, and quickly achieve Guru Vajrasattva's enlightened state. This is my wish.

Thank you very much.

Thubten Zopa

Preface

LAMA THUBTEN YESHE (1935–84) first gave the Heruka Vajrasattva initiation and practice in public to about twenty-five of his Western students at Kopan Monastery, Nepal, in April 1974.

Details of Lama Yeshe's remarkable life can now be found in several places, from Vicki Mackenzie's excellent book *Reincarnation: The Boy Lama* to the introductions to his previously published works, *Wisdom Energy* and *Introduction to Tantra.* Adèle Hulse is also writing an official biography. Perhaps the most eloquent accounts of Lama Yeshe's extraordinary qualities are those given by Lama Thubten Zopa Rinpoche, Lama Yeshe's chief and heart disciple, in the foreword to *The Bliss of Inner Fire* and in his tributes to Lama Yeshe after Lama passed away in 1984.[1]

Lama Yeshe was not only a quintessential vajra master, he was also the inspiration behind the creation of the Foundation for the Preservation of the Mahayana Tradition (FPMT), a worldwide organization of Buddhist meditation and teaching centers, both urban and rural, monasteries, retreat facilities, healing centers, and publishing houses.

I first met Lama in November 1972 while attending the third Kopan meditation course, my first. The teachings were being given by Lama Zopa Rinpoche, and most of the fifty students in attendance were unaware that there was another lama at Kopan. Someone found out that I was a physician, and about a week into the course, I was asked to go see "Lama," who had an infection on his leg. I was taken round the back of the old house at Kopan where a humble Tibetan monk, smiling broadly, greeted me with profuse thanks for nothing I'd yet done. He knew what I didn't—that my life had already begun to change completely.

When my first shot of penicillin squirted all over the room instead of into Lama's buttock, I was invited, with a smile, to return to "try again tomorrow, dear." Thus I saw Lama daily for the next week or so, my Dharma career beginning to flourish even as my medical one began to peter out. Eighteen months later, the now-famous Kopan courses—held twice a year, back then—were attracting well over two hundred people at a time, most of them young Westerners traveling in India and Nepal. Twenty of us, inspired by the peerless example of our teachers, had taken ordination as monks and nuns. In the spring of 1974, just after the sixth Kopan course and several years of sutra teachings on the graduated path to enlightenment, Lama felt we were ready for tantra. He chose the purification practice of Heruka Vajrasattva, and compiled for our use a *sadhana,* or method of accomplishment, from the Chakrasamvara tantra. He then gave a five-lecture commentary on the sadhana and an extensive discourse on how to make a meditational retreat.

This book comprises Lama's commentary on the Vajrasattva practice, detailed retreat instructions based mainly on that initial teaching, six occasional discourses—mostly given as introductions to Heruka Vajrasattva initiations at FPMT centers around the world—and two commentaries on the Heruka Vajrasattva tsok that Lama himself composed in 1982. In the appendices are the sadhana and tsok text in Tibetan script, phoneticized Tibetan, for ease of chanting, and English, and a method for blessing the offering to the local spirits, the *shi-dak torma.* But it must be emphasized, as Lama says in his introduction, that to do the Heruka Vajrasattva practice, you require a highest yoga tantra initiation and instruction from a fully qualified lama.

In this vein, readers should also note that since the teachings in this book are from the oral tradition and aimed at practitioners, Sanskrit and Tibetan terms have not been rendered with scholars in mind but in phonetics approximating their correct pronunciation, devoid of diacritics. Foreign terms are not necessarily italicized within the text, but all foreign terms are defined for the reader in the glossary.

In these teachings, Lama Yeshe frequently uses the word "Westerners," which reflects his audience at the time and has not been edited out. However, non-Western readers should not feel left out, as Lama's wisdom and compassion radiated in the ten directions with complete impartiality.

Lama's 1974 commentary was taped and transcribed by the monks and nuns of the International Mahayana Institute prior to their undertaking the Heruka Vajrasattva retreat in the summer of 1974. I spent more than four months with this commentary in the Charok Cave at Lawudo, not far from the Lawudo Gompa, the site of the hermitage of the Lawudo Lama, of whom Lama Zopa Rinpoche is the reincarnation. This was the high point of my life, and I would recommend making retreat with Lama's commentary to anybody. And having ten or so vajra brothers and sisters up and down the Lawudo mountain around me, doing the same practice, was a great inspiration. It was a wonderful time.

Simultaneously, twenty or so meditators inaugurated group retreat within the FPMT at Kopan Gompa, and three-month Heruka Vajrasattva group retreats are still conducted annually at Tushita Retreat Centre, above Dharamsala, India, and occasionally at other centers.

After the retreat, Lama worked with Ven. Marcel Bertels and Ven. Yeshe Khadro to augment both the initial sadhana and commentary. For almost twenty years, scores of Heruka Vajrasattva retreaters have relied upon Marcel's excellent edition of the commentary, which has been reprinted in transcript form many times by both Kopan Monastery and Wisdom. It forms the basis of parts 1 and 2 of this book.

I began work on this book after Lama Yeshe had appointed me Wisdom's editorial director in 1981. Following Lama's teachings on the Six Yogas of Naropa at Istituto Lama Tzong Khapa in early 1983, seven of us, as detailed by Jon Landaw in *Introduction to Tantra,* got together at an editing retreat near Cecina, Italy, to work on a number of Lama's other teachings for publication. Among many other things, we learned that so unique was Lama's "extremely creative use of English," as retreater Robyn Brentano tactfully put it, that editing his words was akin to translation. The challenge presented by editing Lama's teachings is to come up with a text that is true to his meaning, is grammatically correct, and sounds like Lama. Those of us presented with this challenge do the best we can!

I read my first draft of the main commentary to Lama at Tushita Retreat Centre in April 1983, and he made many corrections, additions, and suggestions. I treasure my tapes of those meetings, as I do my memories of all the other times I spent with Lama. All his suggestions have been incorporated in this book.

I edited the later teachings—Lama's occasional Heruka Vajrasattva lectures and his commentaries to the Heruka Vajrasattva tsok offering he composed—in 1993, at Kinglake, Victoria, Australia.

⌒↻

Lama Yeshe was a great advocate of the Heruka Vajrasattva purification practice. He once expressed the hope that all his students would make the time to do the retreat at least once before they died. After Lama passed away, according to his wishes, a group of students maintained a round-the-clock schedule of Heruka Vajrasattva practice for twelve months at Kopan Monastery, and for shorter periods at Ösel Ling Retreat Center, Spain, and Mahamudra Centre, New Zealand.

Out of Lama's great compassion and his students' somewhat shaky karma, on February 12, 1985, he returned to earth as Lama Tenzin Ösel Rinpoche, and we pray for the day that he will once again teach the Heruka Vajrasattva practice to his disciples and, perhaps, correct whatever errors have been introduced into this book.

ACKNOWLEDGMENTS

"Thank you, Rinpoche, for changing my life," I said to Lama Zopa Rinpoche at the end of my first Kopan meditation course (he just laughed). All of us in the FPMT give continual thanks to Lama Zopa Rinpoche, our shining beacon of wisdom and compassion and a living example of enlightened realizations. When Lama Yeshe passed away, Rinpoche seamlessly maintained the development of the FPMT until it now comprises more than one hundred centers and study groups in thirty-one countries around the world, while continuing to lead an ever-growing number of international disciples spiritually, both by his incomparable demeanor and by his profound teachings.

This project and many others have benefited from the exceptional work done by Peter and Nicole Kedge and Ven. Ailsa Cameron in establishing the archive of teachings by Lama Thubten Yeshe and Lama Thubten Zopa Rinpoche. This computerized diamond mine is now being developed by the Lama Yeshe Wisdom Archive and will continue to produce teachings for the benefit of all sentient beings for a long time to come.

Without detailing their individual contributions, I would also like to thank Ven. Geshe Lama Lhundrup Rigsel, director of Kopan Monastery, Ven. Marcel Bertels, Ven. Yeshe Khadro, Martin Willson, Ven. Connie Miller, T. Yeshe, Ven. Sangye Khadro, Ven. Thubten Pemo, Ven. Thubten Wongmo, Ursula Bernis, Ven. Ann McNeil, Ven. Max Mathews, Jonathan Landaw, Ven. Robina Courtin, Ven. Roger Kunsang, Tim McNeill, Thubten Chödak, Piero Cerri, members of the Cecina Mare editing retreat, Mary Moffat, Cookie Claire Ritter, my mother Beatrice Ribush, Dorian and Alison Ribush, Wendy Cook, Ven. Geshe Tsulga (Tsultrim Chöpel), David Molk, Ven. George Churinoff, and Vincent Montenegro. Thanks are also due to the

FPMT centers where the teachings in this book were given, and to the dedicated students who transcribed the tapes. We are especially grateful to Peter Iseli for the beautiful painting of Heruka Vajrasattva that adorns the cover of this book.

Nicholas Ribush

Editor's Introduction

Purification, the Four Opponent Powers, and the Practice of Vajrasattva

THE PRACTICE OF HERUKA VAJRASATTVA is a tantric Buddhist practice associated with the mother tantra deity Heruka Chakrasamvara. Yet it is also a preliminary to tantric practice generally, for like all Vajrasattva practices, it is primarily concerned with purification, preparing the mind to realize the deepest truths about reality. Without purifying your mind to prepare it for spiritual realizations, you will make little progress toward enlightenment. As Mañjushri advised Lama Je Tsongkhapa: to attain spiritual realizations one must combine meditation on the path to enlightenment with purification, accumulation of merit, and praying to one's guru as a buddha. The yoga method of Heruka Vajrasattva involves all of these, and the methods for purification revealed in this book are among the most powerful ever taught.

Before Lama Yeshe first began giving tantric initiations and teachings to his Western students, he made sure they were well versed in the three principal aspects of the sutra path—renunciation of cyclic existence, the altruistic attitude of bodhichitta, and the right view of emptiness *(shunyata)*. Only after a period of dedicated study and meditation of the sutra teachings did Lama Yeshe agree to initiate them into the purification practice of Heruka Vajrasattva. Lama recognized that a solid grounding in the fundamentals of the Buddha's teachings on the nature of suffering and liberation is essential to gaining any benefit from the practice of tantra.

In Buddhism, purification is a science based on understanding the psychomechanics of karma, or action—the law of cause and effect—and entails the application of what are called the *four opponent powers*.[2] Sometimes referred to as "confession," Buddhist purification is very different from the Christian conception of the term, although parallels certainly exist.

Every action, whether physical, verbal, or mental, leaves an imprint on the consciousness, like a seed planted in a field. When the conditions are right, this imprint ripens into an experience. Positive imprints, or "good" karma, result in happiness; negative imprints, or "bad" karma, bring suffering.

Every action has four aspects that determine whether the action is complete or incomplete: motivation, object, performance, and completion. To be complete, the action of killing, for instance, would require the motivation, or intention, to kill; a sentient being as the object to be killed; performance of the action, either directly or indirectly, that is, doing it oneself or ordering someone else to do it; and completion of the action, with the other sentient being dying before the killer.

If an action is complete in all four aspects, it becomes what is called a *throwing karma,* an action that can determine your state of rebirth by throwing you into one of the six samsaric realms. If one or more of the four branches is missing, the action becomes a *completing karma,* determining the quality of the experiences you will have in this and future lives. A completing karma brings three types of result: the result similar to the cause in experience, the result similar to the cause in habit, and the environmental result. Thus, a complete negative karma has four suffering results. For killing, these four could be rebirth in a hell, a short life plagued with illness, a tendency to kill other beings, and rebirth in a very dangerous place.

Although all this applies equally to positive as well as negative actions, in the context of purification we focus on the latter. The four opponent powers work—and are all necessary— because each one counters one of the four negative karmic results. The first power—taking refuge and generating bodhichitta—is called the *power of the object,* or the power of dependence, and purifies the environmental result. It is called the power of dependence because our recovery depends upon the object that hurt us. For example, to get up after you have fallen over and hurt yourself, you depend upon the same ground that hurt you. Similarly, almost all the negative karma we create has as its object either holy objects or sentient beings. In order to purify it we take refuge in holy objects and generate bodhichitta for the sake of all sentient beings.

The second power is the *power of release,* which counteracts the result similar to the cause in experience. The third power is the *power of the remedy,* which is the antidote to the throwing karma that causes us to be reborn in the three lower realms. Finally, the fourth power is that of *indestructible determination,* by which we overcome our lifetime-to-lifetime tendency to habitually create negativities again and again. Thus, in neutralizing the four different results of negative karma, the four opponent powers purify them completely, preventing us from ever having to experience their suffering results. This kind of explicit logic lies behind all Buddhist practice and explains, in part, why Buddhism is so appealing to the intelligent, well-educated spiritual seeker of today.

The third power embraces many different kinds of remedy, from making prostrations to building stupas to reciting the hundred-syllable Vajrasattva mantra to meditating on emptiness. Ideally, several of these are practiced simultaneously. In the commentary, Lama Yeshe emphasizes realization of emptiness as the ultimate purification and shows how correct practice of the sadhana, which contains the four opponent powers, organically leads up to the explicit remedy in this practice, recitation of the mantra. His detailed explanation of the Mahayana technique of inner refuge as part of the power of the object is both exceptional and unique.

As Lama Yeshe makes abundantly clear, the most effective—although not the only—way to practice the Vajrasattva purification method is in retreat. Therefore, he has given detailed instructions on every aspect of group and individual retreat, instructions that will, in fact, be useful for those making any kind of retreat.

The six discourses in part 3 will be especially useful for retreaters to read during session breaks. However, no one reading these excellent talks will fail to be moved by Lama's uniquely inspiring energy.

Finally, all practitioners of mother tantra are required to offer tsok on the tenth and twenty-fifth days of the Tibetan month, and most do so by practicing the *Guru Puja*. However, the Heruka Vajrasattva tsok that Lama composed is also a perfect means of fulfilling that commitment, especially when in Vajrasattva retreat, and it was Lama's hope that his students and others would include this tsok puja as part of their regular practice.

∽

It is often said that the lamrim teachings are like a meal ready to eat—that the logical way in which they are arranged makes it easy to see the entire Dharma path and to know in which order the vast array of Buddhist meditations should be undertaken in order for the practitioner to reach enlightenment. Similarly, in *Becoming Vajrasattva,* Lama Yeshe has prepared a tantric banquet for all to enjoy.

Prologue:
Intellectuals, Beware!

DURING AN INITIATION, the guru calls upon the divine energy of the universe, which manifests as divine, blissful wisdom in the shape of the particular deity—in this case, Heruka Vajrasattva. This energy activates a force largely dormant in the disciple's nervous system, which now awakens and begins to vibrate. If you generate the proper altruistic state of mind and an understanding of emptiness, and recite the Vajrasattva mantra, you maintain and augment the vibration activated by the guru. If then, through a period of silent contemplation, you induce a calm, reflective mind, free of your usual flow of obscuring, uncontrolled thoughts, your inner wisdom will automatically reveal itself.

But, a word of caution to the intellectual. Reading tantric teachings on your own, without the power of the appropriate initiation, is just an intellectual pastime—only by practicing correctly, under the guidance of a fully qualified and experienced teacher, can you evolve beyond the intellect, beyond conceptual thought, into the true wisdom of a pure, spontaneous being. I am not trying to be mysterious or exclusive here but simply saying that if you think that you can understand, let alone experience, the methods of tantric yoga merely by reading books, you are deceiving yourself—like a terminally ill person doctoring himself with the same methods that made him ill in the first place.

The yoga method of Heruka Vajrasattva should be practiced only by those who have received the initiation and oral commentary from a properly qualified vajra master. Although the commentary published here is potentially of limitless value and should be studied thoroughly before you practice the methods it describes, you must take the initiation and receive some instruction from your guru. Otherwise, instead of giving you the direct experience you seek, it will become a dry, intellectual exercise of relatively little benefit.

ᴄᴖ

The great Tibetan yogi Dharmavajra explained that the highest yoga tantra initiation of Heruka Vajrasattva is a special feature of the Geluk tradition of Tibetan Buddhism. Highest yoga tantra contains methods by which you can reach enlightenment in a single lifetime or even, as in Lama Tsongkhapa's case, three short years. Of course, these profound teachings have never been published, but the methods still exist, undegenerated, in the minds of certain practitioners. These esoteric teachings of Lord Buddha can be transmitted only through unobstructed inner communication between vajra guru and disciple. Few people realize that such powerful methods can still be found in the teachings of the Geluk school.

A whole tradition of Tibetan yogis has made the yoga method of Heruka Vajrasattva a living experience. Before you can actualize the generation *(kye-rim)* and completion *(dzok-rim)* stages of highest yoga tantra, you must purify yourself: practicing Heruka Vajrasattva is one of the most powerful ways of doing so. After taking the initiation, you enter retreat, in which you recite one hundred thousand Vajrasattva (hundred-syllable) mantras. This allows you to practice the two stages of tantra more effectively. If you have not purified the old defiled habits of your body, speech, and mind, even if you put enormous effort into meditating on the path to enlightenment, you will not gain realizations because there are too many obstacles in your way.

Therefore, you should alternate purification with lamrim meditation. Even trying to achieve single-pointed concentration without purification causes you to become frustrated and feel hopeless and discouraged with your lack of progress. This is because you have not recognized or dealt with the obstacles thrown up by your habitual wrong-conception mind and its byproducts—defiled body and speech.

Some misguided practitioners try to experience emptiness simply by reject-ing the existence of all phenomena, obsessed with the idea that shunyata is some kind of vague nothingness. If you want to actualize the right view of emptiness in accordance with, for example, the Madhyamaka or Zen schools of Buddhist philosophy, you have to practice both method and wisdom. Many people have great interest in wisdom but none at all in method. They are like a bird trying to fly with a broken wing.

Whenever you encounter interruptions and obstacles to your practice, don't get discouraged or depressed. Realize instead that you need to purify, and for a time, concentrate more on method than wisdom. In due course you will gain the realizations that you seek.

PART 1
The Main Commentary

1 ~ Why and How We Purify

THIS TEACHING HAS COME at your request, not from my saying, "I want to give you teachings; come here and listen!" In your studies on the graduated path to enlightenment you have come to understand how powerful your minds are and how they create powerful positive and negative actions. Aware of this, you have examined your lives and seen the nature of the actions of your body, speech, and mind. Thus, with knowledge-wisdom, you have requested this teaching to be able to purify the negative forces within you.

The way you requested this teaching is also very good. Based on your understanding of the negative mind, your request is neither ignorant nor emotional. Since you are fortunate, intelligent, and wise enough to be able to practice this powerful yoga method and thereby destroy your negative energy forces completely, I feel that giving you this teaching will be of great benefit.

First of all, you are fortunate just to see that there really *is* a solution to the negative actions that arise from the ignorant mind. Most people are unaware of how they create actions; they also do not understand the difference between positive and negative actions and their results of happiness and suffering. Even when people discover this reality, it is very difficult for them to see how to purify and free themselves completely from the cycle of cause and effect to which they are bound. This is not easy; it takes a long time. You really are fortunate to know all this and to have reached the conclusion that you can purify yourselves.

Furthermore, you are very lucky that your wisdom can grasp the profound methods of tantric yoga. This is often very difficult for the Western mind. How difficult? Well, when Westerners first meet the Dharma they cannot even understand the purpose of making prostrations: "Why should I do prostrations? Sorry, that's not for me." Prostrations are so simple, so easy to understand! In contrast, the profound methods of tantric yoga are extremely deep, much more difficult to grasp.

Let me put this another way. We often find that when we meditate on the *lamrim*—the path to liberation and enlightened realizations—we encounter many hindrances. We cannot understand why it is so difficult to meditate, to control our minds, to gain realizations. "Why do I meet with so many obstacles whenever I try to do something positive? Leading a worldly life was much easier than this. Even an hour's meditation is so difficult." Many such thoughts and questions arise.

It is not just a lack of wisdom. It is that over countless lives the negative energy forces of our body, speech, and mind have accumulated such that now they fill us like a vast ocean. If they were to manifest in physical form, they would occupy all of space. By contrast, our knowledge-wisdom is as weak as the light of a flickering little candle. A little candle isn't much help on a dark and windy night. It is the energy of our wrong conceptions, our negative mind, that makes it difficult for us to actualize the everlasting peaceful path of liberation and to receive realizations. Therefore, we need a powerful purification practice like the tantric yoga method of Heruka Vajrasattva to destroy both the energy of the ignorant mind and the negative actions of body and speech that arise from it.

The yoga method of Heruka Vajrasattva has the power to purify all negative energy, which is the main thing preventing you from actualizing the path. This impure energy creates both physical and mental hindrances, and also leaves certain imprints. Philosophically, we say that these are neither mind nor form. The negativity I am talking about is conceptually different from your previous understanding of the term. Most Westerners think that negativity refers to just the gross level of the emotions. It goes much deeper than that.

Take, for example, the physical body. The first time people come to a meditation course they have great trouble just sitting. Something in their nervous system pulls their energy down to the base of their spine. The reason we recommend the classical cross-legged meditation posture is that when you sit with your back straight, the psychic energy flows properly, and thus it is much easier for you to control your mind. However, this change in the alignment of the nervous system makes it feel as if all your energy is falling down from your crown chakra to your lower chakra. This gives some people the terrifying sensation that they are losing their minds. Not only do new students have trouble sitting, but they also have difficulty concentrating for long periods while listening to totally new and often unsettling ideas. These physical and mental problems may make them wonder why on earth they are sitting there.

The pressure in the lower chakra is caused by negative physical energy, which comes from the negative mind. In Mahayana Buddhism we place less emphasis on such physical reactions and focus on the root of all problems, the ignorant, negative mind.

While insight meditation on the graduated path is the actual way to liberation, when you feel that you cannot meditate—there are too many interruptions, you cannot concentrate, you cannot solve your problems— remember that there is something else you can do to remove obstacles: purification. In the experience of Tibetan lamas, sessions of insight meditation on the path should alternate with sessions of a powerful purification practice, such as the yoga method of Heruka Vajrasattva. This combined approach ensures that you will gain the realizations you seek without frustration.

Do not, however, have unrealistic expectations: "If I meditate today, tomorrow I'll be completely pure." You cannot purify yourself overnight, not even in retreat. Such expectations themselves become obstacles. Just relax; all you need to feel is that in this life you will act as positively as possible. If you can do that, good results will come whether you expect them or not. You won't have to keep asking your lama for a prediction, "If I control my body, speech, and mind, avoid all negativities, and do only good, will I experience positive results?" If you understand karma, you will always act wisely and keep your actions positive. What need is there to ask?

Just think: "From now until I die, whether realizations come to me or not, I shall act as positively as I can, trying to make my life as beneficial as possible." What more can you expect? That sort of expectation is far more reasonable and logical than thinking, "If I meditate for a month I'll become Heruka Vajrasattva." Such expectations only disturb your mind.

In order to gain higher realizations, it is most important to practice the powerful methods of purification found in the Vajrayana path. Many lamas have found that purification overcomes the hindrances of both negative energy and its imprints. While other Vajrasattva practices emphasize physical purification, the Heruka Vajrasattva yoga method emphasizes mental purification. This makes it especially powerful.

THE FOUR OPPONENT POWERS

The Heruka Vajrasattva sadhana is divided into three parts: taking refuge, generating bodhichitta, and the actual yoga method. Why are taking refuge and generating bodhichitta parts of this purification practice? Because negative actions are usually created in relation either to holy objects such as the Three Jewels of refuge, or to other sentient beings.

You can see for yourself that this is true. Most of your problems arise from the people around you, not from bricks, rocks, or trees. And the most common problems can be found between people who are close to each other—the closer the connection, the more mental complications arise. For example, if you stay away from tar, you'll be okay; but if you touch it, it will get all over you, will be hard to get rid of, and will cause you much difficulty. In the same way, proximity to other people can lead to sticky situations.

Some simple examples of common negativities will clarify this. We ourselves, the subject, act under the influence of our negative minds, but we usually need an object upon which to act. For example, when we kill, there has to be another being whose life we take; when we steal, there has to be an owner of the thing we take; when we lie, there has to be someone to lie to. Of course, our ignorant, dissatisfied, greedy, selfish mind is always there, but other beings have to be there, too. In this way we create negativities in dependence upon others. We purify this kind of negative karma by generating bodhichitta.

We also create negativities in dependence upon holy objects. Sometimes, with a negative mind, we might criticize a buddha, denigrate a bodhisattva, treat books or statues disrespectfully, or complain about monks or nuns. There are countless ways to create such negative karma, and we purify it by taking refuge in Buddha, Dharma, and Sangha.

To generate bodhichitta we must feel unbearable great compassion for all sentient beings, irrespective of their species, race, nationality, or philosophical and religious beliefs. As well, we must have the strong, enthusiastic will to lead them to perfect enlightenment, taking the responsibility for doing so upon ourselves alone. Simply having this attitude releases us from a great deal of negativity.

For example, your karmic connection with your parents is very strong, but it is out of control. Although they have been so kind to you, you cause them great suffering. You cannot cut the connection with your parents by saying that you are completely fed up with them and running off to the mountains. Separating yourself from them physically is not enough. To exhaust the negative karma with your parents you have to purify it by experiencing great compassion for them and generating bodhichitta with them in mind. Similarly, your karmic connection with other people can't be cut intellectually, by just saying you're finished with them. These bonds have to be severed by purification.

The best way to purify negativities is by using the four opponent powers.

The first of these is the *power of the object,* which means taking refuge and generating bodhichitta. In the practice I am describing here, the object of refuge is Heruka Vajrasattva, who is one with the Three Jewels of refuge: Buddha, Dharma, and Sangha. We can also say he is one with the guru, the absolute guru, but I'll discuss that more fully later. His divine wisdom understands the nature of both positive and negative energy. He becomes your liberator, and you go to him for refuge.

The second power is the *power of release.* It is sometimes called the power of regret, but this is misleading, for this power derives from wisdom, not from some kind of emotional sorrow or guilt. Such feelings actually reinforce our negative propensities. Think instead of a person who suddenly realizes that he has just swallowed poison: he wants to take the antidote right away. The power of release is the wisdom that understands the negative repercussions of unwholesome actions so well that the moment you become aware that you have created a negative action, you want to purify it immediately.

The third is the *power of remedy.* It is with this power that you counteract the force of your amassed negativities. With single-pointed concentration on Heruka Vajrasattva—the manifestation of blissful, transcendental, divine wisdom who is one with your guru—you do the yoga method and powerfully recite the purifying mantra. This practice is the actual remedy.

I'm not sure that the fourth power can be succinctly translated into English. It is something like the *power of indestructible determination.* It is not so much a vow or a promise or a resolution or a decision. Simultaneous with the power of the remedy you have this great determination never to create any negative actions again. There is something complete about it. It is firm and strong and comes from wisdom. Within you there is a subtle energy that protects you from moral falls. It is far more than an intellectually motivated decision; it is a force that totally counteracts the old habits, a realization that instinctively protects you. Of course this power has degrees, but when fully developed it offers perfect protection.

For example, when you take the eight Mahayana precepts for a day, in the early morning you generate the great determination to keep the vows intact. From that moment on you must practice perfect awareness to maintain them throughout the day. Determination to keep the precepts at the time of the ceremony alone is not enough; it has to be maintained minute by minute for the duration of the commitment. Otherwise, as soon as the ordination ceremony is over, you will fall straight back into your old samsaric ways, as if unconscious, completely unaware of what you are doing.

Vows are not broken spontaneously. The motivation for an action that will break a vow evolves gradually in the mind. You have a long history of similarly uncontrolled energy patterns. Therefore, if your early morning determination is accompanied by exceptional continuous conscious awareness, there is no way you can break your vows. Within you there is that very subtle, accumulated energy that completely protects you from defiled actions.

KARMA

The same thing applies to following the law of karma. When we take refuge, our main obligation is to keep our karma straight, to avoid defiled, negative actions. But often we cannot do so, even though we understand on an intellectual level that if we keep on creating such actions again and again, we shall continue endlessly in the cycle of suffering and conflict. This is because we do not have a deeply integrated understanding of karma. Those with such an understanding never recklessly create negative actions.

I know Westerners quite well. They are intelligent, but their minds are divided. On the one hand they desire to have perfect wisdom and to keep their karma straight. On the other they are impelled by the force of their bad habits, which prevents them from keeping their karma straight. This causes them a lot of suffering. When difficult circumstances arise, the negative energy overpowers the positive because many Westerners have never built up within themselves the force of good habits; they also lack deep, internal understanding of the nature of karma, of cause and effect.

Some people argue that karma is experienced only by those who believe in it; in other words, those who don't believe in karma don't experience its effects. This is completely incorrect. The laws of karma function whether you believe in them or not. If you act in a certain way, you are sure to experience the appropriate result, just as surely as taking poison will make you sick—even though you think it is medicine. Once you've created the karma to experience a certain result, that outcome is inevitable.

Cows, pigs, and scorpions have no ideas about karma—no beliefs one way or the other—but they must still live out their karma. All their actions are motivated by either greed, ignorance, or hatred, and each definitely brings its own result. Therefore, you must never think that karmic actions and reactions are only a Buddhist thing, a lama thing. Karma is a natural law governing all physical and nonphysical phenomena in the universe. It is extremely important for you to understand this.

When I teach about karma, I don't usually give technical explanations such as those found in Tibetan texts. I simply tell students to look at the way their minds are working at that very moment. They can easily see how up-and-down their minds are, especially during a meditation course. Once they are aware of this phenomenon, it is easy for them to understand how it has come from their previous experiences, and that karma is exactly that. Simply put, the uncontrolled body, speech, and mind are manifestations of karma.

Thus, we are all under the control of the true law of karma, whether we believe in it or not. Don't think that followers of Christianity, Judaism, and Islam are beyond the reach of karma and do not need to be mindful of it. It's not true. For example, Jews and Arabs have accumulated karma with each other, and now there are all sorts of problems in the Middle East. Even though butchers may not believe that killing animals will have any negative repercussions, whether they believe it or not, giving such suffering to other beings will definitely come back upon them.

When you first come to Kathmandu you enjoy yourself and make yourself very comfortable. Then when you come up here to the monastery, you feel agitated. You think it's very dirty and that there are no proper toilets.[3] Your agitation is the result of your previous attachment to comfort. That, too, is karma. If you weren't attached to your earlier experiences of comfort, you wouldn't care so much about your surroundings. You can get a clear understanding of karmic action and reaction simply by analyzing your everyday experiences.

I think this is a far better and more powerful way of developing mindfulness of your actions than by becoming obsessed, as so many Westerners are, with the cultivation of single-pointed concentration *(samadhi)* and mindfulness meditation. If that happens, you run the risk of thinking that sitting meditation is the only form of Dharma practice and that all other activities, such as eating, talking, and sleeping, are completely samsaric and negative. When you believe that these things are negative, they become negative.

There are many ways to meditate. Mindfulness is not the only kind of meditation. Insight can be gained by meditating on any phenomenon in the universe. You don't have to sit cross-legged to meditate: guarding your karma day in and day out is also meditation and can be a powerful way to develop insight. In this way your entire life can be used to bring you closer to the wisdom of egolessness.

When you understand the nature of karma, you are constantly aware of everything you do. Thus, wherever you go, you cannot escape from meditation.

You know that if you do not maintain awareness of the actions of your body, speech, and mind, you will create one negativity after another and will have to experience the resultant suffering of confusion and dissatisfaction. This makes you conscious all the time: when interacting with others, eating in restaurants, shopping in a supermarket, or working at your job.

Usually our dualistic minds interpret the ordinary activities of daily life as being samsaric, dissatisfactory, full of suffering, and undesirable—impossible to use as objects for insight meditation. This is a gross misapprehension. Mahayana Buddhism teaches that if bodily sensations such as physical feelings can be used for the development of insight, then so can any other form of sensory experience, such as the taste of food on the tongue.

Some people say that visualizations cannot be used for insight meditation because they are a mental projection, implying that one's breath or feelings in the body are more real. Sensations and feelings are just as illusory as visualizations of the Buddha. Bodily sensations are not permanent. They change from moment to moment because the relative mind is constantly changing. The feelings of the body and mind, especially those caused by the negative mind, are projections of ignorance. Your dualistic mind automatically projects a dualistic view of whatever you experience.

Ordinary people who start to practice what they consider to be mindfulness meditation believe that the world of bodily sensations is real. But no matter whether they use an internal or an external object of meditation, it still exists only in their imagination and in the view of their relative mind. Fundamentally, there is no difference between inner and outer phenomena: either both are true or both are hallucinations. Until you have realized nonduality, shunyata, then whatever you experience, either physically or mentally, is a hallucinatory wrong view.

Actually, the taste of food on the tongue is also a physical sensation. To think that it is not is incorrect. The Mahayana tradition contains meditation practices for every action. Tantric yoga teaches us that when we eat, we should first offer and bless the food. While eating, we should be relaxed and aware of whatever we are doing, constantly remembering the dependent nature of ourselves and the food, and not grasping at the sensory pleasure of eating, as we usually do. Any sensory experience can be used for the development of insight.

Mantra recitation can also be a great help in insight meditation. It makes the mind focus single-pointedly, thereby counteracting mental scattering and distractions. However, the recitation does not have to be verbal. Mantra is a sound that has existed within your nervous system since before you were born; it is audible if you listen wisely. Mantra is not something that you receive, all of a sudden, from a lama. Without the natural vibration of sound within your nervous system, you would be deaf—each kind of energy has its own natural sound. This is not religious dogma, but something you can verify empirically. You cannot abandon the natural sound of your nervous system. You might as well try to abandon your head!

However, it is the experience of countless lamas that the unstable, transitory objects of the five senses are more of a hindrance than a help in the development of single-pointed concentration. As long as you continue to perceive things with your relative mind and to grasp at objects of the five senses, you will not be able to realize single-pointed concentration. You will be neither a samadhi meditator nor a mindfulness meditator. Check to see whether or not this is true.

You can understand then how ridiculous it is to think that sitting, trying to gain samadhi, is the only way to practice Dharma, and that anything to do with living in the world is totally negative. You should constantly take care of every aspect of your life—waking, working, eating, sleeping—with understanding wisdom. Whether you are close to your guru, to the Sangha, to your parents, or all alone, you must take care of your karma as best you can. It is quite wrong to believe that you can outsmart karma by locking yourself in your room, thinking that when you are by yourself, you can do whatever you like. There is no escape! Whether you are with others or not, karma-creating reactions come automatically.

If I told you that the only way to meditate was to sit and think of nothing, you would find no time to practice. Karma ensures that most Westerners have to spend their lives either working or doing other external activities. Since you couldn't find time to sit, you would think that your Dharma practice was history. But meditation is not blank navel-gazing. When you have an understanding of the fundamentals of Dharma, you will see how much there is for you to do and how much you can grow. This gives you constant resources to maintain your practice, and even though you cannot concentrate, you know that you can still practice Dharma. Wherever you go, whether you are with other practitioners or with more worldly people, you know how to make your life one with Dharma. This ability comes from wisdom.

Without wisdom, how can you make the unavoidable activities of eating, sleeping, and excreting one with Dharma? When you have wisdom, you don't always have to be around your guru to receive teachings. You can see the teachings in everything around you. You can learn from the movement of the planets, the weather, the growth and decay of plants, and all other phenomena. This is what happens when you have wisdom. In fact, your own wisdom that understands reality is your real guru. This is what Tibetan Buddhism teaches.

Integrate your whole life with the experience of Dharma. That is the most powerful thing you can do. That is the way to reach enlightenment in one lifetime, because you do not waste a moment. It's perfectly logical. If you believe that your one-hour daily meditation is the only chance you have to practice Dharma and that the other twenty-three hours of your day are completely dark, impure, and samsaric, you will definitely take three countless great eons to reach enlightenment! What your mind believes becomes reality for you, whether it is reality or not.

2~ Taking Refuge

So far I have been talking about why we need purification and how it works. I have also emphasized that we are unable to stop continuously creating negativities of body, speech, and mind because we have not yet understood the cause, karma.

There is a big difference between an intellectual understanding of karma and one based on the living experience of it. Some students have word-perfect understanding of the teachings on karma and some superficial faith—"It must be true because my lama said so." But because they do not have any experiential understanding of karma, when their understanding is tested, they fail. They have no solution when serious problems arise. They are satisfied with being able to talk about karma, as if being able to tell their parents and friends all about it were enough, but they cannot *do* what they talk about because they haven't practiced.

Other students, however, are not satisfied with the mere intellectual understanding but attempt to understand through practice what they have been taught. They may not be able to give extensive discourses on karma, but because they are always mindful of their actions, they get a true taste of Dharma, an experience as real as the sweetness of honey on your tongue. When problems arise for such practitioners, they know how to apply the solutions. Be clear about this. It is very dangerous to be content with the intellectual explanation of Dharma and not to practice. That cannot help you.

Many Western and Eastern professors and scholars who admit they don't practice can speak at length on all aspects of Buddhist philosophy. Ask them a question and they can answer. But their explanations are very superficial. When an experienced practitioner talks, his words have a blessed energy. He may be talking about the same thing that the scholars are, but the way he expresses himself touches your heart. The talk of those without experience is like the empty wind whistling about your ears.

If you understand cause and effect through your own experience, there is no way you can be careless about anything you do. Although those whose knowledge is only intellectual can express their conceptual understanding of karma in perfect language, they do not really understand what they are talking about—they have not tasted the honey of what they know. They do not live by the ethics they discuss. Personally, I find this rather painful. When asked a practical question about how karma works, such scholars can answer only by quoting some book or text. Since they have no experience, they cannot explain precisely how to observe karma, what to do in practice, or how observing karma leads your mind in a positive direction. Since practical questions go beyond these scholars' philosophical framework of karma, they can't relate to them. All they can say is, "You can't ask that question. Buddhism doesn't deal with that."

I am sure that most of you understand clearly how defiled actions of body, speech, and mind are cyclic in nature, bringing the results of suffering, confusion, and more defilement. In your minds there is no question about the truth of this. You can probably explain it much more clearly than I can. When you hear my broken English, you may think to yourselves, "What kind of language is that? If he'd let me talk, I could give a much better explanation." All this is true. But why can't you put a stop to your negative habits? Theoretical knowledge alone is not enough.

Many Buddhists with little learning have attained high spiritual realizations through earnest practice. Many great scholars who can lecture at length have reached nowhere. Therefore, I advise you to be careful. When you talk about the teachings it is not what you say but how you have gained your knowledge that is important. Your speech must carry the vibration of personal experience and convey that energy to your listeners.

In Tibet, when skillful, realized lamas gave teachings on the graduated path to enlightenment, often they would emphasize the practical aspects of the teaching rather than the philosophical doctrine; they would even make the students meditate while they taught. As a result, some students would receive realizations during the discourse. By the end of a twenty-day teaching, they would understand the entire path from beginning to end and, full of energy, would want to rush off from the monastery into mountain caves for long meditation retreats. On the other hand, scholars could teach you the same subject for twenty years without touching your heart.

I have also seen Westerners so energized by the lamrim teachings that they too have wanted to rush off into the mountains. However, continuous practice over many years is a much more powerful way of purifying negative actions and much better for you than impulsive bursts of meditation in solitary retreat.

Thus, when you take refuge and generate bodhichitta, there should be no gap between them and your own mind. If refuge and bodhichitta are not one with your mind, they cannot purify. When you take refuge, your mind should be inseparable from refuge; when you generate bodhichitta, your mind should become bodhichitta. You should not be sitting down *here* on your cushion dualistically doing something out *there* in front of you. Your mind needs to become the Dharma that you practice. It is difficult but possible, and it is essential if practice is to benefit your mind.

If in a teaching situation the teacher is just like a radio and the audience like the walls of a room, how can there be any benefit? The natural skepticism of Westerners that does not allow them to accept what they hear until they understand it makes them exceptionally well qualified to listen to Mahayana teachings. I like it when they say, "You said so-and-so. I don't accept that." Those who have guru devotion based on emotional faith instead of understanding wisdom are not properly qualified to take teachings.

Taking refuge and generating bodhichitta

Forever, I take refuge in Buddha, Dharma, and Sangha, and in the Sangha of the three vehicles, the dakas and dakinis of secret mantra yoga, the heroes and heroines, the gods and goddesses, the bodhisattvas, and, in particular, my guru.

"Vehicle" is the way we translate the Sanskrit word *yana*. It connotes that certain actions will transport your consciousness to a higher level. For example, if you cultivate bodhichitta and practice the six transcendental perfections, you will definitely achieve enlightenment. The Great Vehicle, the Mahayana, carries you from the beginning, bodhichitta, through the six transcendental perfections and the ten bodhisattva levels to the goal, enlightenment. If you begin perfectly and act correctly, your vehicle will definitely carry you to your desired destination. *Yana* also has the connotation of "path": the right path will lead you to the right place. If out of ignorance you follow the wrong path, you will get lost.

The three Buddhist vehicles are the two Hinayana vehicles and the one Mahayana, and we take refuge in the Sangha of all three. Even though we are following the Mahayana—and in particular its profoundest aspect of tantric yoga—we should not be arrogant, thinking: "I'm a Mahayanist; I don't need to take refuge in the Hinayana Sangha." Although Hinayana arhats do have some attachment to their own liberation, they have transcended their egos with full realization of shunyata and can guide us from samsara. Therefore, without discrimination we take refuge in all Sangha.

Hinayana and Mahayana were not invented by Tibetan lamas. These two Buddhist schools were founded by the Buddha himself and were thus in existence long before the teachings arrived in Tibet. Some people think that the Buddha taught only in Pali and that sutras recorded in other languages are false. Others believe the same of Sanskrit. All such ideas are wrong. When the Dharma spread to other countries, realized practitioners, while retaining the essence of the teachings, adapted them to the minds of the people of their own country for the purposes of clear communication. After all, there are great differences between Tibetans from the snowy mountains and Indians from the hot plains, so you would expect some changes in the mode of expression of the Dharma when it went to one place from the other.

Once, a king who was a disciple of the Buddha had a dream in which eighteen people were fighting over a roll of cloth, each trying to get it for himself. Finally, each person finished up with a complete roll. The king went to the Buddha and asked him what it meant. He told the king that the roll of cloth symbolized his teaching and that the dream meant that after the Buddha's death, eighteen schools, each with its own, slightly different interpretation of his philosophy, would develop. Each person's receiving a complete roll meant that each of these schools would contain the correct, complete path to liberation. Thus, the establishment of the eighteen Hinayana schools was prophesied by the Buddha.

The Theravadan school is one of the eighteen. Some followers of the Hinayana feel insulted when they are called "Hinayanists" and insist on being called "Theravadins" (which doesn't make much sense, because as only one of the schools, Theravada does not contain the entire Hinayana philosophy, and thus, the two terms are not equivalent). And then again, there are others whose egos swell with pride when they think of themselves as "Mahayanists." Such dualistic reactions arise from ignorance and are entirely contrary to the inner peace of Dharma wisdom.

The main difference between Hinayanists and Mahayanists lies in their states of mind. The principal concern of a follower of the Hinayana is his own liberation; that of a follower of the Mahayana is the enlightenment of all sentient beings. Some may feel that wearers of yellow robes are Hinayanists and wearers of red, Mahayanists, but such superficial categorizations are usually wrong. Those who live by the great enthusiastic determination to lead all sentient beings to supreme enlightenment by themselves alone, giving not a thought to their own liberation, are Mahayanists, no matter what they wear. If those robed in red, overwhelmed by insight into the suffering and confusion of their own samsaric existence, are motivated solely by the wish to liberate themselves, they are Hinayanists. We take refuge in the Mahayana as well as the Hinayana Sangha: dakas, dakinis, heroes, heroines, gods, goddesses, and bodhisattvas—all those who have realizations of the completion stage of highest yoga tantra. You should not think that bodhisattvas always look peaceful; some manifest wrathfully. Even on the first of the ten bodhisattva levels, which is called *Joyous One,* they can manifest simultaneously in one hundred different bodies. With these they can take teachings directly from the sambhogakaya aspects of one hundred different buddhas or transform into one hundred different manifestations for the benefit of sentient beings. As bodhisattvas progress, their abilities increase tenfold with each level; what they can do is beyond our comprehension. Thus, bodhisattvas manifest in the aspect of peaceful and wrathful dakas, dakinis, and so forth, and we take refuge in them.

Actually, bodhisattvas can manifest as Easterners or Westerners, as dark- or light-skinned people, as Christians, Muslims, or Jews—in any aspect whatsoever. These days, many so-called religious people are narrow-minded. They would not go for spiritual guidance to a teacher whose race, gender, skin color, or nationality was different. When they align themselves with a particular guru, they become partial, believing that all other gurus and their followers are evil. I call this "guruism." That's wrong; it's taking refuge in a dualistic way. That is not the Buddhist way of taking refuge.

Of course, some so-called gurus claim that they are the best and only guru in the world, and their disciples naturally believe this. In this way, instead of becoming a vehicle for liberation, the religion they teach suffocates their followers, who become narrower and narrower and end up as fanatics. It would be better to be nonreligious than to end up like this. At least nonreligious people don't have such extreme views; for them, simply being human is enough.

We take refuge in the buddhas and bodhisattvas of the ten directions, in whoever has the realization of shunyata, no matter what their color, nationality, or creed. Remember, a first-level bodhisattva can be an African man or woman, a Saudi Arabian camel driver, perhaps even a terrorist, taking such a role to serve others better.

Finally—but, as it says in the prayer, *in particular*—we take refuge in our guru, especially our root guru, who has shown us the blissful path to the everlasting realization of enlightenment. Remember always that your guru is completely one with Heruka Vajrasattva. *Lop-pön* means the one who shows us the true path and guides us along it, straightening the actions of our body, speech, and mind and leading us away from blind, ignorant actions. He can lead us to enlightenment in one lifetime, or even in three years. Recalling our guru's inconceivable kindness, we take refuge in him forever.

The visualization we use when taking refuge is as follows. Your father is to your right, your mother, to your left. Your worst enemy, the sentient being who agitates you the most, is in front of you. Your dearest friend, the person to whom you are most attached, is placed behind you. All other sentient beings surround you on all sides.

This visualization is a good example of Mahayana psychology. If we were asked where we would like to put our best friend, we would normally say, "Oh, here! In front of me!" Similarly, we would prefer to put our enemy behind us, out of sight. Instead, when we take refuge we put our enemy right in front. Look at him or her; examine his or her life sincerely. Think of the problems that your own uncontrolled mind causes, and realize that your enemy is in exactly the same predicament. Analyze the way you feel toward this person.

"I think he is the worst person on earth, but his problems are the same as mine. Why should I feel angry whenever I see his face? The main thing wrong with him is his ego-grasping ignorance. If I'm going to be angry with anything, that's what I should be angry with. But his ignorant mind is invisible to my sense perceptions, so why do I react to his physical appearance? His body is merely the agent of his negative mind. His negative mind is the actual source of everything I don't like about him. May he realize this, purify his ignorance completely, and receive perfect realizations."

Thus, you should generate great compassion for your enemy and, with that, take refuge. This is the best way of taking refuge. The practice of taking refuge in this way is itself a solution to your problems of ignorance, attachment, and hatred. Otherwise, you run the risk of being too worried about your own problems, and your taking refuge becomes simply a new way of augmenting your self-attachment and concern for your own realizations. You will say that you are practicing Dharma, but the Dharma that you practice will be nothing but another means of increasing your attachment. Because of your attitude, Dharma wisdom will become just one more material possession instead of the solution to your problems. Then, if someone says, "Your Dharma is kaka," your ego will explode in rage.

Wisdom is wisdom. Why should it bother you if some ignoramus tells you it is excrement or calls your lama a demon? You cannot make things into excrement and demons simply by calling them that! Therefore be careful. If you get upset when someone criticizes your Dharma practice, it means that you have made Dharma wisdom into something material. This applies not only to Buddhism but to all other religions as well. If the followers of any religion are angered by someone's telling them that their religion is no good and they want to burn their critics at the stake, then their conceptions are completely wrong. Check now how you would react to such abuse—once you're angry, it's too late to check.

Visualizing all mother sentient beings around us while taking refuge is a very powerful way to overcome excessive concern for our own problems. Many of us are obsessed with our problems. We cannot forget them and never stop to think what others are experiencing. When we finally realize that others have exactly the same troubles that we do, we start to feel, "I'm not the worst person in the world after all; nor am I alone in my suffering. There are many just like me. I should have exactly the same sort of compassion for them as I do for myself."

How do the Buddha, the Dharma, and the three vehicles' Sangha save us from the confusion of samsara? It depends on our attitude. We have to understand the nature of our samsaric existence and the great power and ability those holy beings have to guide us out of it. "I am truly helpless. Although I am intelligent enough to make my life comfortable and even enjoyable, I do not have the knowledge or wisdom to overcome the gravitational pull of my attachment to sense pleasures, which binds me to samsara. There is no way I can free myself. But those holy beings can guide me. They have the method, the solution, the light of wisdom to dispel my ignorance, the key to open my mind so that knowledge-wisdom can grow. I am so sick of being uncontrolled, of endlessly going on and on. The buddhas show the perfect way from darkness into light. The Sangha guides me and all others from our confusion. And Dharma wisdom is the actual guide, the true path and the true cessation of suffering."

There are many levels of meaning in the word *Dharma,* as I am sure you have learned. When you take refuge in the Dharma, your actual object of refuge is the wisdom that fully understands absolute nature and is completely one with shunyata, totally free from dualistic view. We always talk about Dharma, but what is Dharma? Dharma is wisdom—Dharma wisdom. However, it takes a long time and the accumulation of many realizations to attain the ultimate wisdom. We have to work at this. To run properly, an automobile depends upon many parts, none of which is the complete automobile itself. Similarly, perfect wisdom is composed of many different sorts of knowledge, each of which is an integral part of the path of wisdom.

Thus, you can understand that there is a difference between the Dharma refuge we are talking about here—perfect wisdom, which fully understands absolute nature, shunyata—and the usual Dharma we discuss—the wisdom solution to mental problems. That perfect wisdom is the ultimate object of refuge. Many of my students complain that they have been waiting in vain for me to teach shunyata, but I have been teaching it all along. It is just that I did not call it shunyata: "Come, I'll show you shunyata, and by tomorrow you'll be enlightened!" I have been camouflaging it in simpler terms.

The buddhas show you the Dharma and how it works within you to bring the true cessation of suffering. Through putting Dharma into practice you become a buddha. The Sangha help you to create the right conditions for practice and make sure that you purify your negativities and gain true cessation. As I said before, bodhisattvas manifest in numberless ways for the sole purpose of helping us in our practice. When they show a wrathful aspect, we should not get upset and think that they no longer love us. Instead we should think, "This bodhisattva is showing me how awful I look when I'm angry. If he hadn't done that, I would never have known. I should be grateful for his kindness." Whenever anybody is angry with us, we should think that he or she is a manifestation of a bodhisattva teaching us not to be angry. Similarly, whenever anyone around us is peaceful, we should think with joy that this person too is a bodhisattva, showing how others get great pleasure when we behave well.

You must have noticed that the moment you see certain people you feel happy, while with others you immediately feel uncomfortable. This is karma at work. Within you there is some energy that causes this to happen; there is almost nothing you can do about it. Handsome men and beautiful women are spontaneously treated well wherever they go; ugly ones are treated poorly. This is their karma: even though they don't want it, it is very difficult to change. What kind of scientific explanation are Westerners going to offer for this common phenomenon? Karma makes your life difficult; karma makes it easy.

This is not to say that karma is permanent or fixed. Karma is changeable. All the same, until the energy of a certain karma is expended, you have to tolerate your situation.

Take, for example, Gomchen, the monastery dog. We all love him; Lord Buddha loves him; Jesus loves him, too. Despite all this, none of us can communicate to him the absolute nature, shunyata. Until his body changes into a more suitable one it will be impossible to connect with him in this way. That's his karma. All samsaric sentient beings have to accept what they are going through until the power of the karmic energy behind that experience has run out. Everything in your life depends upon this kind of energy. Each sentient being lives according to his or her own way of thinking, level of conscious energy, attitude, and environment. That is karma. I am using the word *karma* a lot here. I hope you understand what I mean.

In conclusion, then, all buddhas show you the true path and true cessation, the Dharma that liberates you from samsara. They try to make you realize that what really benefits you is acting in accordance with the path. This means that you, not the buddhas, are ultimately responsible for your liberation. You have to understand this clearly.

The Sangha of the three vehicles, including protectors such as Mahakala and Kalarupa, are your friends; they help you whenever they can. Thus you should know what Sangha really means. Most people think that Sangha refers to those who have taken robes, but there's no text that says that only those in robes are Sangha. However, we *can* say that those who have dedicated their lives to Dharma by taking ordination are *relative* Sangha. The ultimate Sangha are those who have the perfect realization of absolute nature, shunyata, in their minds; regardless of the clothes they wear, the color of their skin, or anything else, they are the real Sangha—your best friends.

You often feel lonely, but there is no need. Your true, everlasting Sangha friends are always with you: the dakas and dakinis, the peaceful and wrathful bodhisattvas, and the other Sangha of the three vehicles. They can guide you out of worldly agitation and confusion. When you realize this you will never miss friends or feel alone. Meditate; go within: that's where your real friends are.

VISUALIZING THE OBJECT OF REFUGE

The way we take refuge in the Heruka Vajrasattva practice is different from the way we do it according to the teachings on the graduated path to enlightenment, where the principal refuge object is Shakyamuni Buddha. Here the Buddha refuge object can be either Heruka or Vajradhara, whichever is easier for you to visualize.

Visualize a standing blue Heruka, embracing his consort, red Vajravarahi. Around them are many dakas and dakinis, the sixty-two deities of the Heruka mandala, and countless buddhas, bodhisattvas, and arhats, all of whom have attained the realization of everlasting peace.

If you prefer to visualize Vajradhara, he is seated in the full-lotus position embracing his consort, Vajradhatu Ishvari (Tib. Ying-chug-ma). Again, he is blue and she is red, and they are surrounded by the same manifestations of divine wisdom as Heruka, except for the sixty-two deities of the Heruka mandala. However, whether you visualize Heruka or Vajradhara, remember that it is actually your guru appearing in that aspect; that the deity you visualize as the principal object of refuge is completely one with your guru. Thus Heruka (or Vajradhara) is Buddha; the dakas, dakinis, and other Sangha of the three vehicles are Sangha; and their wisdom is Dharma.

One benefit of visualizing Heruka in the standing position is that it blesses your nervous system and activates the kundalini energy within it. This helps your practice of highest yoga tantra.

Visualizations are not objects of the eye consciousness; you cannot see them by staring in front of you. Heruka's divine body is a manifestation of his divine transcendental wisdom, which transforms into that divine form and appears instantaneously in the space in front of you. Since this visualization is a transformation of and one with the blissful omniscient mind, it is in the nature of consciousness. We cannot perceive divine transcendental wisdom with our eyes or our other physical senses. Thus, in order to communicate with us, the energy of the ultimate wisdom manifests in this profound, clean-clear divine form, which is in the nature of light. Also, it does not appear gradually but with the suddenness of a movie instantly projected onto the screen, or a person suddenly appearing in a doorway. Through visualizations such as this we can easily communicate with the dharmakaya.

After you have taken refuge, the Buddhas and the Sangha of the three vehicles—the dakas and dakinis, the peaceful and wrathful bodhisattvas, the protectors such as Mahakala and Kalarupa, and so forth—melt into light and dissolve into the principal deity, Heruka. Vajravarahi also becomes light and absorbs into Heruka. Finally, Heruka himself melts into light, which dissolves into his heart. This ball of light comes to the crown of your head and descends through your central channel, passing through your throat chakra to melt into your heart chakra. You become absolutely one with this light, which is in essence Heruka and your guru. Remain concentrated on that for as long as you can, allowing no dualistic thoughts of *this* and *that* to disturb you.

With practice, you might be able to remain in this single-pointed concentration on nondual oneness for half an hour. When wrong conceptions begin to arise, leave this meditation and generate bodhichitta:

> *I must become Heruka in order to lead all sentient beings to the sublime state of Herukahood.*

THE THREE WAYS TO TAKE REFUGE

There are three ways of taking refuge: outer, inner, and secret. Most people think that the sutra, or *Paramitayana,* way of taking refuge is the only one. This is what we call *outer refuge* and is the method usually explained when teachings on refuge are given. In outer refuge, the Buddha in whom we take refuge is somebody other than ourselves: a person who has attained buddhahood, an enlightened being such as Shakyamuni Buddha. The Dharma refuge in this system is the teaching given by that enlightened being. The outer Sangha includes the ordained and realized followers of the Dharma teachings, as I explained before. Understanding that the already-existent Buddha, Dharma, and Sangha have the power to guide us, and fearing the sufferings of samsara, we take refuge in them.

The other two ways of taking refuge are tantric methods. *Inner refuge* is taking refuge in the buddha you yourself will become. The wisdom of that, your own future buddha, is the inner Dharma refuge object. When you have attained that state, you yourself become Sangha: that is the inner Sangha refuge object. At that stage, you not only become Sangha, you attain unity with all Three Jewels of refuge and no longer need to take refuge in something separate from yourself.

When you take inner refuge, your mind becomes transcendental omniscient wisdom; this transforms into the divine aspect of Heruka (or Vajradhara), along with the dakas and dakinis, the peaceful and wrathful bodhisattvas, and so forth, and you take refuge in that. To do this you need to have at least a deep intellectual understanding of the false conceptions and projections of your ego so that you can somehow purify these at the moment of taking refuge. You can see that this is quite difficult.

Secret refuge is the third way of taking refuge. This way of taking refuge is the most difficult of all. You have to recognize that your nervous system is pervaded by blissful daka-dakini energy instead of the usual ridiculous energy of gravitational attachment to sense pleasures, and you take refuge in that.

Here you are utilizing your nervous system's energy resources to generate simultaneously born great bliss, which you unify with the wisdom of nonduality, taking it as the blissful path to liberation. This experience is really what liberates you from dissatisfaction and dualistic thinking. Most people are not aware of the blissful energy that lies within themselves. But when they create the right situation through practices, such as this yoga method or tumo meditation, for example, they can experience an explosion of blissful energy that they would never have thought possible.[4] I also heard recently that some people experienced incredible blissful energy within their nervous systems while doing the fasting retreat with my *chulen* pills.[5]

These three ways of taking refuge are entirely noncontradictory and have been taught so that practitioners can choose the method that best suits their level of mental development. Outer refuge is for the least developed, secret refuge for the fortunate, highly intelligent few.

If you understand the true meaning of taking refuge, you will know what a positive effect it has on your mind and experience its great benefits. You will really enjoy taking refuge, and every time you do, the pure energy of your innermost heart will grow. If you do not know how to take refuge properly, whatever meditation you do will be like snow on the road, which looks very impressive as it falls, but quickly disappears. Like that, your meditation will have no lasting effect. With a deep understanding of taking refuge, you will begin to taste the honey of Lord Buddha's wisdom.

3~ Inner Refuge and Meditation on Emptiness

UNDERSTANDING SHUNYATA

WHY IS THE PRACTICE of inner refuge emphasized by tantric yoga so difficult? Because it is mainly done by the mind. To begin with, refuge has to be taken from the heart. It is not something superficial where you just repeat a few words while your mind remains unmoved. Some people take refuge as a social custom. They chant "Namo gurubhya, namo buddhaya, namo dharmaya, namo sanghaya" with no understanding of the practice or the meaning of the words and no change in their minds. Others chant the refuge formula "Namo gurubhya..." just because they are with other people who are reciting it. That is not taking refuge—it has no more to do with the path to liberation than eating breakfast every morning or going to church on Sundays out of ingrained habit or social obligation.

As I mentioned above, when we take inner refuge, our mind should become the wisdom of the greatest transcendental bliss and transform into the divine aspect of Heruka. Then we take refuge. Do not look outside for the object of refuge! I know you will think it should be somewhere out in front of you. That is your dualistic way of thinking: "*I* am taking *refuge.*" *You* are sitting down *here,* doing *something* out *there.* Your dualistic mind immediately discriminates between subject and object. As soon as you think you are doing something you automatically think of external activities. This happens because you have so many dualistic imprints on your mind.

So, when taking inner refuge, your mind itself becomes the greatest blissful transcendental wisdom. While you generate great faith in and devotion to that wisdom, it simultaneously transforms and appears to you as Heruka. Feeling completely one with Heruka, you take refuge. This psychological method is extremely beneficial. It may be hard to understand, but you should try.

To be able to understand this way of taking refuge we have to understand shunyata. If we do not, the transformation of our minds into the greatest, everlasting, blissful transcendental wisdom becomes just a dry intellectual concept instead of a powerful inner experience. If we have a proper understanding of the absolute nature—if our minds have been touched by the experience of shunyata—it is relatively easy for our minds to become the greatest transcendental wisdom, to transform into Heruka, and for us to feel oneness with this. In this way our minds mix with the transcendental blissful energy of Heruka instead of the usual hatred, desire, and attachment.

If your mind is truly mixed with the great transcendental blissful energy of divine wisdom, you do not need to say the words of the refuge prayer, "Namo gurubhya...." Words are not refuge. All the same, weak people do need words as a way of communicating; words have some meaning for them. But if you have the realization of the constant, blissful feeling of oneness, you do not have to take refuge with your mouth. Wherever you go, whatever you do, you are taking refuge all the time; because of your constant faith, your very being is in the nature of refuge. You know that the everlasting, blissful transcendental wisdom is most profound, most pure. Whenever you eat, whenever you drink, your mind is one with the blissful energy of Heruka, so you are always taking refuge. Taking refuge does not mean sitting cross-legged in meditation. Thus you make constant progress on the path no matter what you are doing, and in that way, can quickly reach enlightenment.

The realization of shunyata has the quality of everlasting joy. Samsaric pleasures, on the other hand, are transitory and painful: here one minute, gone the next. Because they suddenly disappear, they cause us pain. If we weren't attached to samsaric pleasures, we wouldn't be hurt when they disappeared.

If we do not have a perfect understanding of shunyata through realization, we should at least have a clear conceptual knowledge of it, in order to overcome the wrong conception of the way we exist, which is deeply imprinted upon our consciousness. The ordinary, relative idea we have of ourselves is very physical. I think, "I am Thubten Yeshe," and in my mind there is this extremely thick image of a head, arms, legs, and grasping sense organs. As long as you see yourself like this you cannot mix your consciousness with the everlasting, blissful transcendental wisdom. An understanding of shunyata automatically causes this ordinary, relative image to disappear.

If you have sharp intelligence it is not so difficult to understand shunyata. You do not have to learn tremendously complex philosophies or study volumes of texts under many lamas. Of course, you *can* learn from teachers and books, but if you are skillful, you can learn through a very simple method: do not believe what your senses tell you. It is not necessary to search far and wide for what stops you from seeing shunyata. Simply realize that the way you perceive the sense world every day of your life is completely wrong, that it is the misconceived projection of your ego. The moment you realize this, your deluded view will disappear. One reason that the yoga method is so powerful is that it allows you to see very quickly how your ego's projections are wrong and to cut through them completely.

We often feel insecure. On the way to meet someone we think, "Maybe she won't like me," "Maybe he won't like me," "I wish I were better looking," "Maybe she won't like the way I speak," and things like that. All such insecure thoughts derive from wrong conceptions and misinterpretations. As soon as we realize that everything has been painted by our ignorant mind, that our illusory views, thoughts, and feelings are not even relatively true, let alone absolutely, we shall stop feeling insecure. Even if others abuse us, call us thieves and the like, we'll have control and won't suffer. Such are the practical benefits of this kind of understanding.

We live in the sense world believing that the misconceptions and projections of our ignorant mind are true. We think that seeing is believing; "I saw that; it must be true." Some people believe passionately that their philosophy is the ideal one for their society. Communist or capitalist, both are wrong; both are hallucinations! If we go on like this, we shall never discover shunyata; it will always be somewhere else. When we realize that our view of the world is a hallucination, that our view of reality is obscured by the heavy blanket of delusion, the wrong view disappears, and we are left with its opposite, the right view of shunyata. The moment we extinguish the dualistic mind, we experience shunyata.

Thus, you can study shunyata every day, because every day your five senses' gravitational attachment to the sense world has you believing that whatever you perceive really exists as it appears. If you continuously investigate your perceptions and beliefs, there is no time that you are not studying shunyata. Sometimes books and philosophies can be more of a hindrance than a help in your understanding of shunyata, because if you do not know how to integrate words with experience, they can cause conflict in your mind. If you *do* know how to do this, then even one word can become a great teaching for you.

Those who think that understanding shunyata necessitates studying vast numbers of scriptures and committing to memory thousands of words of text are liable to get discouraged. They feel that trying to understand shunyata in their lifetime is a hopeless task. But you can easily understand shunyata by realizing that your ignorant mind's view of any object is completely illusory, not even relatively existent, even though for countless lives your ego-grasping and self-attachment have made you believe "this is really this" and "that is really that," and caused you great suffering. As long as your mind is ignorant, you will perceive any object dualistically. Any object perceived in that way is actually nonexistent.

However, you cannot say that nothing exists: "My nose, my tongue, my mouth—nothing of me exists." How can you say that there is no light, no table? This form of intellectual negation is completely wrong. Better, investigate whether or not *your view* of a table really exists. You will find that it definitely does not. Investigate your views of anything—you will find that none of them exist as they appear. You always say things like, "Nepal is like this," "America is like that," "Europe is like this." You are talking nonsense. The Nepal, America, and Europe you are talking about do not exist. You think, "Oh, this meditation course is too heavy," or "This retreat is such suffering." You are living in a dream world of dream projections. Your dreaming mind is making you suffer.

All the same, this does not mean that you can deny the existence of the sense world. That is totally illogical. You should not concern yourself with whether Nepal exists or not; your business is to discover whether your mind's interpretation of Nepal exists or not. The problem is that your wrong conceptions build up a view of Nepal that has nothing whatsoever to do with the true nature of Nepal, even relatively, and you cling to it. My ignorant mind builds up its view, "Thubten Yeshe is like this, like this, like this"—which has nothing whatsoever to do with my true nature—and I cling with attachment to this unreal, self-pitying projection. Sentient beings have developed attachment over countless lives because they believe that without something to cling to they are lost. When sentient beings *believe* they are lost, they really get lost. For example, during the death process they panic in terror because they feel they are losing everything.

To realize the right view, shunyata, first you have to search for and discover it within your own mind. If you start by searching for ultimate nature in external phenomena, such as trees, tables, and other persons, you will never find it. In the experience of the great Indian pandits and Tibetan lamas, shunyata can never be found like that.

Samsaric beings are by nature very outward looking. We always think that we can understand reality by looking at what other people are doing. We try to assess our own progress by checking out our neighbors. What do they possess? How did they get it? This approach itself makes it impossible to find reality.

If this is your attitude, you'll never find shunyata, even if you study it your whole life.

To discover our inner nature, to have the inner realization of shunyata, we must begin by searching for the absolute nature of our own minds. When we have discovered reality within, it will be much easier to discover the reality of external phenomena. The principal means of realizing shunyata is not through intellectual exercises, such as studying the words of other teachers or engaging in logical debate. Through such methods alone we cannot discover shunyata. We also have to investigate our own minds to identify our wrong concepts and views and practice methods of purification.

Why have we not yet discovered the ultimate nature, shunyata, that lies within our minds, even though we may have studied it for years? Because the vibration of mental defilements and impurities prevents us from doing so. Therefore, to allow shunyata wisdom to grow within us, it is very important that while we study the teachings on shunyata and investigate our minds, we cleanse these hindering negativities through purifying methods, such as prostrations and the Vajrasattva yoga method. In other words, to make progress in understanding shunyata in order to fully realize it, we must do two things: develop our intellectual understanding of shunyata and purify our mental hindrances, including the wrong concepts and views we have discovered through analyzing our minds. The power of this combined approach will make it much easier for us to realize shunyata.

Once, the great Tibetan teacher Lama Tsongkhapa was studying and analyzing shunyata according to the teachings of the Madhyamaka school, when Mañjushri appeared to him and said, "At this point, nobody on earth can teach you shunyata." So Lama Tsongkhapa went to an isolated place, made powerful purification, and meditated, and in that way finally received direct, nonconceptual knowledge of shunyata according to the view of Nagarjuna's Middle Way philosophy. Thus the yoga method of Heruka Vajrasattva is not solely for purifying negativities but is also a method for making possible the quick discovery of the ultimate nature, shunyata, within our minds through its powerful destruction of wrong conceptions.

This long discussion on shunyata has come about from the explanation of inner refuge. To take inner refuge properly, we must understand shunyata and purify the wrong view of ourselves projected by our ego. The moment we start to think, "I am so-and-so, born there, brought up like this...," problems begin. Our ego's projections are a natural source of problems. For example, when someone is born into a Jewish family, he identifies with the Jewish race, and thousands of years of historical problems come to him. As long as there's ego, there will automatically be problems.

The marvelous quality of Lord Buddha's psychology is that it can eradicate all problems and their cause completely and forever. In this it is the exact opposite of Western psychology, which merely alleviates symptoms; as the root of problems is left intact, the removal of one set of symptoms simply results in the growth of another. We should understand and appreciate the psychological mechanism by which Lord Buddha's yoga method works in the treatment of human problems.

When you actualize the evolutionary yoga method and generate yourself in the divine form of the deity, you should understand that it works through the power of your wisdom of shunyata. It is absolutely nothing like your becoming, for example, a candle. The two things are completely different. You must be really clear about this; it is very dangerous if you are not. I think Western understanding of this process has a long way to go. You must understand the difference.

When you understand shunyata, you have the power to bring your mind into oneness with the blissful transcendental wisdom that is totally beyond projections of ego. That wisdom transforms into the deity. You can see what a vast difference there is between your becoming Heruka Vajrasattva and your becoming a candle! If you do not have a deep understanding of how the evolutionary yoga method works, then when somebody disputes your practice—"What's the difference between becoming Heruka Vajrasattva and becoming a candle? You'd be better off becoming a rose. At least you'd smell good!"—you have no answer. You start to doubt what you are doing: "That's a powerful argument. I have no answer. Perhaps my whole practice has no greater benefit than does trying to become a candle." If this is the level of your understanding of the practice, it is less than nothing. You must know the difference.

Most of you practice meditations where you have to visualize Shakyamuni Buddha or a deity such as Avalokiteshvara. If you have at least an intellectual understanding of shunyata, you find visualization easy. If you do not, your wrong conceptions project in such a physical way that it is very difficult for you to visualize the divine wisdom transforming from shunyata into the divine form of the deity. On the other hand, if you are aware that the all-embracing divine wisdom of the buddhas is everywhere, your understanding faith makes it easy for you to visualize the divine form of the Buddha suddenly appearing in the space in front of you. As I explained before, the full visualization appears at once: you do not have to start with a baby Buddha that gradually grows to completion.

Thus, the way of taking refuge in the practice of tantric yoga is not easy. It is much more difficult than taking outer refuge as explained in the sutra teachings on the graduated path to enlightenment. However, once your mind has reached a certain stage of development, you can definitely practice inner refuge. Also, you should understand that these different ways of taking refuge are not contradictory. The tantric yoga method is not implying that the sutra method is no good, or wrong. These different methods have been taught because people's minds are at different stages of development. At this time I do not think it is necessary to give any further explanation of secret refuge.

Generating bodhichitta

After meditating on refuge, we generate bodhichitta according to the methods of tantric yoga. This means feeling the greatest enthusiasm for reaching Herukahood quickly—as quickly as possible—so that we can lead all mother sentient beings to Herukahood in the shortest possible time. If we feel like this we can never be lazy.

For example, what if your dear mother were caught in a blazing fire. You would not relax and say, "Let her burn. I don't have time to get her out right now. I'll do it later." Of course you would stop whatever you were doing at the time, no matter how important, and immediately rush to rescue her without wasting a moment. Similarly, when you realize that mother sentient beings are trapped and burning in the fire of wrong conceptions and negativities, there is no way to be lazy. You have to transform every action of your life—eating, sleeping, working—into Dharma wisdom. You cannot allow yourself to lapse into samsaric behavior for even a moment.

But we *are* lazy. Our impure mind lets us live life as if it were a tea party: "Let my mother burn—I'll pull her out of the fire when I've finished enjoying myself." Of course, we do not say these words, but our inner feeling, beyond words, reflects this attitude. Be careful; we often behave like this. Imagine: I'm at a first-class restaurant having a good time, when all of a sudden one of my students comes rushing in to tell me that my mother is in flames. I just sit there and reply, "Later; I have a dessert to finish!" I mean, you'd want to beat me for my selfishness, wouldn't you? Of course, this is a bit of an exaggeration, but it shows the sort of attitude we have.

All the same, we should not get emotional about all this. If I pump you up too much, you'll get over-excited and not want to do anything but run off to the mountains to meditate. That becomes another problem. I am not trying to excite you; it is much better to have calm, understanding wisdom. As I mentioned before, often in Tibet, after lamrim teachings, the students would be so full of energy that all they wanted to do was leave their studies at the monastery and rush off into the mountains, to live and meditate like Milarepa. Actually, many of them did go, but of course, most of them came back a few days later.

Nevertheless, this shows how powerful the Dharma can be. Sometimes people feel that the lamas are powerful, they change your life. But it is Dharma wisdom that changes the human mind. Dharma wisdom comes into your consciousness, and your mental attitudes change. That is the power of the Dharma, not the magic of the lamas. We don't even know any magic!

When you practice the sadhana of Heruka Vajrasattva, the refuge and bodhichitta prayers are recited three times. Why these repetitions? To ensure that you have time to meditate and imbue your mind with the meaning of the words. Otherwise, there is the danger of your just rushing through the prayers and your mind remaining unmoved by them.

However, as I have already mentioned and as I always explain to Westerners, taking refuge is not simply reciting prayers. You can take verbal refuge, in either English, Tibetan, or Sanskrit, or you can do it silently; the main thing is what is happening in your mind. If you have perfect devotion and continuous understanding that the everlasting, blissful transcendental wisdom is your ultimate goal, with the joy of constantly striving to discover it in your heart, there is no such time that you are not taking refuge. But if you do not have this understanding, even though you say "Namo gurubhya, namo buddhaya..." a million times, nothing happens. It is just a waste of time and energy.

In the Mahayana Buddhist tradition we have the preparatory purifying practices of taking refuge one hundred thousand times, offering one hundred thousand mandalas, doing one hundred thousand prostrations, and so forth. This is to make sure that we do these things not only with our bodies and our speech, but also with our hearts. You can rattle off "Namo buddhaya, namo dharmaya, namo sanghaya" and think that you have finished taking refuge, but it is possible that while your mouth has been taking refuge, your mind has been taking Coca-Cola. Then what benefit have you derived from the words you have been chanting? Perhaps certain words do have some power of their own, but even so, it is questionable that they would have had much effect on you if your mind has been fully occupied by attachment and you have been saying them unconsciously.

Thus, you can see that it is not necessarily easy to take refuge. And when a group of people take refuge together, each person is doing something different. The way one takes refuge depends upon one's understanding and realizations, and these differ from person to person. Even though we all chant the same words or recite the same mantra, each of us feels a unique vibration, which accords to the level and experience of the individual mind.

When you start actualizing bodhichitta, you will find many ways to help other sentient beings. The bodhisattva's duty is to complete the six transcendental perfections, but it takes a long time to gain full realization of these. It is not just one or two days' work. When you practice the perfections, you feel that you are making good use of your life. If you feel that you are not doing anything useful and that you cannot help any sentient being, you are most unwise. Your concern for your problems alone will make you narrower and narrower. You will obsess, "I have so many problems…this problem… that problem…my problem…my problem," and thus remain unaware of the problems faced by mother sentient beings throughout the extent of space. As a result, you will feel no compassion for them.

Such self-obsession causes people to commit suicide. Don't admire them because you think they have finally understood their own problem. People who commit suicide do not understand their problem at all. That's why they kill themselves. Their view is narrow. Suicide is never the result of realizations.

In ancient India there was a king who killed his father. When he realized what he had done he was overcome with remorse, completely depressed, and almost unable to think. Finally, he sought advice from the Buddha, who told him, "Killing your parents is worthwhile." Somehow, he was jolted awake by these words, and his mind started functioning normally again. He thought deeply about what the Buddha had said, and finally realized that what the Buddha was really saying was that he should kill the attachment and deluded mind that give birth to his samsara. Through that realization he became an arhat. The point here is that he became so worried and obsessed by his own problems that these ignorant emotions filled his mind and left no room for understanding wisdom. If our minds get so narrow that we cannot benefit even ourselves, how can we possibly expect to be able to benefit others?

THE VASE MEDITATION: THE NINE-ROUND BREATHING EXERCISE

After you have taken refuge and your objects of refuge have melted into light and dissolved into you, meditate single-pointedly for as long as you can on being one with Heruka or Vajradhara, depending upon which of these deities you visualized as your object of refuge. When dualistic thoughts start to arise, generate bodhichitta, as I explained before.

From this point of the sadhana, you no longer visualize yourself in your ordinary form; instead, you appear in the divine aspect of Heruka or Vajradhara. Thus, you no longer feel, "I am so-and-so..." or imagine that your body is made of flesh, blood, and bone—but neither do you hold the divine pride of being the deity. This means that you visualize yourself as the deity but do not generate the belief that you *are* the deity. Later, you will do the same thing as you recite the purification mantra when practicing the power of the remedy.[6]

Now, while holding the divine appearance of yourself as the deity, you do the vase meditation. In this practice, breathe only though your nose; keep your mouth closed. Inhale and exhale slowly, naturally, and completely, but a little more strongly in the middle of the breath than at the beginning or the end. We say that the pattern of each breath resembles the shape of a barley grain, which is pointed at the ends and wide in the middle. We do not use the forceful method of breathing found in some of the practices of Hindu yoga.

There are many psychic energy channels in your body. Here, we visualize the three main ones. The central channel is a transparent tube in the nature of light about the width of your little finger in diameter running straight down the center of your body from your crown chakra to the chakra at the base of your spine, just in front of your spinal column. The right and left channels are also transparent tubes in the nature of light but are narrower than the central channel. They run from your nostrils up toward the crown chakra, where they curve over like an umbrella handle to run down alongside the central channel, parallel with it, to a point about four fingers' breadth below the level of your navel, where they curve inward and join the central channel.

Having visualized these channels, first breathe in through the left nostril: slowly, then slightly more forcefully, then slowly again. Visualize that the air enters the left channel, filling it completely, and passes down and across into the right channel, up through it and out of the right nostril. This air pushes out all the energy and impressions of your desire and attachment, and these are pushed out beyond the earth's gravitational field, out of this solar system, to disappear forever. Do this three times.

Concentrate fully on the passage of the air through the channels, letting your mind become one with the movement of the air energy. Don't think about what your neighbor is doing or anything else. Do not regard your channels as physical, made of flesh and blood. Remember: you are visualizing yourself in the pure aspect of the deity and the channels are in the nature of consciousness. But since you are not holding the divine pride of being the deity, you can still purify the delusions as I have described.

Repeat the exercise three times, now breathing in through the right nostril and expelling the air through the left. As the air goes down through the right channel and up through the left it pushes out all the energy and impressions of your hatred and aversion—whatever makes you feel dark and uncomfortable. These also pass out of the solar system and vanish into emptiness.

Now breathe in through both nostrils together, bringing the air down through the right and left channels to the point where they join the central channel. To help you concentrate on this you can swallow some saliva as the air goes down. When the air reaches the central channel, tighten the inner pelvic muscles and draw energy up from the lower chakra through the central channel to the navel chakra, where it meets and mixes with the air energy from above. Hold your breath and concentrate on the blissful energy you can feel at this point. This is important. As soon as you no longer feel comfortable, exhale naturally through your nostrils, but visualize that instead of going out, the air you have been holding goes up and dissolves inside the central channel. Do this three times.

This exercise is very helpful for generating blissful energy within your nervous system. The experience of bliss is an integral part of the method of tantric yoga, and thus, this exercise is also helpful for your tantric practice. It is this blissful energy, which is in fact your mind—and it is *your* mind, not somebody else's—that transforms into the lotus seat and the syllable HUM when you go on to practice the rest of the sadhana.

Therefore, make sure that by the end of the vase meditation you feel calm and blissful and that your mind is in no way involved in thoughts of samsaric activities or old familiar places. You should feel that you have such control over your mind that you could place it on any meditation object you choose. If your mind is bothered and agitated, you cannot meditate. Another benefit of this exercise is that it destroys your exaggerated, emotional superstitions, which keep you from accomplishing the yoga method.

Thus, it is important to experience bliss at the navel chakra as you are holding your breath and concentrating there. And simultaneously, you are clearly, consciously aware of that blissful feeling. This is the exact opposite of ordinary samsaric pleasure, which you normally experience unconsciously, without awareness. Why are these two experiences so different? Because one derives from wisdom, the other from ignorance; one becomes the path of liberation, the other brings more attachment, desire, and conflict into your mind. But through practice, you can discover all this for yourselves; there is no need for me to tell you.

Visualizing the energy dissolving within the central channel when you exhale is an essential aspect of the practice of kundalini yoga. Therefore, it is important to do this and not feel that you are losing the energy at that time. When you have finished the nine rounds of the vase meditation, you can then go on to the actual yoga method.

4 ~ The Actual Yoga Method

THE INITIAL VISUALIZATION

Out of the void, about six inches above the crown of my head, appears the seed syllable PAM, *which transforms into a thousand-petalled lotus. On top of the lotus appears the seed syllable* AH, *which transforms into a moon disc. In the center of the moon disc stands the seed syllable* HUM. *Suddenly, the* HUM *transforms into a white five-pronged vajra that has a* HUM *at its center. Much radiant light emanates from both the* HUM *and the vajra, going out into the ten directions and completing the two purposes. The whole universe melts into light. This light then returns to and is absorbed by the* HUM *in the vajra. The* HUM *and vajra also melt into light and transform into Heruka Vajrasattva.*

Vajrasattva is white. He has one face and two arms. He holds a vajra in his right hand and a bell in his left. He is sitting in the full lotus position with his hands in the embracing mudra. His consort, Dorje Nyema, embraces him, her legs encircling his body. She is white and has one face and two arms. She holds a curved knife in her right hand and a skull cup in her left.

They are both dressed in robes of heavenly silk and adorned by precious jewel ornaments. [They both have seed syllables] OM *at the crown chakra,* AH *at the throat chakra, and* HUM *at the heart. Brilliant light radiates from the* HUM *at the heart, invoking the divine supreme wisdom energy of all tathagatas.*

OUT OF THE SPHERE OF SHUNYATA, a few inches above the crown of your head, appears the white syllable PAM, which transforms into a white, thousand-petalled lotus. On the lotus appears a white syllable AH, which transforms into a white moon disc. This moon is nothing like the physical moon that scientists examine, but is in the nature of radiant light. On the moon, at its center, appears a white syllable HUM, which transforms into a white five-pronged vajra, marked at its center by a HUM. The vajra is in the nature of transcendental blissful wisdom.

From the vajra, and especially from the HUM at its center, radiant light shines forth in the ten directions, filling the entire universe. This light accomplishes two purposes. It becomes an offering to all the gurus and buddhas, filling them with a feeling of great blissful energy and joy. The light also reaches all mother sentient beings, purifying their body, speech, and mind of all defilements and negative imprints. All sentient beings and their environments—all animate and inanimate phenomena —melt completely into light, which returns to dissolve into the HUM at the center of the vajra.

The vajra also melts into light, out of which Heruka Vajrasattva suddenly appears. He is white and has one face and two arms. He holds a vajra in his right hand and a bell in his left. He is sitting in the full lotus position with his hands crossed in the embracing mudra.

He embraces his consort Dorje Nyema, who is also white and sits with her legs encircling his hips. She has one face and two arms. She holds a curved knife in her right hand and a nectar-filled skull cup *(kapala)* in her left. The knife symbolizes wisdom; its purpose is to cut wrong conceptions, the ego's projections, and gravitational attachment to sense pleasures. The nectar-filled kapala shows that she has attained the everlasting blissful realization of enlightenment and is not simply an up-and-down worldly woman. Although she is just symbolic, she really gives a great impression.

If you check back through history, you will find that women have usually been considered worthless, nothing but mere servants for men. But they are not. The greatest of Lord Buddha's psychological methods, tantric yoga, shows clearly that women and men are equally capable of discovering the everlasting peaceful transcendental wisdom that lies within the minds of all. Furthermore, women have a special potential to generate the power of wisdom and can thus give great blissful energy to other yogis. At the same time, they receive blissful energy back. Therefore, if you have the inner experience of what the consort symbolizes, every time you see a Mahayana painting, a deep positive imprint is placed upon your mind, and you receive transcendental wisdom. In fact, these paintings are talking to you, beyond words.

Our ignorant, limited mind always thinks, "I can't do anything…I can't do this…I can't do that…," which is completely untrue. You can do whatever you want! Your precious human rebirth offers you so much: you can communicate, think intelligently, and develop yourself infinitely. If you think you are lazy, you will become lazy. You will waste your whole life and will do nothing, simply because you believe that you are incapable of doing anything. You keep pushing yourself down. But this is not true; you are capable of so much!

Tantric yoga shows you the powerful qualities that exist within you and stops you from thinking that you cannot do anything. You are extremely fortunate to have met and understood these teachings and to be putting them into practice. It would be very wise of you to take as much advantage of this opportunity as possible.

If ordinary people saw a painting of Dorje Nyema holding the kapala full of the nectar of blissful energy, symbolizing her attainment of the realization of everlasting joy, they would think that she was some kind of blood-drinking demon. They would be revolted and afraid, thinking that the kapala held human blood and that Mahayana Buddhists believed in human sacrifice. They might even be scared of our cutting their throats! If they saw paintings of Yamantaka wearing human bones, they would feel sick; their superstitions would project that he kills human beings. Contrary to their superstitions, however, these symbols have deep significance and reflect the supreme, highest realizations.

During the sadhana of Heruka Vajrasattva or the six-session guru yoga, there is a part where you have to visualize yourself as Vajrasattva embracing the consort. Now, monks and nuns have vowed not to have sexual contact, and it might be thought that they should not practice this kind of sadhana. However, the consort is not a physical female but a samadhi female, and therefore, it is permitted for monks and nuns to engage in these meditations. Women can visualize themselves either as Vajrasattva embracing the consort or as the consort, Dorje Nyema, herself, who is completely one with Heruka Vajrasattva and his blissful transcendental wisdom. Thus, we transform our negative energy into the blissful transcendental wisdom of Vajrasattva.

The purpose of consort practice is to develop the blissful transcendental wisdom of shunyata. This is the exact opposite of the purpose of the ordinary male-female embrace. In order to be able to embrace with blissful transcendental awareness, it is necessary to gradually develop the mind of blissful transcendental awareness. Therefore, yogis and yoginis first cut any physical contact and practice the yoga method with a samadhi female until they have gained higher realizations. Only when they have reached a higher stage of development can they embrace physically, but it has nothing to do with unconscious samsaric pleasures. There is a long way for us to go to reach that point, and it may not even be necessary for us to do those practices. Therefore, I do not need to give any more details about them now.

Here, the point is that the consort symbolizes helping other yogis to develop everlasting blissful wisdom. If women can do this, it's fine, but if their effect on men is to make them agitated, depressed, discouraged, and unhappy, then everything just becomes samsaric. Naturally, the same can be said about the effect of men upon women.

Both Heruka Vajrasattva and his consort are dressed in garments of heavenly silk and adorned with beautiful jeweled ornaments. Of course, "beautiful" here is relative. What people from one country might find beautiful, people from another might find ugly. According to Buddhist philosophy, beautiful and ugly and good and bad depend on sentient beings' minds. What is ornamental and what is not is all in the mind.

You can understand this simply by looking at the development of Western civilization and how at different times people have considered certain things beautiful and others ugly. You probably understand all this much better than I do. I only know about these things through having studied Buddhist philosophy; you know about them through direct observation of reality. All you have to do is watch how shopkeepers keep changing their displays all the time. What was beautiful yesterday is ugly today, and so it goes. You are lucky! You can see Buddha's philosophy right there, simply by looking at what is going on around you all the time. You don't have to bother so much with technical terms and scriptures. You can enjoy life in your own country and come to understand reality at the same time.

Since people from different countries have their own ideas about what ornaments are beautiful, you might not like the way I describe those adorning Vajrasattva and his consort. Perhaps you'd like to visualize their ornaments in a way more attractive to your tastes. But the ornaments symbolize particular inner realizations and should therefore be visualized as described in the text. Certainly, you should not leave them out just because you think they are too complicated to visualize.

Heruka Vajrasattva has six different kinds of ornament, his consort five. The sixth is a white substance that is applied to his body in a certain way to indicate that he has the kundalini energy realization; it is not smeared all over his body in the way that you might have seen Indian sadhus cover themselves with ash. Some men look like men but are impotent; their male energy does not function. This sixth ornament shows that Vajrasattva's kundalini energy is functioning, that he has the kundalini energy realization and can have the experience of transcendental, simultaneously born bliss. (I say "kundalini energy" instead of just "kundalini" so that you will not think that I am referring to the ordinary male energy.)

Both Heruka Vajrasattva and his consort have the syllables OM at the crown chakra, AH at the throat chakra, and HUM at the heart chakra. The HUM is standing at the center of a moon disc. This moon is completely full and symbolizes transcendental great bliss. When you feel hot and go outside to cool off under a full moon, you automatically feel cool and happy. This is one of the reasons that a full moon has been chosen to symbolize great bliss. Around the edge of the moon disc stand the syllables of the Heruka Vajrasattva mantra, reading counterclockwise. Usually in tantric sadhanas, the mantra reads clockwise—from left to right; here, it reads counterclockwise, from right to left, to show that Heruka Vajrasattva emphasizes female energy more than male. It is said that women use the energy of the left side of their body more than the right, while men use the right more than the left.

When Buddhists circumambulate a stupa, they usually walk clockwise, keeping the stupa to their right. As a practitioner of female tantra, conscious of what you are doing, you could go around in the opposite direction. People who don't have a higher understanding might just think you are wrong, and simply trying to be different; those who do understand might be very impressed by your obvious knowledge of secret mantra. However, it is not good to show off, and you should just try to be simple and act conventionally.

From the HUM at the divine heart of Heruka Vajrasattva, much radiant light goes out in all directions, invoking the supreme pure energy of the wisdom of all buddhas, which returns in the form of light to dissolve back into the HUM.

MAKING OFFERINGS TO HERUKA VAJRASATTVA

OM KHANDA ROHI HUM HUM PHAT

OM SVABHAVA SHUDDAH SARVA DHARMA SVABHAVA SHUDDHO HAM

All is void. A seed syllable AH appears out of the void. It turns into a huge white kapala containing the five meats and the five nectars. They melt, becoming an ocean of the amrita-energy of divine transcendental wisdom.

OM AH HUM HA HO HRI

Next you recite the mantra to purify and bless the offerings and make their energy inexhaustible (OM KHANDA...). It is similar to making the inner offering. You are in the aspect of Heruka Vajrasattva, and you bless the offerings.

Then recite the shunyata mantra (OM SVABHAVA...). All becomes empty. With the shunyata mantra and the right view of emptiness, you transform the offerings and all other phenomena in the universe into blissful transcendental wisdom. Out of nonduality appears the white syllable AH, which turns into a huge white kapala. Inside this there are the five kinds of meat and the five nectars. They melt, blend, and become a vast ocean of nectar, the essence of which is blissful divine wisdom.

Then recite the mantra OM AH HUM HA HO HRI three times. Here, we purify the impure energy of the offering ingredients, removing faults of taste, smell, color, and power, or potential; we transform it into nectar; and we increase it, making it inexhaustible.

I am sure that many of you could have some kind of shunyata experience in meditation, but the trouble is that whenever you perceive a sense object your dualistic mind automatically grasps at it, and you fall back into your old habitual samsaric mind patterns. It is completely different if you have blissful divine wisdom. No matter what you perceive, your mind does not move, grasp, or cling; you have complete, joyful freedom. You see the absolute nature of all phenomena in the universe and experience everything with bliss.

OM VAJRASATTVA ARGHAM...SHABDA PRATICCHA HUM SVAHA

Thus, we make the eight offerings to Heruka Vajrasattva. One needs transcendental wisdom to make them perfectly; we should at least have deep understanding and intelligence.

Ordinary tourists who see altars in Tibetan temples and monasteries judge everything by external appearances and worldly modes of thought. They really believe that we offer food, paper, water, and cloth to graven images and other physical objects. They even get upset by some of the statues, such as those of wrathful deities grasping human beings between their fangs, and cannot believe how the stupid heathens could possibly make offerings to such hideous figures. Be careful: if your wisdom is a little weak you too could think like this.

However, making material offerings is a highly beneficial practice. It stops you from being lazy and hypocritical, rationalizing, "Oh, I make offerings mentally," and never reaching into your pocket to give even a few cents. I'm sure you know what I mean. But if you offer only one candle with correct understanding and the proper visualization, it is as if you were offering the entire universe and everything in it. Also, most of us have small minds and cannot visualize. It is difficult for us mentally to offer the entire universe. The eight material offerings make it easier by serving as a base that we can transform into everything magnificent in the universe.

You should not see any offering as an ordinary, samsaric object of enjoyment; instead, transform it into blissful transcendental wisdom that then manifests as nectar-like water, light, sound, taste, smell, and touch. Through this practice you can realize that anything on earth, whatever its outer form, is a transformation of blissful transcendental wisdom. Western science has already shown that all energy is in a constant state of flux; one form of energy is always changing into another. For example, the energy of the sun interacts with that of a plant, and a beautiful flower emerges. Everything in the world is capable of change.

Whenever you visualize blissful transcendental wisdom in any of its aspects, your mind reflects it automatically; all the negative, foggy, obstructive energy of your wrong conceptions is displaced by wisdom. Joyful energy arises spontaneously in your mind, without your having to depend on chocolate and cake! If you experiment, you will easily discover how this exceptional psychology works.

Many people want to kill themselves. Their problem is their visualization. All they can see is suffering and conflict; they cannot forget their worries, they cannot sleep. Suicide is their only solution; they slash their wrists. It is important that you understand the psychology of suicide.

It is just as important that you understand the psychology and the real purpose of making offerings. If you do not understand the transcendental nature of the materials you offer, they remain physical objects, and your offering is an empty ritual. But if you understand their nature, you can see how making offerings is a profound and perfect treatment for the deluded mind: peaceful, gentle, and full of wisdom. If you train yourself in this kind of visualization, you will never have a depressed or pessimistic view of the world.

Do not look down on the practice of transformation. A drink turned into blissful nectar tastes far better than any drink samsara can offer. Even the best tea or coffee gives you only a little bit of pleasure between your mouth and your stomach. Its energy is fleeting, and soon after drinking it you have to go to the toilet. Divine nectar, on the other hand, dissolves into your entire nervous system, giving bliss to all five senses, and the energy you get from it is beyond compare. Really! I am not exaggerating.

Some people think that monks and nuns have to renounce music. We renounce nothing! We enjoy and offer every beautiful sound in the universe. We do not miss out on singing and dancing either. We can sing and dance as much as we like, as long as we remain in single-pointed concentration, conscious and liberated, and do not shake or upset our nervous systems. In Tibetan monasteries and nunneries they play musical instruments in pujas and do religious dances, too. We don't miss out on life, we gain from it!

Of course, if you try to explain all this to Westerners, they will think you are either crazy or dreaming. But it is neither madness nor a dream; it is reality. If they disagree, ask them, "What, then, is reality?" They cannot answer. They think they are very intelligent; that what they are doing is reality, while what we are doing is a fantasy. This is a wrong conception. If you analyze with skillful wisdom, you will find that basically we are both doing the same thing—they're hallucinating; we're hallucinating. So what's true for one is true for the other.

The offerings you make have three characteristics: their essence is blissful transcendental wisdom; this wisdom manifests as the various objects of offering; and each object gives its own kind of inexhaustible, everlasting pleasure to the senses.

You can visualize that the eight offerings are being made by eight goddesses. When you snap your fingers at the beginning of each offering mudra, the appropriate goddess emanates from your heart and makes the offering, after which she dissolves back into your heart as you finish the mudra with a second snap of your fingers. The goddesses are manifestations of divine transcendental wisdom; when they dissolve into you, their immaculate purity and beauty brings indescribable bliss into your heart. Each has four arms: their first right and left hands hold a vajra and bell; their other two hold the appropriate offering.

The eight offerings and their goddesses are:

argham	Nectar Goddess	(*Chö-yön-ma*), white in color
padyam	Foot-bathing Goddess	(*Zhab-sil-ma*), white
pushpe	Flower Goddess	(*Me-tog-ma*), white
dhupe	Incense Goddess	(*Dug-pö-ma*), smoke-colored
aloke	Light Goddess	(*Nang-säl-ma*), red
gandhe	Perfume Goddess	(*Dri-chab-ma*), green
naivedya	Food Goddess	(*Zhäl-sä-ma*), multicolored
shabda	Sound Goddess	(*Dra-chog-ma*), blue

JAH HUM BAM HO. *[The wisdom beings] become nondual [with the symbolic beings].*

Having made the offerings, we recite the mantra JAH HUM BAM HO. With JAH, the divine wisdom is invoked; with HUM, the divine wisdom enters; with BAM, it becomes nondual unity; and with HO, it becomes blissfully indestructible.

Thus, the energy of the divine wisdom of all buddhas that we invoked before is magnetically attracted by the light that radiates from the HUM at the heart of Heruka Vajrasattva. Instantaneously and effortlessly, it dissolves into his heart, becoming blissfully one with his divine wisdom, like a drop of water merging with the ocean, no longer separate or dual.

Actually, Heruka Vajrasattva has no need to invoke divine wisdom; he is already one with all buddhas. It is quite wrong to think that Heruka Vajrasattva is one thing and that all buddhas are something else. But the problem is that your dualistic mind does not understand that the divine form you are visualizing above the crown of your head and the divine wisdom from which it manifests are perfectly one. You instinctively distinguish them as separate. Therefore, you need to trick your dualistic mind with this kind of visualization.

Also, it is no good simply saying, "Oh yes, they are one and the same," if your knowledge is merely intellectual. This does not help your mind develop. However, when you experience the real meaning of oneness through your practice of the yoga method, your realization of it becomes entirely intuitive. Heruka Vajrasattva is the combined pure energy of all buddhas manifesting in that divine aspect to communicate with you. When you have fully purified your dualistic mind, you too will be one with this blissful transcendental wisdom.

THE INITIATION

Again, brilliant light radiates from the HUM at the divine heart, invoking all initiating deities of the five families.

OM PANCHA KULA SAPARIVARA ARGHAM...SHABDA PRATICCHA HUM SVAHA

"All tathagatas, please bestow on me the [Heruka Vajrasattva] initiation." Upon this request, all the tathagatas hold up their initiation

vases, which are full of the amrita energy of divine transcendental wisdom, and the amrita starts to flow. As the mantra OM SARVA TATHAGATA ABHISHEKATA SAMAYA SHRIYE HUM *is said, the initiation is conferred.*

The divine body of perfect absolute wisdom, Heruka Vajrasattva, is completely filled by the amrita energy of blissful transcendental wisdom. Some amrita overflows and turns into Akshobhya, who adorns his crown.

The seed syllable HUM *stands at the center of a moon disc at the divine heart, encircled by the hundred-syllable mantra [standing counterclockwise around the edge of the moon disc].*

Once again, much light radiates from the HUM at the divine heart of Heruka Vajrasattva, filling all of space in the ten directions and invoking the principal initiators—the five dhyani buddhas—and all other buddhas, in their tantric aspects, for the initiation. Again, magnetically attracted by the light, they come in an instant into the space above and around Heruka Vajrasattva's head.

Now, before requesting these buddhas for the initiation, make them the same eight offerings as above. When you say PRATICCHA HUM SVAHA you are asking them please to accept each of these offerings, whose nature is divine wisdom, and experience the joy of blissful transcendental wisdom in their holy minds.

Having made the offerings, you request the initiation. As you recite the mantra OM SARVA TATHAGATA..., the initiators then grant your request, conferring the initiation by lifting up the initiation vases and pouring the purifying nectar of divine transcendental wisdom into the central channels of Heruka Vajrasattva and Dorje Nyema through their crown chakras.

It looks to you as if you are down here visualizing Heruka Vajrasattva up there, taking the initiation on your behalf. Again, this is because of your dualistic imprints of, "I am this, he is that." To destroy the ordinary conceptions and projections of the dualistic mind, you need purifying visualizations such as this.

The whole point of this yoga method is to purify your own mind. Although you visualize Heruka Vajrasattva being purified, psychologically you are purifying yourself. Your visualization of Heruka Vajrasattva is your own impure vision. By purifying him with the most profound, pure, clean-clear energy of enlightenment, you yourself become pure. This leaves a deep imprint on your consciousness and automatically releases you from negative energy.

After the initiation, the divine body of Heruka Vajrasattva is completely full of the energy of the nectar of blissful transcendental wisdom that the initiating buddhas have poured through his crown chakra into his central channel. If you have the great wisdom of tantric yoga, you can have the same experience yourself.

You should realize, however, that your entire nervous system is, in fact, *already* full of the energy of blissful nectar. But instead, you always think you are poor, that something is always missing from your life: "I don't have this, I don't have that, I don't have the other." Then you think, "If only I had this, I'd be happy." You are constantly dissatisfied and always looking for whatever it is that you think you do not have.

Your lower chakra is dark, blocked, painful, and devoid of blissful energy. Your naval chakra is dark, depressed, and closed. Your broken heart chakra is drowning in the blood of emotions of hopelessness. Your throat chakra is completely defiled, and nothing you say is positive. And your frozen head chakra is as hard, cold, and inflexible as an igloo, unmelted by the fire within. You are too impure, and give blissful energy to neither yourself nor others. Everything is dark, blocked, and defiled.

However, through this yoga method you can realize the greatest wisdom and bring its everlasting blissful energy into your innermost heart. You can use the techniques of this highest yoga method from now until you die. Even after death we can use them, because we are constantly developing. If we do not develop, our minds will always be up and down, dualistic, and we shall never be happy. Look at how we are: we have studied so much Dharma but still we are running around doing this and that. Samsaric activities are endless. Even those of us who live in monasteries and meditation centers, which are supposed to be places of peace and quiet that everybody likes, are busy, busy, busy. Life is sure to finish soon, that's all.

In the sadhana there is the Tibetan word *ku; kaya* in Sanskrit. We translate this term into English as "divine body" or "holy body," but perhaps "pure nervous system" would be better. I don't know what the right scientific term should be to translate these Tibetan and Sanskrit words, but I'm sure that we have all had some experience of what these words connote. Ku implies that the pure nervous system of Heruka Vajrasattva is pervaded by everlasting blissful kundalini energy.

Our nervous systems are pervaded by this blissful energy too, but we don't recognize it. However, we have all had feelings of joy in our minds and physical nervous systems, when our negative energy has transformed into bliss and we have not clung to any external object, and have been able to maintain control. But despite such experiences we continue to act under the influence of the old imprints of our wrong conceptions. Of course, I know these conceptions are strong, but we should try to overcome them as hard as we can, according to our understanding of these pure blissful experiences. It is simply a question of taking advantage of the opportunities offered us. We should learn from our small experiences of bliss.

For example, if someone were to ask you to choose between lunch at a beautiful five-star hotel and chapatis in a dirty Indian tea shop, you would not hesitate to choose the big hotel. In the same way, here we have the chance to experience within our nervous systems the everlasting bliss of the internal five-star lunch, but we still choose the dirty chapati. Why? Because of our grasping emotional attitude and wrong conceptions. This shows clearly how ignorant and neurotic we really are. Check up, you'll see!

Now not only does the nectar completely fill Heruka Vajrasattva's pure nervous system, but it also overflows, the excess nectar turning into the dhyani buddha Akshobhya, who adorns the crown of Vajrasattva's head. There are different ways of interpreting the significance of this, but here it shows that Heruka Vajrasattva is in the energy stream of the buddha Akshobhya. You will remember that during an initiation there is a part where you discover to which of the five dhyani buddhas you are most closely connected, and after that, you are supposed to maintain your contact with that buddha's energy stream. This visualization relates to that.

Having given the initiation, all the buddhas melt into the divine heart of Heruka Vajrasattva, their blissful transcendental wisdom becoming inseparably one with his. Again, this visualization of the initiating buddhas not returning to their original places but dissolving into Vajrasattva's heart has profound psychological significance and benefit in terms of your developing the realization of union-oneness.

At the center of a moon disc at Heruka Vajrasattva's divine heart stands the seed syllable HUM, surrounded by the letters of the hundred syllable Heruka Vajrasattva mantra standing counterclockwise around the edge of the moon disc.

OFFERINGS AND PRAISE TO HERUKA VAJRASATTVA

OM VAJRASATTVA ARGHAM...SHABDA PRATICCHA HUM SVAHA
OM VAJRASATTVA OM AH HUM
*Nondual divine wisdom, magnificent inner jewel ornament of all
mother sentient beings; supreme, unchanging, everlasting great bliss;
indestructible, magnificent wisdom mind that releases all sentient
beings from all negativities of body, speech, and mind, especially broken vows and pledges: to you I prostrate.*

(Optional: long or short outer mandala offerings.)

SECRET MANDALA

*The right view of shunyata is one with the wisdom of great bliss. This
wisdom transforms into Mount Meru, the sun, the moon, and all
other phenomena in the universe. I offer everything magnificent to
you, ocean of great kindness, the one who is liberated and who liberates all others as well.*

INNER MANDALA

*Please bless me and all other sentient beings to be released immediately
from the three poisons, for I am offering without the slightest hesitation
or attachment all objects of my greed, hatred, and ignorance; friends,
enemies, and strangers; and my body and all possessions. Please accept
all this.*

Make the eight offerings as you did before. These are followed by the inner
offering (Tib. *nang-chö*).

Our samsaric mind views all phenomena as either pure or impure, and
dualistically we grasp at and cling to the objects that constitute our impermanent five aggregates. Through the yoga method we transform our five
aggregates into blissful transcendental wisdom, which is beyond duality and
of the nature of the five dhyani buddhas, and offer it. That is why it is called
the inner offering.

Next, we praise the divine wisdom of nonduality, the magnificent inner
jewel ornament of all mother sentient beings, whose nature is unchanging,
everlasting great bliss. This is Heruka Vajrasattva, who by the power of that

blissful wisdom releases all mother sentient beings from all the negative energy of broken vows and nonvirtuous actions of body, speech, and mind. We prostrate to that sublime indestructible mind of wisdom.

Then we offer the mandala. In the secret mandala offering we are saying that the understanding of the ultimate nature, shunyata, is one with blissful, simultaneously born wisdom. This wisdom is transformed into Mount Meru, the sun and the moon, and all other phenomena in the universe. We offer the magnificence of all existence to Heruka Vajrasattva, the ocean of great kindness who is himself liberated and who liberates all others as well.

5~ The Purification

"Bhagawan Vajrasattva, please purify all negativities and broken and damaged pledges of myself and other sentient beings."

Because of this request, brilliant light radiates from the mantra rosary and the HUM *at the divine heart. It purifies all negativities and obscurations of all sentient beings and becomes an offering for all buddhas and bodhisattvas. The essence of the perfect qualities of their holy body, speech, and mind returns in the form of light, which dissolves into the* HUM *and the mantra rosary.*

[From the HUM *and the mantra rosary] a stream of blissful white amrita energy begins to flow down through the chakras of the divine couple. It flows out through the chakra of union and enters my crown chakra. This stream of amrita of transcendental wisdom fills my whole body, destroying all the negativities and obscurations of my body, speech, and mind. These are completely purified.*

FIRST YOU REQUEST Heruka Vajrasattva—destroyer of all defilements, who possesses all realizations and has transcended this world—to purify you and all other sentient beings of all negativities of body, speech, and mind and all broken and degenerated tantric pledges and commitments.

Much light radiates from the HUM and mantra rosary at the divine hearts of Heruka Vajrasattva and his consort, filling all of space in the ten directions, purifying the negativities of all sentient beings and making offerings for the enjoyment of the buddhas and their sons, the bodhisattvas. The pure essence of the transcendental wisdom of all holy beings' body, speech, and mind returns in the form of light, dissolving into the HUM and mantra rosary at the hearts of Vajrasattva and his consort. From these, vast quantities of blissful white kundalini *(amrita)* energy pour down his central channel. The essence of this kundalini energy is his blissful transcendent wisdom. Its energy is inexhaustible—the exact opposite of our limited energy, which always runs out quickly and requires us to eat to replenish it. When you are doing this visualization, you should also visualize the blissful white kundalini energy pouring down the central channel of Heruka Vajrasattva's consort, Dorje Nyema.

The blissful white kundalini energy pours down their central channels, past their navel and sex chakras, and leaves their pure bodies from the point where they are joined in union. It continues down through the moon and lotus seats, which, being in the nature of transcendent wisdom, offer no resistance. It enters you through the crown chakra, rushing down through your central channel with the force of a powerful waterfall. It is very important that you visualize this torrent of white nectar as overwhelmingly powerful. It surges into your body and spreads through your entire system. This white energy is not physical, but somehow it feels incredibly real. You are also filled with radiant light and almost totally overcome with bliss. All defilements of your body, speech, and mind disappear without a trace.

MANTRA RECITATION[7]

> OM VAJRA HERUKA SAMAYAM ANUPALAYA. HERUKA TENOPATISHTHA.
> DRIDHO ME BHAVA, SUTOSHYO ME BHAVA, SUPOSHYO ME BHAVA,
> ANURAKTO ME BHAVA. SARVA SIDDHIM ME PRAYACCHA. SARVA KARMA
> SUCHA ME CHITTAM SHREYAM KURU, HUM! HA HA HA HA HOH!
> BHAGAVAN VAJRA HERUKA MA ME MUNCHA. HERUKA BHAVA MAHA
> SAMAYA SATTVA AH HUM PHAT!

Now recite the hundred-syllable mantra of Heruka Vajrasattva. There are three different meditation techniques for you to use while you recite it. The first is called *yän-de*. The blissful white kundalini energy rushes into your central channel. It spreads throughout your nervous system, flushing out all negativities through the openings and pores of the lower part of your body. There are various ways of visualizing the negativities as they leave your body; you can choose that which is most effective for your mind. You can visualize the three poisonous minds of ignorance, attachment, and aversion coming out in the form of pigs, chickens, and snakes, respectively. Or you can simply visualize all your negative energy in the form of what you consider to be the worst kind of sentient being, such as scorpions, crabs, snakes, and worms, or as thick black tar or dirty sump oil.

Some people might think it strange to be flushing insects, reptiles, and crustaceans from their bodies, but in fact, there are many sentient beings living inside us. We have a symbiotic relationship with some of these and would not survive without them.

Our bodies also harbor worms: long worms, short worms, and many other kinds as well. It is not through chance but through karma that they are there. We are repaying them our karmic debt. In the past we took from them; now they are taking from us. We took their food and left them none; therefore, they have come into our stomach to eat ours. Even the greediest people in the world, who through great attachment cannot share anything with others, have no choice but to share their food when the worms move in. Karma is strong; there is no way out. Even when you get rid of the worms, they return. They take your health and, sometimes, even your life. There are many ways you can lose your life; don't think it needs someone to attack you with a knife or something like that.

Feel that you have been completely purified, especially of gross negativities. We often say that our old habits are difficult to get rid of, but that's not true; at least, the reasons are not physical—it is our minds that make things difficult. We always feel bliss physically; we are so physically oriented. We believe things to be physically difficult for all sorts of external reasons. When things aren't going well we blame our parents: "My mother did this; my father did that. My mother is like this; my father like that...." It is not our bodies but our minds that make life difficult.

If it really were your body alone that caused problems, how could you sit cross-legged for as long as you do? You were not brought up to sit like that. It is your mind that allows you to do so. When you sit cross-legged and meditate, you feel comfortable, your mind is more easily controlled, and that small experience gives you enough interest to continue. As you do so, you feel increasingly comfortable. This does not come about for physical reasons; such control comes from your mind. Therefore, the process of the yoga method is for the blissful transcendental energy to wash away your ego and gravitational attachment to sense pleasures, leaving you completely purified.

The next technique to use while reciting the mantra is called *män-de*. Here, the blissful kundalini energy fills your entire nervous system, starting at the bottom and going all the way up to the top. As it rises, all your negativities float up on the surface of this blissful energy and exit through the openings and pores of the upper part of your body. It is similar to the way that garbage lying at the bottom of a bucket rises to the top as you fill it with water. As the nectar fills your body, you experience great bliss. Feel that you have been completely purified, especially of subtle negativities.

The third visualization is called *pung-de*. Here, the emphasis is on light instead of the white kundalini energy. Limitless blissful radiant light emanates from Heruka Vajrasattva's heart in a powerful beam that bursts through his sex chakra and your crown chakra and enters your central channel. It is white but has a rainbow-like quality with red, yellow, green, and blue in it as well. The instant this brilliant light enters your body it completely dispels the darkness of your doubt-wracked, indecisive mind and your ignorance, attachment, and aversion; all of these disappear forever. It is like switching on a light in a dark room, where the darkness vanishes instantly and no longer exists anywhere. It doesn't go out the window, does it? It simply vanishes. Thus, there is no space for darkness or impurity anywhere in your brain, throat, or any other part of your nervous system. You are as clear as crystal. Feel that you have been completely purified, especially of the most subtle negativities.

When you are in retreat, you can do each of these purifying techniques in each session by dividing the period for mantra recitation into three, or spend an entire session on each method separately, using the next technique in the following session.

When you are not in retreat, it is highly beneficial for you to practice this meditation every day, reciting the Heruka Vajrasattva mantra twenty-one times with each of the three techniques. The best time to do it is at night, just before you go to bed. During the day you are so busy that you are likely to meditate distractedly. Therefore, as the last thing at night, you completely purify all the nonvirtues you created during the day and go to sleep feeling free and liberated instead of sad and bothered by the day's negativities. Because we are constantly involved in so much activity, we need a powerful yoga method such as this. There is so little time to purify.

The weight of unpurified negative karmic imprints increases exponentially, but if we recite the Vajrasattva mantra just twenty-one times at the end of each day, even the negative karma of tantric vows broken that day will not increase. If this method has the power to prevent from increasing the negative karma that results from broken tantric root vows—which are the highest vows and most serious transgressions of all—of course it can stop the increase of negativities from actions that are nonvirtuous by nature (natural negativities), such as killing and so forth, and other broken vows. Moreover, if we recite this mantra properly one hundred thousand times, all negativities whatsoever can be completely purified.

While you recite the mantra, it is essential that you remain in single-pointed concentration; do not allow any samsaric thoughts to interrupt your meditation. If you can do your practice with good concentration and stable penetrative insight, it will be tremendously effective in eradicating impure concepts and the darkness of emotional obstacles. That purification comes from the power of your concentrated meditation, but the mantra too has power of its own. Sometimes it brings you telepathic visions of things that are happening on the other side of the planet. When you purify the obstacles of narrow emotional concepts, you will discover a whole new world.

Mantra can also enable you to read the minds of others. That can cause you pleasure or pain; it depends what the other person is thinking! Many other things can happen too—it all depends upon the individual; when people retreat, they have different experiences and receive different realizations. It is very difficult for us to tell who has realized what. Some become American Vajrasattvas, some Asian Vajrasattvas, some European Vajrasattvas, some Australian Vajrasattvas...who knows!

6- The Concluding Practices

OM VAJRASATTVA ARGHAM...SHABDA PRATICCHA HUM SVAHA
OM VAJRASATTVA OM AH HUM

Nondual divine wisdom...to you I prostrate.

Through ignorance and delusion, I have broken and damaged my pledges. Holy Guru, who has the power to liberate me, my inner master, holder of the vajra, whose essence is great compassion, Lord of all migratory beings, to you I go for refuge.

Vajrasattva says, "Oh son (or daughter) of good family, your negativities and obscurations and damaged and broken pledges are cleansed and purified." Then he dissolves into me. My three doors (of body, speech, and mind) become inseparably one with Vajrasattva's holy body, speech, and mind.

FOLLOWING THE RECITATION of the mantra we again make the eight outer offerings and the inner offering, offer praise to Heruka Vajrasattva as before, and make the prayer of supplication.

You declare to Heruka Vajrasattva that because of unawareness caused by ignorance, you have not known what you have been doing and have acted contrary to the pure energy of your *samaya,* your sacred pledge. Actually, while you are living at a monastery or a meditation center, you can't really assess the progress you have made. It's when you get back home or into the city that your reality shows. While you are practicing in a group, you feel very strong and think that it will be easy to maintain a daily practice, get up for meditation early in the morning, and so forth.

But when you're back home, you sleep late, get up slowly, talk, plan the day with your friends, have breakfast...and all of a sudden it is nine o'clock, and there is no time for meditation because you have to rush off to work. Then, it is lunchtime, teatime, dinnertime, and finally—too late for meditation—bedtime. And so your life finishes. What you really want is wisdom, but you are not doing anything to get it. You spend all your time working for money. You don't give wisdom a chance. Analyze your day and you will see how ridiculously samsaric your life is.

It is not that you really want to destroy yourself; you are not so ignorant that you want to miss out on the blissful energy of transcendental wisdom. But you make your outer world so interesting that you have to spend your whole time watching it. Thus, you never give yourself a chance to sit and meditate on your internal world. The outer world runs day and night; it will rotate forever. And although you don't want it to, your Dharma wisdom declines.

This is like what happens at our Kopan Monastery in Nepal. In the monsoon it rains so much that there is too much water. Then, the sun shines and gradually the water dries up until we are left with dust blowing in the wind. Your Dharma wisdom is like this water: it evaporates until all that is left in your mind is the dust of the defilements. You wonder, "I really thought I had something but there's nothing there. What went wrong?" You feel empty inside. There is wisdom there, but you are not giving it a chance. Wisdom cannot come in a day. First you have to cut your old conceptions, and then slowly, slowly, the vibration of wisdom will grow to guide you.

When students who have lived and studied Dharma in the East go home to the West, that is what happens. Whatever wisdom they have gained decreases without their even noticing. They cannot understand how it happened and can hardly believe that it has. Then, they rationalize, "Oh, what I learned from the lamas must be an Eastern thing. It doesn't work in the West." What doesn't work? If you don't use something, how can it work? If you use Lord Buddha's wisdom, it works; if you don't use it, it doesn't work. It gets rusty! Also, it is very difficult to detect small increases and decreases in wisdom; you have to be very sensitive and watch carefully. Then, you will notice how your mind goes up and down.

If you are not sensitive, if you do not observe your mind, you will never notice what it is doing. This is how dogs behave. A dog's mind is up and down a thousand times a day, but in the evening there is no way for him to analyze his day's experiences. He cannot remember. A dog has no idea whether his mind is developing or degenerating, and neither do you. You should not be like that. While you are preoccupied with your ego's illusory projections, your life is running out.

In the second half of the prayer of supplication you take refuge in your lama, who has the power to liberate other beings. Indians and Nepalis use the word "lama" to refer to any Tibetan. Here it has its true meaning of spiritual master, or guru. He holds in his mind the inner vajra of the great blissful transcendental wisdom, his nature is great kindness and compassion, and he is the leader of all sentient beings.

Then Heruka Vajrasattva replies to you, saying, "My son (or daughter), all your negativities, obscurations, and broken samayas have been completely purified." After that, Dorje Nyema melts into light and dissolves into his heart. Heruka Vajrasattva also melts into light, which enters your central channel and dissolves into your heart. Your three doors of body, speech, and mind and the holy body, speech, and mind of Heruka Vajrasattva become inseparably one. You remain in union-oneness, enjoying the bliss of the shunyata experience with full single-pointed concentration, completely beyond all dualistic views that differentiate between subject and object. This is the highest possible enjoyment.

While you are saying the prayer, you should meditate. After you have finished the prayer, continue meditating with single-pointed concentration on the feeling of unity and avoid all dualistic thoughts of *that-this* and "I am...." You might have noticed that in pujas, Tibetan monks chant and stop, chant and stop. Some people probably think it's weird, but they are meditating on the important points of the practice, not just rushing through it without pausing to think. When you practice the sadhana of Heruka Vajrasattva, you should also do it in this way. And after the dedication, you should not jump up immediately and rush out of the room, but remain a while in single-pointed concentration on your oneness with Heruka Vajrasattva, who is also completely one with your guru.

Make sure that you understand the divine wisdom of Heruka Vajrasattva's holy body, speech, and mind, without projecting, "I am." And also, as I emphasized before, don't have expectations, such as, "Oh, maybe today I'll see Heruka Vajrasattva." Not only is this unnecessary, but it also helps develop your superstitions. So, abandon such thoughts. Also, especially in retreat, don't worry that you're going to get sick. The worry itself will make you sick. Just relax, and have great faith in Guru Heruka Vajrasattva and karma.

DEDICATION

Because of this merit, may I quickly become Heruka Vajrasattva and lead each and every sentient being into his divine enlightened realm.

PART 2

Retreat Instructions

7~ *Getting Ready for Retreat*

WHAT QUALIFICATIONS ARE NECESSARY for a person to retreat on the maha-anuttara yoga tantra aspect of Vajrasattva? The basic requirement is that you must be a serious, sincere practitioner, free from hypocrisy and enthusiastically determined to attain the everlasting peaceful realization of enlightenment. You should be practicing what your teacher has shown you—not a misinterpretation projected by your own mind.

In the experience of yogis and yoginis in the Tibetan tradition, it is necessary that, as a general qualification, you have received teachings on the graduated path to enlightenment in a perfect manner and have put them into practice. As a specific qualification, you must have received initiation into the maha-anuttara yoga tantra aspect of Vajrasattva. If you are so qualified, it is possible for you to actualize this practice.

The reason that knowledge and experience of the graduated path to enlightenment are essential is that the three principal aspects of the path—renunciation, bodhichitta, and correct understanding of shunyata—are indispensable prerequisites for the attainment of tantric realizations. Without them your practice of the yoga method will not be effective. It will remain superficial and intellectual, and it will never become one with your mind. If on this basis you receive the necessary initiation from a perfectly qualified master, you are fully equipped to make a successful retreat on Heruka Vajrasattva, and you are most fortunate.

WHERE TO RETREAT

Where should a properly qualified person retreat? Not just any place will do. The ideal place to retreat is one that gives you a sense of reality, not one that is a big hallucination, a polluted projection of the deluded mind.

Sometimes we are unwise; we try to meditate in a place that's like a furnace and complain when we can no longer stand the heat. A fire's nature is to burn, so if you stick your finger into a fire, then it'll get burned. It's up to you to choose the appropriate mandala for the way in which you want to develop—just like you should choose shoes that fit your feet!

Of course, if you have great mind control, you can retreat anywhere; your controlled vibration will even affect others. But if you are weak, the uncontrolled vibrations of others will affect you; your small candlelight of wisdom will be blown out. In retreat we try to gain control over our minds—but we are babies with a long way to go. Baby minds need ideal conditions. Actually, our minds are worse than those of babies. Babies grasp at whatever they see, but we not only grasp at things we see, we intellectualize about them as well. As our wisdom is limited, we must put ourselves in the right environment. If our minds were free from confusion, we would have no need to worry about the environment; we wouldn't even need to retreat on Vajrasattva.

It is very important to think carefully about the place in which you are putting yourself—not only where you are going to retreat, but also where you are going to live. Decide what you want to learn, and live near where you can be taught. In Western cities you can choose your environment quite easily. If you want to spend your time at the movies, you can live near a cinema. You have the freedom to do that. In other words, you have some control over your karma, the way your life develops. You are not powerless; through your choices, you create your karma. If you want to retreat, you arrange the circumstances accordingly. That is creating karma.

In the lamas' experience, the ideal place is a beautiful, natural environment where the atmosphere is quiet, peaceful, and relaxed. You can see snowy mountains, and there are wild flowers, medicinal plants, pleasing, natural smells, and fresh, clean water. Avoid places that are dirty, close to roads, traffic, and people. Environments that are dangerous and those where poisonous plants grow should also be avoided. Do not retreat in a place where you automatically feel insecure and nervous.

Places where holy beings live are excellent: they have a good vibration that I am sure Westerners, who are very sensitive, can feel. Such ideal places are usually very isolated. In Tibet we used to study in the monasteries and qualify for retreats as explained above, and then go to an isolated place to meditate. These places were extremely simple, not like the Western luxury "retreats" to which rich people escape when they do not want to meet anybody. Westerners really know how to enjoy themselves, even in isolation! However it is all done out of self-cherishing. Ascetics' retreats are exactly the opposite. Many Tibetan yogis would abandon the world for years—or even a lifetime—in order to ensure the perfect retreat conditions. Some even sealed themselves into doorless caves, receiving food through a small hole in the wall. You can also retreat in a monastery or at a Dharma center. In the East many meditators used to retreat near cemeteries. Such places are usually quiet. You build your hut away from the part of the cemetery frequented by visitors and, with deep understanding of impermanence and death, retreat.

So choose carefully. The best place is one in which you feel secure in the knowledge that from beginning to end, there will be no distractions. Of course there is no real security in our samsaric lives, but somehow you should feel that the place you have chosen is as good as it is possible to find and that you will be able to retreat there effectively.

WHEN TO START RETREAT

Generally, the type and purpose of a retreat determine its starting time. Since Heruka Vajrasattva is a mother tantra, a retreat on this deity should start on the tenth or the twenty-fifth of the Tibetan month. These are auspicious dates for tantric yoga, when there is much movement of the dakas and dakinis and your nervous system can easily be blessed. Because of the intensity of the daka-dakini energy at those times, you can discover everlasting blissful energy within the chakras of your nervous system simply by starting on either of these days. For the same reason, it is best to start retreats on deities of the mother tantra class in the evening after sunset.

SOME GENERAL PREPARATIONS

If you are doing retreat alone, you may need someone to help with the shopping and cooking. Your helper should be totally positive toward you and what you are doing, and you should have a good relationship with this person. If your helper thinks that you are ridiculous or that what you are doing is evil, it will be a great disturbance to your mind. Similarly, if you are retreating with a group, it should not include people with whom you cannot get along. It is important that you create the best possible conditions for your retreat.

If you don't have a helper and are not in a group retreat where eating arrangements are usually made for you, you should try to obtain most of the food you'll need for the duration of your retreat beforehand. Don't get too much; rather, limit yourself to basic things. This is what we used to do in Tibet.

Before starting retreat you should cut your connections with the outside world and abandon whatever expectations you have of it. Although you are retreating in order to cut off your ignorance, this internal separation is a gradual process that begins with detaching yourself from the outside world. You must finish all your letter writing and other business before you begin, otherwise your retreat will constantly be disturbed by distracting thoughts of, "I have to do this," "I really should do that...." Even if a beautiful present arrives, you should not accept it until the retreat has finished. Make sure that while your body is in the retreat room, your mind doesn't wander back home.

You should do your retreat as strictly as possible, continuously keeping your mind in the sphere of the transcendental process. Sitting in a cave while your mind keeps wandering back home is not being in retreat. Your body, speech, and mind should be focused on the same thing. Most of the time your mind is split and agitated, and you cannot do mundane things without coming down from a state of higher awareness. In retreat you must learn how to unify the two—the mundane and the transcendent.

Before your retreat starts you must decide who you will allow yourself to meet and how far from the place of retreat you can go. Thus you might decide, "During this retreat I shall talk to my parents but no one else," or, "During this retreat I shall go as far as the spring to wash but no further." Such decisions are very helpful for your mind. In Tibetan we call it *tsam war gyu* ("putting retreat"), which means you'll meet certain people if necessary, but no others. Even if your best friend turns up unexpectedly, you should not meet him or her. The more outside people you meet, the more samsaric information you collect, and you gain mental pollution instead of wisdom. It is best not to talk to even the other people in your retreat until lunchtime, and then the conversation should be only about Dharma—not all your past experiences, future plans, or other gossip. If you are feeling very tense and need to talk to relax, as a kind of therapy, perhaps that is acceptable, but you should be careful not to waste your own energy or that of others. If there is something urgent or important to say, you can write a note.

You should be careful about what you read in retreat and avoid all samsaric literature completely: newspapers, magazines, novels, technical books, poetry, and astrological charts. Even certain Dharma books should be avoided during retreat. Those that deal with philosophical doctrine are too dry and may only add to your confusion and superstitions instead of enhancing the psychological process that retreat is supposed to be. You can read books on the graduated path or commentaries on the yoga method; however, even these should not be read too much. Read only books that help you. Doing glance meditation on the graduated path during the breaks is especially useful because it directs your energy into the right channel. Sometimes in retreat your mind can veer toward extremes; the graduated path can bring you back to center.

One of the most important preparations is your determination to succeed. You should feel, "I am so fortunate to have this perfect human life in which I have the opportunity to receive the everlasting blissful realizations of Heruka Vajrasattva. Therefore no matter what samsaric experiences I have during this retreat, be they good or bad, I shall control my mind." Thus whether you experience samsaric happiness or difficulties, you do not overreact but take the middle way.

For example, one morning you might wake up with a headache and think that you are too sick to go to the session. A little headache won't kill you! You are here for retreat. That means you have to exercise control. You can meditate with a headache. Or perhaps a beautiful, ego-breaking present from your parents suddenly arrives, and you lose control and get very excited: "Wow! I've been waiting for this for more than a year; I must take it right away." You should not do this. Do not get excited. It doesn't matter; have control.

What to eat

One of the most important things you can do to ensure the success of your retreat is to stay healthy. Some people think, "Oh, I'm doing Dharma; I don't need anything." That's wrong. When you're in retreat trying to develop Dharma wisdom, it makes more sense to feed yourself even better than you normally do—and you know how much you usually need to take care of your samsaric body. Some people equate retreat with what they imagine to be asceticism: uncomfortable conditions, an unhealthy environment, poor food, feeling hungry and thirsty, not sleeping, wearing rags, and so forth. This is completely wrong. First, these are not the signs of asceticism. Second, tantric yoga has the methods of transforming all pleasures and comforts into the rapid path to enlightenment. Therefore, as long as you can use it wisely, you can have whatever you like. You should stay in a clean, healthy place, have a beautiful blissful room, a comfortable seat, a good place to sleep, and plenty of good food. Treat yourself with respect—after all, you are Heruka Vajrasattva! Offer yourself nice clothes and eat well.

This does not mean you should overeat. When you are doing a kriya tantra retreat, the food restrictions are quite inflexible. In a highest yoga tantra retreat you have a bit more latitude but should still avoid what we call "black" foods—meat (especially chicken, pork, and fish), eggs, garlic, onions, and radish. Garlic is very heavy and disturbs your nervous system either by making it feel too full or by causing too much movement within it. If the onions are not too strong, they're probably okay. The problem with radish is that it causes gas and makes you break wind. Fruit and vegetables are good, as are so-called "white" foods like milk, yogurt, and cheese, which are considered pure. The food you eat should be clean and healthy. You should not accept food from people suffering from contagious diseases, like tuberculosis. You can also have muesli, chocolate, and even Vegemite, which, despite its color, is not a black food! Some people like to fast during retreat; however, in a long retreat you should fast with moderation.

If you do not eat properly, there is the danger that your nervous system and the energy winds of your body will become disturbed. A strong retreat itself has the tendency to do this, and a poor diet compounds the risk. Such disturbances manifest as nervous breakdowns, "spacing out," or physical pains, especially in the heart chakra. Sometimes you will get pain in the heart because your visualization of the nectar that rushes down from Vajra-sattva's heart into your central channel is too concrete. You are concentrating strongly at your heart and think that something physical is hitting it. This is a fundamental error, but it is much easier to develop such symptoms if you do not take care of your health.

Sometimes retreaters experience so much bliss and joy in a session that they want to keep going without food. This is the baby mind speaking—don't trust it. Take your meals as scheduled. While breakfast and lunch are fine, there's a question about whether or not you should eat dinner. It's better to avoid eating in the evening because a full stomach impairs concentration. It depends on the individual—we're all different. Some people can eat only a little at a time; for them, I'd say dinner is okay. Those who can manage a good breakfast and lunch should keep the evening meal very light or, preferably, skip it altogether. Be flexible; food is not all that important. Just stay healthy.

Sometimes people take the eight Mahayana precepts during retreat.[8] On those days, of course, you can't have breakfast or dinner. You can choose whether to take them every day or not; it's up to you. In my opinion the best days to take them are the full and new moon days. Taking precepts gives you great energy and is another excellent way of taking action to purify yourself.

Cleaning the retreat place

Since you are going to clean yourself inside, you should also clean your external environment. To give yourself the best chance of success you must keep environmental distractions to a minimum. You have to create an environment that suits your needs. When you do worldly business, you set up your office in a certain way. Since your business is now retreat, you should act accordingly.

The meditation room should be comfortable, clean, and very tidy. Do not leave things lying all over the place; their disorderly vibration will agitate your mind. Nor should you distract your mind by having objects of attachment in your room. No animals, including dogs, should be allowed to enter. After cleaning your room you can sprinkle it with saffron, sandalwood, rose water, or any other kind of perfume. Instead of putting perfume on your body with attachment, put it around the retreat room—just walking into the room becomes a completely blissful experience. You should also sprinkle some blessed inner-offering nectar around the room. This should all be done before you start retreat and then again every morning. Similarly, the room in which you sleep should not be decorated with pictures or other objects that stimulate your delusions.

The meditation seat

The next thing to do is arrange your meditation seat. It should be as comfortable as possible; you should feel as though you could sit there for twenty-four hours without a break, experiencing only bliss. The seat should not be flat; rather, you should have a small pillow beneath your buttocks, making them higher than your knees. This will help you keep your back straight and prevent you from getting pins and needles in your legs. A thin, lumpy, uncomfortable seat does not necessarily signify renunciation.

Beneath the seat there should be a right-pointing swastika drawn on the floor in chalk or rice, or on a piece of paper. The swastika is an ancient Indian symbol of auspiciousness. The word comes from the Sanskrit *svasti,* which means well-being. It also symbolizes the indestructible, or *vajra,* seat that Buddha sat upon at Bodhgaya when he became enlightened. The buddhas of this fortunate eon attain enlightenment at Bodhgaya. Since we ourselves are retreating in order to reach enlightenment, we too should have a vajra seat, not an up-and-down, here-today-gone-tomorrow, yo-yo seat. If you're in a boat, you follow the rise and fall of the ocean's movement. Your meditation seat should not be like that. Since we cannot put an actual vajra beneath our seat, we use this symbolic representation. The combination of an indestructible seat with an indestructible, pure, enlightened attitude makes your retreat really worthwhile.

You can also put two kinds of grass under your seat. One is *kusha* grass, the grass that some Indian brooms are made of. Two bits of this can be arranged so that their tips point toward the center of the swastika from the back, their stems pointing backward. At Bodhgaya, Buddha sat on a cushion of kusha grass. Using the same grass reminds us of Lord Buddha's meditation experiences, especially his decision to remain seated on that grass until he reached enlightenment, no matter how difficult it was or how many hardships he had to bear. Kusha grass is composed of hundreds of slender strands, all lying parallel, orderly, close together, and pointing the one way. It symbolizes strong, single-pointed concentration and clear visualization—all your energy flowing in one direction.

The other kind of grass is called *tsadurwa* in Tibetan; it is like couch or *kikuyu* grass. This is arranged in the same way as the kusha grass, two bits pointing in toward the center of the swastika from the back. The pieces you choose should have as many joints as possible. This type of grass is considered auspicious for a long life.

Once you have arranged your seat, you should not move it for any reason. Westerners always want to shake out their cushions or leave them in the sun, but in retreat this is not allowed. Do not move your seat to another part of the room once the retreat has started. You have to control your schizophrenic mind.

In a group retreat there should be plenty of space between one person and the next. You don't have to squash up like Tibetans in puja. I remember a student once having trouble because he put his seat on a damp section of the floor, and his small carpet became moldy and rotted. Therefore it is important to be careful at the beginning, when you are first deciding where to put your seat.

At home you should also try to have a special meditation seat, preferably not in your bedroom, which tends to have a strong samsaric vibration. If you can set up a shrine in a separate room or in a quiet corner of your house and use it only for meditation, it will help you a lot. The Dharma trip and the samsara trip are completely different—unless you have a great realization of bodhichitta, they don't go together at all.

In front of you there should be a small table for your vajra *(dorje),* bell *(drilbu),* damaru drum, kapala, and, if you need it, sadhana text. The kapala contains the inner-offering liquid, which is usually black tea with a special, blessed inner-offering pill dissolved in it. However in a group retreat it is not necessary for everyone to have these things. It's enough if just one or two of the retreaters have them. If you don't have an actual dorje and bell, a drawing of them will do.

THE ROSARY

You should have a special rosary that you use only in retreats and do not allow other people to see. This rosary should be treated with great respect. Some retreats require you to use a rosary made of bone or some other specific substance. It should not be worn around your wrist or neck, and once the retreat has started, it should not be taken out of the room—leave it on your table. You must never take your rosary into the bathroom. Before the retreat starts, the rosary should be blessed by a lama, and each morning, at the beginning of the first session, you should bless it with the mantra OM RUTSIRA MANI PRAWA TAYA HUM. Say this mantra seven times and blow on the rosary.

How to arrange the altar

Arranging the altar

After you have cleaned the room, arrange your altar. Put your image of Heruka Vajrasattva on the altar, or, if it is a picture, hang it on the wall above. You should not put other images on your altar. During this retreat Heruka Vajrasattva is the most important deity—your manifestation of universal reality. You don't need any others.

Ideally you should use three different offering cakes *(tormas).*[9] In Tibet we used to make these out of roasted barley flour *(tsampa),* but in the West you can use chocolate, candy, biscuits, cake, or other foods instead.

The main torma (shown at the top) is your offering to Heruka Vajrasattva. You bless it with the blissful transcendental wisdom of Vajrasattva through the methods of tantric yoga. Leave it on your altar until the end of your retreat.[10] When this torma is made of tsampa, a little alcohol is usually added, which by its nature has the energy of expansion and development. This symbolizes the meditator's development of kundalini energy through the yoga method.[11] The second torma (shown immediately below the first) is for the special wrathful protector of Heruka, who pacifies all uncontrolled energy. Once you place it on your altar, you should not remove it until you have finished your retreat.[12]

No matter where you retreat, there will be local deities, or spirits *(shi-dak),* who possess or control that place. To prevent them from taking offense at your intrusion and causing you harm, it is necessary to make an offering to them. Again, this does not have to be a Tibetan torma (as shown just to the right of the second torma above) but can be rice or any of the other things mentioned before. It also stays on your altar for the duration of your retreat.[13] Visualize your offering as whatever those sentient beings would need and enjoy, and feel that you are also offering your body and speech to these beings, sacrificing yourself for the sake of *all* sentient beings.

As you make the offering think, "Please let me do here what I have to do: purify myself and gain wisdom and compassion for the sake of all sentient beings. I am not trying to take this place away from you; I am just using it for a short time. Therefore please do not worry or be angry, jealous, or afraid. Please have compassion, help me, and do not interfere. Take this offering and anything else you need." Visualize that the spirits take the offering, are very happy and satisfied, and give you permission to use the place in safety. In the Hinayana sutras Buddha explained that before a monastery is built permission should be sought from the spirits who own the land, trees, and other things at that place. Without these offerings, the spirits may get angry and harm us physically or mentally.

Offering bowls, candles, butter lamps or other light offerings, flowers, and food should also be placed on your altar. Change the water and make fresh light and incense offerings before each session. The light you offer symbolizes the inner light of wisdom that you are trying to develop; incense represents your pure morality.

Why do we offer so much water? It's not because Vajrasattva is always thirsty; there's no such thing as a deity actually taking your offerings. No, the problem is our miserliness. We usually give with the spirit of attachment; this sneaky spirit is somehow completely unified with our gift. Water is so freely available that when you offer it, you don't grasp at it, and in this way you get used to giving without attachment or expectation. Therefore offering water is very useful: it costs you nothing, and you get great benefit for just a little work. Also, water has many precious qualities and contains the energy of all kinds of precious jewels.[14] Bless the water you offer with the mantra OM AH HUM, which symbolizes Vajrasattva's enlightened body, speech, and mind. Although it looks like you're putting water on your altar, because of the blessed transformation, you are actually offering the blissful nectar of transcendental wisdom and compassion.

As I mentioned before, it is highly beneficial to make physical offerings as often as you can. The lazy mind will say, "Real offerings are internal; I don't need to go through the ritual of making all these external offerings on the altar." Don't be fooled by laziness—it is much better for you to engage in the action of giving. The only exception to this is if you are completely in samadhi. Spending your time absorbed in single-pointed concentration may be more important. When you have plenty of time to do other things but no time to make a decent altar, it shows how misconceived your samsaric value judgments really are.

A small portion of your food or drink should be blessed and offered on the altar before you take it yourself. Offer a little of your morning tea in a small bowl and a portion of your lunch on a plate. This is very useful for loosening attachment and developing the perfection of generosity.

At the end of the day, the food you have offered can be taken off the altar and eaten the next day. You do not have to restrict your offerings to the material ones I have been talking about. You can transform them mentally into infinite offerings of the best kinds of nectar, flowers, incense, lights, perfumes, food, sound, and so forth. Along with these, offer everything else in the universe transformed into sublime blissful offerings, as we do when we offer a mandala.

There are many disciplines that help preserve the pure energy of retreat. You shouldn't take things in and out of the meditation room, especially your rosary and ritual implements, such as your vajra and bell. Animals and those not in retreat should not enter the meditation room. No one else should sleep in your bed or sit on your meditation seat. You cannot take your seat outside to air or clean it; all you can do is brush it off. You should not touch weapons or put knives, arrows, and so forth in your mouth. You should not use others' plates, cups, and cutlery or allow them to use yours. And one of the worst things you can do is to fight with other members of the group. That really breaks the retreat.

There are also many things that you can do during retreat. In a group, "karma yoga" is good. Each person has a little work to do, helping the Dharma center or serving the other members. All this should be worked out before the retreat starts and rosters drawn up so that everyone knows what his or her job is. People are needed to clean the meditation room and arrange the altar before each session. Help may be needed in the kitchen or with serving food. Some people might like to do gardening. Others might like to transcribe tapes or edit teachings for publication. These activities are good and help keep you balanced, but while doing them, you must maintain the mindfulness that I have already described.

During the breaks you can also do other practices: your daily commitments, prostrations, and so forth. You can also recite Vajrasattva mantras, but remember, these don't count toward your retreat total.

All these practices may not be the most important thing you can do, but they are very useful in your spiritual development.

8~ The Retreat Session

THE DAILY SCHEDULE

IN GENERAL it is best to start your retreat with sessions of an hour's duration at the most. These are recommended because, if a session is short, you will do it well. Sessions in which you are alert and your concentration is strong are obviously better than ones in which your mind is tired and sleepy. We have been asleep for countless lives, now it's time to wake up!

The length of sessions throughout a retreat should resemble the shape of a grain of barley: pointed at the ends and wide in the middle. Thus sessions at the beginning and end of a retreat should be short and those in the middle, longer. As your retreat progresses and your meditation gains in strength, you gradually increase the length of the sessions. Toward the end of the retreat, as you prepare to face the world once more, shorten them again. If you finish your retreat still doing long, intensive sessions, your first contact with the outside world may upset you or make you sick. The vibration will be too different from what you have been experiencing.

Short sessions give you much energy. You may not want to stop meditating when the session reaches an end; nonetheless, you should. If you stop meditating only when you are exhausted, you will have no enthusiasm for the next session. The mere sight of your meditation cushion will nauseate you. This is obviously not good. Or, as I mentioned before, you might feel so blissful and energetic that you want to continue meditating all day. If you do that, the next day you will almost certainly feel the opposite and not want to meditate at all. Gradually increasing the length of your sessions ensures that you always finish with an alert mind eager for more meditation. Treat your baby mind wisely.

One Tibetan lama recommended eighteen sessions a day! Perhaps we could begin with a more modest eight. Get up early enough to ensure that your first session finishes before sunrise. Take a coffee break and do another session before breakfast. Between breakfast and lunch you can do two more sessions separated by a fifteen-minute break. After lunch you can rest, work, study teachings on the graduated path or the Heruka Vajrasattva commentary, or do your daily commitments and other meditations. Then you can do two more sessions separated by a fifteen-minute break before afternoon tea. After tea do another session, have dinner, and do the final session of the day. The best time to conduct a discussion group is after lunch, prior to the first afternoon session. It should definitely not be after or instead of the last session of the day. That is the wrong time to stimulate discursive thought. Of course this is just a rough guide. As sessions get longer, there will be fewer each day.

By the middle of the retreat you could be doing four sessions a day: one before sunrise, one between breakfast and lunch, one between lunch and dinner, and the last one after that. However you should not be in session at sunrise, noon, sunset, or midnight. At those times the changes in the vibrations of the external environment affect your nervous system, automatically causing your mind to be distracted. Therefore, you should avoid meditating during these periods.

Tibetan monks would rise at two or three in the morning when in retreat. However in hot countries it is difficult to do without sleep. Since you are not used to this kind of discipline, if you get up too early, you will get tired very easily and that will spoil your meditation. You should stay healthy and do your sleeping in bed, not on your meditation cushion. Whatever you do, do it well.

In conclusion, it is best not to push yourself unreasonably. You cannot imitate Milarepa—don't even try. Be comfortable and relaxed, take your retreat easy, and make it worthwhile.

JUST BEFORE THE SESSION

Washing. Before each session you should clean your teeth and wash your body. If you cannot wash your whole body, you should at least wash your face, neck, arms, armpits, and feet. This will prevent your mind from getting sluggish and sleepy during the session. Having washed, you wake up, feel more comfortable, and are able to meditate with fully awakened wisdom.

Coming on time. Make sure that you come into the meditation room at least five minutes before the start of the session, especially if it is your job to arrange the altar. Do not rush in, out of breath, puffing and sweating just as the session is about to begin. Come in slowly and mindfully, do three prostrations, and sit down gently. Collect and calm your mind. Think: "On this seat I shall purify myself completely in order to attain the enlightened state of Vajrasattva for the sake of all mother sentient beings." Then, with awareness, purify your nervous system with the blessed inner offering. Dip the tip of the ring finger of your left hand into the inner offering in your kapala, touch it to your tongue, and feel the blessed energy flowing throughout your nervous system, purifying it of all negativity and filling you with blissful wisdom.

Do not disturb others. Do not talk to or disturb the members of your group when you come into the meditation room. It is best to keep the meditation room a silent area for the duration of the retreat. If you have things to do in the room, such as cleaning or arranging the altar, do them without involving others.

Arranging the altar. As I said before, make fresh offerings before each session. In a group retreat I recommend that you make an offering of five candles or butter lamps each time. Make your offerings with the pure, sincere thought that, "I am making this offering for the everlasting, blissful, divine wisdom of Heruka Vajrasattva to grow within me so that I will be able to lead all mother sentient beings to the discovery of this realization in their own minds."

BEGINNING THE SESSION

Once the session begins, there must be absolutely no talking in the meditation room. Start by taking refuge and generating bodhichitta with the prayers in the sadhana, but remember what I said before: taking refuge and generating bodhichitta are states of mind beyond words; make sure your mind becomes one with them. When the prayers finish, do not go immediately to the breath-holding exercise, but stay a while in meditation on refuge and bodhichitta. If you combine these attitudes with your mind properly at the beginning of the session, their energy will pervade your entire practice, making it far more beneficial.

SESSIONS IN GENERAL

I have already stressed the great importance of single-pointed concentration during recitation of the mantra. This cannot be overemphasized. Most of the time our minds are fully occupied by superstitions and wrong conceptions that influence everything we do. Be very careful to ensure that for the duration of the retreat your mind is completely free of these delusions; otherwise, you shall not receive the realizations that you seek. This is even more important with respect to the session, and crucial while you are reciting the mantra.

You must also avoid other activities that might disturb the session, such as talking, eating, getting up from your seat, and leaving the room to go to the toilet. Make sure you go to the toilet before the start of the session.

The great ancient yogi Padampa Sangye said that there are five things to which you must pay special attention if you want to do a perfect retreat. He said that if you do not take care of these, your retreat will be almost useless.

The first is the *power of body*. During the session you must maintain your visualization of the deity continuously. If you lose it and allow your wrong conceptions' samsaric projection of yourself to arise—"I am so-and-so; I am hungry and thirsty"—you have lost the power of body. The second is the *power of speech*. If you speak during the session, you have directly interrupted this power. Next is the *power of mind*. You lose it as soon as your single-pointed concentration is broken. The fourth is the *power of signs*. During retreat signs appear in your mind. If you come into contact with people who are not in retreat, this power is lost. Finally, there is the *power of energy:* there are negative repercussions from letting people who are not in your retreat see the image of your deity or the blessed way in which you eat. Therefore, do not allow them to do so.

We also talk about body, speech, and mind retreats. *Body retreat* means that you cut the connection with your deluded projections of your body. During retreat you are not allowed to lose the power of your body. For example when you are meditating on a samadhi female, you must not lose semen.

Speech retreat means that you avoid any ordinary conversation, which only induces mental agitation. You must retain the power of speech, which will be explained below when we discuss mantra recitation. You are not even allowed to spit.

Mind retreat means that you cut off all superstitions, the actions of the deluded mind. You keep the power of your mind by preventing any deluded, superstitious thoughts from arising.

THE SADHANA

I have compiled a Heruka Vajrasattva sadhana for the purpose of retreat [see appendix 1]. You can do it in English or Tibetan. If you do it in Tibetan, make sure you have the translation handy so that you will understand the meaning. You can do it in English, but somehow the Tibetan has a very good feeling and a kind of blessed energy associated with it.[15]

Mantra recitation

The mantra of Heruka Vajrasattva is extremely powerful. Reciting it even once shakes the very foundations of your negativities. However, for it to be effective, you must say it very clearly; one mantra recited with perfect sound has more power than a hundred mumbled indistinctly. Each syllable should be articulated cleanly, clearly, and smoothly, with a uniform rhythm and pitch. It should not be slurred or irregular, with some phrases fast and others slow, or some syllables high and others low. When you recite the mantra, whisper it quietly so that you can hear it, but the person sitting next to you cannot. Make sure your recitation doesn't disturb others.

If you do this mantra properly—with single-pointed concentration and clear visualization—it becomes transcendent, transforming your body into the bliss-pervaded divine body, your speech into divine, blissful speech, and your mind into divine, blissful wisdom. If, on the other hand, your mind is occupied by negative energy, there is not much power in your retreat, and everything remains ordinary. Therefore you should know which factors, in addition to unclear recitation, prevent your mantra from becoming transcendent.

To maintain awareness and to ensure that the mantras you count in your tally have all been said correctly, there are a number of penalties that you incur when certain faults interrupt your session. If you leave the room, get up from your seat, or speak, you cannot count any of the mantras in that session. Ideally once the session starts you should not move your legs at all. If you fall asleep, drop your rosary, lose concentration, get angry, or find yourself saying the wrong mantra, you cannot count any of the mantras that you recited on that round of the rosary. You have to go back to the first bead and start again. Losing concentration is one of the worst faults. All of a sudden you find that your mind has wandered back to your home, into a supermarket, or to a meeting with your friend; you must not allow these kinds of things to happen.

If you break wind, there is a penalty of seven mantras: you must go back seven rosary beads and continue from there. Similarly there is a penalty of five if you cough, sneeze, clear your throat, blow your nose, hiccup, or belch during recitation of the mantra. The mantra blesses your speech and breath, so you should not waste this precious energy. You should also avoid wasting your breath by blowing out candles and lamps, blowing on fires, whistling, and so forth during your retreat.

There are two ways of deciding the length of a retreat: by time or by number of mantras. The length of a Vajrasattva retreat is usually three months or the time it takes to recite one hundred thousand mantras. Actually, you should increase the number of mantras you are committed to do in any retreat by ten percent to compensate for those recited badly. Thus in a Vajrasattva retreat you should recite one hundred and ten thousand mantras.[16] This can usually be done in three months.

The problem with having a commitment to do a certain number of mantras is that you may become obsessed with the "score," which disturbs the peace of your retreat. It is better to do fewer mantras properly than to do more in a sloppy fashion. Of course, you can only count full rosaries of mantra and the mantras you recite in session toward the total, not those done during the breaks.

I was once in a group retreat of one hundred monks in our refugee camp in West Bengal. We were committed to counting a certain number of mantras, and the retreat could not end until each monk had completed his total. One of the monks had great trouble articulating the mantra, and by the time the rest of us had finished he still had a long way to go. He was so embarrassed that he could not show his face, so he covered his head with his robes while he recited the remaining mantras. We had to sit there for about five days waiting for him to finish! I don't think his reaction was appropriate. Just reciting a certain number of mantras is not the point. You can do some other meditation instead. The important thing is to take advantage of the retreat situation and do what suits your individual needs.[17]

ENDING THE SESSION

At the end of the sadhana, just before the dedication, Heruka Vajrasattva dissolves into you and you become one with him. At this time, it is good to do a short glance meditation on the graduated path, such as Lama Tsongkhapa's *Three Principles of the Path, Concise Meaning of the Stages of the Path,* or *The Foundation of All Excellence,* all of which can be found in Geshe Wangyal's book *The Door of Liberation.* In a group retreat the leader reads the meditation aloud and everybody else meditates. After that, you dedicate your merits. Your dedication at the end of the day's last session should be particularly strong. Then remain seated for a few more minutes, single-pointedly contemplating your blissful unity with Heruka Vajrasattva's holy body, speech, and mind, not allowing a single dualistic thought to arise.

9 ~ More Retreat Advice

BETWEEN SESSIONS

FOR THE SERIOUS RETREATER the session breaks are just as important as the sessions themselves. Actually, session breaks should *be* sessions. You put so much effort into creating a beautiful environment in the meditation room and developing your mind during the sessions, so make sure that between sessions you do not destroy all that you have gained. During the sessions you have good concentration and feel blissful, but when you come out, you become unaware and ordinary. You are like someone who walks along a sandy beach trying to smooth out his footprints as he goes, while making new ones all the time.

During the session you are concentrating fully on the deity, and your mundane thoughts cannot intrude—for that time your mind is free of them. You should maintain such concentrated awareness after the session, too. In this way you can totally eliminate your samsaric mind. The old habits are there, waiting for the chance to arise, so you have to be mindful not to give in to them.

The short breaks should last at least fifteen minutes, giving you a chance to get some exercise—walk, stretch your legs, and relax your body. However, do not relax your gentle awareness; try to keep your mind even and stable, at the level you attained during the session. This is relatively easy in the short breaks, but much more difficult at mealtimes and at night. Therefore you should use the short breaks as opportunities to practice this kind of session break meditation.

As I said before, at the end of the session, Heruka Vajrasattva dissolves into you, and you become inseparably one with him. Before you get up and leave the room, sit for a few minutes or more meditating on this blissful union—your body, speech, and mind being one with Heruka Vajrasattva's holy body, speech, and mind. You should have the clear appearance of yourself as the deity and the divine pride of *being* Vajrasattva himself. This is the concentration that you must maintain between sessions. You must never think, "I am so-and-so; I am this or that," as your ego habitually projects. As soon as you start to think that, problems begin. If you cannot maintain the thought, "I am Heruka Vajrasattva," you should at least think, "I must attain the divine state of Heruka Vajrasattva as quickly as possible for the sole purpose of enlightening all sentient beings."

Throughout the retreat you should feel highly fortunate to have the chance to practice this highest tantric yoga method and to actualize the six transcendent perfections for the sake of all sentient beings. Realize with joy that for almost the first time in your life you are doing something truly meaningful. If you analyze your life honestly you will see that most of it has been spent in an effort to satisfy your hallucinating, craving mind with illusory objects of the senses. Your dualistic misconceptions have never given you the time or space to exercise your wisdom.

From the moment you wake, craving coffee and other objects of the senses, to the moment you sleep, craving the pleasure of unconsciousness, your day is filled with actions motivated by ignorant, grasping attachment. You enjoy without awareness the few small pleasures you find and believe that the illusory projections of your dualistic mind and the perceptions of your defiled senses are reality itself. You do not allow your wisdom to function. Thus goes your life and thus it finishes, in misery.

Now that you have the opportunity to change, it is imperative that you do not waste a moment. Therefore you must remain aware throughout the entire day, not only during sessions. If you feel that the time in the sessions is Dharma and that all else is samsara, there is something wrong with your understanding. Tantric yoga is so powerful because it gives no time for samsara. There is no way that a proper tantric practitioner can say at one moment, "Now I'm practicing Dharma," and at another, "Now my actions are samsaric." Tantra contains all the methods required to transform every single action into Dharma wisdom.

If you believe that meditation is Dharma and that eating, drinking, shopping, and so forth are samsara, then you will never be able to attain liberation. The amount of time you spend for what you believe to be Dharma, the path to liberation—meditation—will be negligible in comparison to the rest. However, if you are skillful in your application of wisdom and method, everything you do, even the things you consider worldly, can become the path to enlightenment. Thus, your whole life becomes tantric yoga, and there is no space for samsara. Once you have stopped your samsaric mind from functioning, it is impossible *not* to quickly attain perfect liberation.

In the Paramitayana, desire is considered bad. The Vinaya says, "You cannot do this; you must not touch that." Sometimes you feel that you cannot have even a drop of water. The powerful methods of tantric yoga see desire as just another resource on the rapid path to enlightenment. Any pleasures that you have are transformed into experiences of the blissful wisdom of the deity. You should not feel guilty because you are enjoying the things you have or because others don't have them. Guilt does not help anyone.

Enjoy with bliss whatever you do. When you eat and drink, bless the food and drink with the mantra OM AH HUM, thereby transforming it into the nature of the holy body, speech, and mind of Heruka Vajrasattva. Offer it to yourself, identified as the deity. Feel the blissful energy of the blessed substances pervade your entire nervous system. If you do this with wisdom, it can help quickly bring you the realizations of transcendent bliss. If you eat and drink only with desire and interpret the experience in an ordinary way, you will have a very samsaric experience. It all depends upon your mind. When you go to sleep, do not allow your ego's projection of yourself to arise, but sleep feeling blissfully, one with Heruka Vajrasattva. When you wash, visualize yourself as Vajrasattva and think, "Heruka Vajrasattva's holy body is free from all defilements, but I am washing to purify my dualistic mind."

Your view of yourself is usually projected by your ego. Between sessions you have to recognize yourself instead as the manifestation of blissful transcendent wisdom, Heruka Vajrasattva. Whatever you perceive is from the perspective of this nondual mind and is in the nature of nonduality. In this sphere of nonduality the whole world passes by. It is almost like a television show. The world is no longer concrete in appearance; therefore, it cannot disturb you. It seems like an illusion or a dream. Thus you should determine that whatever appears to your senses is not real, contrary to what you have always believed. When you see others, you should see them not in their ordinary form but in the aspect of Heruka Vajrasattva. Treat them with the utmost respect.

RETREAT IN GENERAL

You may have thought that retreat was easy. Now you can see that, if done properly, it is not. However it is worth doing strictly: the more strictly you retreat, the better the results you can obtain. Retreat is the only way to really transform your mind, since in retreat you are putting the teachings into action, not merely collecting more information. With transformation, the solution to your problems comes. You become the Heruka Vajrasattva method—you are not *here* looking at the printed sadhana *there*. When there is that kind of separation, your mind may start telling you, "You are a Westerner; this is Tibetan…why are you doing this?" All sorts of doubts will arise. When you practice and achieve results, there is no doubt.

Our minds are somewhat crazy and out of control; therefore, we need to treat them firmly. However, change must be sought voluntarily, gently, and skillfully. Sometimes retreaters are unskillful. They imagine that they are great ascetic meditators and want to become famous for their efforts. They change their appearances and push themselves until their nervous systems explode. You cannot change your mind as simply as you change your clothes. Discipline yourselves wisely.

If you want your retreat to be successful, you should have the right attitude toward it. You should not feel that it is some kind of prison sentence during which you are locked up, unable to go to the movies, see friends, converse freely, and so forth. Instead you should feel joyful and fortunate that you have the chance to do something highly beneficial for yourself and others, a rare opportunity that you have not had before and may not have again. All the same, you should not expect Heruka Vajrasattva to appear to you and say, "My son…my daughter…." This is unrealistic and a hindrance to your meditation. You should be relaxed while maintaining the strong determination that, "On this seat I am going to actualize the yoga method of Heruka Vajrasattva. Until I have received the signs of success I shall not break this retreat."

Be kind to yourself. When you do a good session, pat yourself on the back and congratulate yourself. Offer yourself good food as a reward! If you do badly, scold yourself gently and make yourself promise to try harder. Make sure you get enough sleep. It is much better to sleep properly at night and do strong sessions than to fall asleep while trying to meditate.

If you experience many hindrances during your retreat, you can do a Mahakala protector puja or emphasize meditation on shunyata, which is actually the best protection. You should recognize bad signs and bad dreams as illusory and not read too much into them. Keep a written record of whatever good or bad experiences you have. Later this will be useful both for you, as a reminder of what happened in your retreat, and for others who will be doing this retreat in future.

If you do this retreat conscientiously, observing all the strict conditions laid out above, it is guaranteed that you will receive signs of realization. The sadhana has been specially arranged to lead your mind gradually, so that by the time you reach the mantra recitation, your mind is naturally focused. You cannot jump straight into single-pointedness; you have to build up to it. If you do this properly and observe all the other disciplines described, there will be signs—if not during the day, then in your dreams at night. Not that you should be expecting them. Just relax in the certainty that you are extracting the essence from your precious human life and feel highly fortunate to be doing something that is not dedicated to samsaric pleasure. Do your best without pushing yourself. When signs come, be detached, steady, and controlled, and do not grasp at them emotionally. Do not tell others about or brag of your realizations. Be simple, humble, down-to-earth, and practical. Life is much easier that way.

Group retreat

In my observations of Western students over many years I've noticed that they are more successful when they do group retreats than when they retreat alone. This may not apply to all students, but it certainly does to most. Especially when students are new to retreat, or when the retreat is a long one of, say, three months, it is better to retreat with a group. When you are alone, it is too easy not to follow the schedule. One day your meditation might be going well, so you will try to meditate all day and not stick to the sessions. The next day you will be down and unable to do any meditation. One morning you may feel tired and skip the first session to sleep in. Perhaps your leg or head might hurt, so you'll make another excuse not to go. These things don't happen when you are a member of a group because you have a responsibility to the others to attend all sessions.

In a group retreat everybody benefits from shared energy—you help each other. If you are feeling depressed you consult your friend, whose sympathetic advice restores you. When someone else is having some difficulty that you have experienced and overcome, you can explain what should be done. We are not completely stupid; in fact, we can be of significant help to each other. Therefore I recommend group retreat until you have had enough experience to retreat alone.

Conclusion

If you get the chance—or make the time—to retreat, you are extremely fortunate. Few things are as beneficial. With strong renunciation of samsara, you will realize that you have been everywhere, done everything, and that it's useless to do the same old things again and again, getting absolutely nowhere. That realization stops your mind from wandering. If you find yourself in retreat dreaming of your hometown or some other desirable place, you can tell yourself, "I know what I'll do if I go back there. I've been doing it for lifetimes. Essentially, there's nothing new. Why keep getting caught in that old, crazy samsaric trip?"

Therefore, by recognizing the nature of samsara and having the enthusiastic determination to completely cut its root, you will have no expectation of pleasure from worldly things. Even if your best friend shows up, "Hey, come on! Let's go out and have a great time," you can say, "Sorry. I've had enough of all that."

You're not just emotionally locking yourself away. Rather, with strong wisdom, you are really renouncing samsara. You know the sort of nonsense you're likely to get involved in with your family and friends, so you generate the strong motivation: "I'm not going to break this retreat until I have unified my body, speech, and mind with Heruka Vajrasattva."

We often do things halfheartedly. This is because our minds are split. When opposing mental tendencies come into conflict, we are susceptible to a nervous breakdown. So you need to know very clearly why you are retreating and to make sure that your motivation is strong. You should feel that it is necessary and worthwhile, and that you are extremely fortunate to have the opportunity to do it. You are so blessed to have the chance to retreat, acting for once under the strong influence of wisdom instead of constantly running from one thing to another, touching honey. Do you know what I mean by touching honey? When you touch honey, it tends to stick to your fingers and to everything else you touch. It makes a mess, and it is very difficult to get rid of. Samsaric actions are a lot like that.

Therefore start your retreat with great determination and no expectations. It doesn't matter whether or not you receive all the realizations of enlightenment. It's enough that you are trying to control your mind and relax in this peaceful, tranquil atmosphere. To reach this conclusion just once is the result of great fortune. All samsaric trips are a complete waste of time; they produce only more and more problems. If you are deeply aware of the nature of samsaric life, you will have no obstacles or distractions during your retreat. But if you are halfhearted, your mind will wander and bother you constantly: "Oh, if I were back home, I could be going out to dinner and the movies with my girlfriend…."

To the samsaric way of thinking, that's having a good time. In fact, it is just confusion. Check it out with wisdom. Even though you say, "I had a great time," if you are honest, you will admit that it was just another old samsaric trip. We have had these experiences over countless lives, but our minds are still ignorant, out of control, and undisciplined.

Therefore, don't be halfhearted. Cut off the wandering, confused mind by generating strong, enthusiastic motivation: "I am extremely fortunate to have come to the conclusion, at least this once, that it is worthwhile to discipline my body, speech, and mind, and to have the opportunity to decisively put myself on the path of perfect peace."

When you take your seat before each session, you can think, "For the sake of all mother sentient beings, I must attain enlightenment on this very seat. I shall not move from it until I am one with Guru Heruka Vajrasattva."

PART 3

Discourses

10 ~ No Negativity Cannot Be Completely Purified

THE MOMENT THE SUN RISES, the darkness of the night vanishes automatically. Similarly, when the light of wisdom appears in your mind, the dark shadow of ignorance naturally disappears.

Whenever you are depressed, anxious, or afraid, your view of the world becomes more distorted than ever, and your wrong conceptions multiply. Whenever your confused, dissatisfied mind arises, you become foggy and unclear. Even if you are outside in the sun or under a spotlight, there is darkness in your mind.

Therefore, it is highly beneficial to practice such a powerful tantric method as the yoga of Heruka Vajrasattva, which facilitates the growth of wisdom in your mind.

Most spiritual practitioners have taken vows and commitments as part of their religious practice. Those who lack wisdom feel that when they have broken some of their promises, they have done something irreversibly negative and become permanent sinners: "Oh, I promised not to do that, and now I've gone and broken my vow! Now I'll never be saved." That's a big misconception. All relative phenomena in the realm of the senses are impermanent, changing all the time. By their nature, they will cease of their own accord.

Another misconception is the depressed thought that you are hopeless. "Try as I might, I am always making mistakes." That's not true. Nobody is completely negative. We all have a positive side and a negative side.

In his Vajrayana teachings, the Buddha explained that although the root infractions of tantra are the highest vows of all, even they can be restored when broken. Such transgressions are extremely negative, but since they are psychological phenomena, they can be purified.

In his Vinaya teachings, which are part of the Sutrayana path, the Buddha taught that there are certain unwholesome actions, such as murder, that cannot be fully purified in this lifetime. Thus, if you have broken one of the five precepts, you might feel that you have become permanently stained and get terribly upset. But you must remember that Lord Buddha gave his numerous different teachings according to the varying psychological needs of his many disciples. Sutra teachings were given to followers of a certain level of intelligence.

In the Vajrayana, the Buddha taught that there is no negativity that cannot be completely purified by the powerful methods of tantric yoga. Thus, you should never feel that because you have broken your vows or, for example, committed one of the so-called five inexpiable sins, you are a hopeless sinner beyond redemption.[18]

On the other hand, you should not rationalize that just because any negativity can be purified, you are free to do whatever you like. A broken cup can be repaired, but it's never the same as it was. Therefore, even though your vows and commitments can be restored when breached, it is better to keep them intact.

The best way to practice the Heruka Vajrasattva purification is in a three-month retreat, during which you recite the mantra one hundred thousand times. I usually ask students who want to take the Heruka Vajrasattva initiation to make a three-month retreat commitment. Also, it is easier for them to do this in the East than in the West, where the busy environment makes it almost impossible to find the time.

The retreat should be conducted under the right conditions, as explained in the retreat section of this book. Very few, if any, students have been able to follow these instructions to the letter. It is very difficult to adhere strictly to the ideal retreat discipline. Nonetheless, many conscientious and sincere Westerners have tried to do so, and although their concentration may not have been that strong, their three-month retreat has definitely changed their minds for the better.

Therefore, it is of great benefit to undertake this retreat, but make sure that the conditions you create are conducive to success. If I'm sitting here and someone is poking me with a needle, saying, "Come on, Lama, meditate, meditate," it's impossible. In the same way, it is hard to retreat in the middle of a city vibrating with the energy of aggression and desire. That's why Tibetan lamas always tried to find peaceful, isolated settings for their retreats. Good vibrations automatically help your practice.

If you can practice the Vajrasattva yoga method according to this commentary, there is no doubt that you will receive a most powerful purification. Why do you lack knowledge-wisdom and realizations? Because your mind is thickly clouded with the negative vibrations of delusion. The heavy obstacle of your ego concepts and an emotional inability to cope with problems allow no space. Wisdom cannot grow in this unclear atmosphere.

The Mahayana tradition emphasizes a combination of purifying and wisdom-generating meditations, rather than a preponderance of one over the other. When you purify the obscuring hindrances, your innate wisdom has a chance to develop. Thus, far from being contradictory, meditations on the graduated path and Vajrasattva purification are in complete harmony, and if you practice them together, you will quickly gain realizations.

Of course, I understand that not everyone is able to find the right circumstances for a three-month retreat at this time. Each of us has prior commitments and responsibilities according to his or her individual karma. If you can't commit yourself to the retreat, you shouldn't take the initiation and then feel as if you're somehow a prisoner of the Dharma. Lord Buddha's teachings are for freedom, not bondage! And those of you who cannot devote yourselves to intensive practice should not feel inferior to those who can. You have to accept your present situation. The time will come when you will be able to find an ideal retreat situation. At that time you can take the Vajrasattva initiation with a three-month retreat commitment. Don't feel that you are unlucky or bad. It's not true. You are still very fortunate. You can maintain a daily practice on the graduated path to liberation, and do shorter retreats as time permits.

To develop your loving kindness, you can do Avalokiteshvara retreat. For wisdom, you can retreat on Mañjushri. To overcome weakness and feelings of inadequacy, you can do Vajrapani retreat. There are many different retreats you can do according to your need. Retreats are like therapy. In the West, when you are sick you get therapy to cure your illness. Retreats are similar: you put yourself into a certain situation depending upon what the particular problem is. That's why I say that retreat is like medicine: an antidote to both the disease and its symptoms.

Why is purification so powerful? Because your wisdom and method are powerful. There is not some supreme power up in the sky washing your sins away. Power comes from your mental approach, the psychological key to the yoga method.

As I said before, the Heruka Vajrasattva tantric yoga method can purify the worst negativities you can imagine, including broken tantric, bodhisattva, and pratimoksha vows. It also purifies the symptoms of dissatisfaction, such as anxiety neuroses, inferiority complexes, and arrogant pride. Therefore, whenever you find you have broken your vows you should not get emotionally upset and feel hopeless or depressed. That's not wise. Instead, just be aware of what has happened, understand the interdependence of your uncontrolled negative mind and the conditions that caused you to break your vows, and skillfully apply the methods of purification.

You can learn a lot from such experiences. Analyze your mind. Intellectually, you do not want to do things that you have vowed not to do, but your uncontrolled mind interacts with the conditions and forces you to do them. Hence, you can understand your karma and see how powerful it is. You know from your studies on the graduated path that your precious human rebirth gives you the potential to do anything. How can you feel hopeless or depressed?

Do not belittle the teachings on the graduated path, thinking that they are too simple for you, the great practitioner of tantra. They are not at all simple but really most profound. This is not the hyperbole of a true believer but a scientific fact that you can prove for yourself by understanding and practicing the graduated path. In this way you can extract the essence from your precious human life, and instead of degenerating, you can progress. It is entirely in your own hands.

When you understand the graduated path clean-clear, you can see the benefits of purification retreat. At that time you are ready and qualified for such a retreat. If you don't know who or what you are, you can't practice even the graduated path properly, let alone the profound methods of tantric yoga.

Once you understand the nature of your life and the possibilities offered you by Dharma practice, you can choose your direction with wisdom instead of blindly following your ignorant wrong conceptions, as you've been doing for countless lives. You can choose your future because you now know how to create its causes. The past is finished, done with. What's the use of getting emotionally distraught over broken vows and other nonvirtuous actions? You are not only wasting your time, but you are also piling negativity upon negativity. If, instead of applying the antidote when you recognize a nonvirtue, you become emotionally disturbed, you are doubling your bad karma. You should be purifying your negativities, not becoming more sick.

Recently I read about a banker who committed suicide because he was caught embezzling funds. Was that the way out? He stole, felt guilty, got emotionally disturbed, and killed himself. That's a good example of what I'm saying: he has already created the negativity of stealing, but what are they going to do to him? Jail him, perhaps. Maybe confiscate his property. But they're not going to kill him, are they? Nevertheless, he couldn't bear the loss to his reputation, so he took his own life. We're the same. We do something negative then almost kill ourselves with guilt and worry. What's the use? It's completely self-destructive.

New experiences now lie ahead, and you can change direction to meet or avoid them as you choose. I'm not suggesting that you have the psychic power to see telepathically the details of your future, but I am saying that through analyzing your past experiences and drawing upon your understanding of the law of karma, you can deduce what you should and should not do. Checking in this way is very useful; worry is ridiculous.

Also, it is not enough simply to feel distress over and want to purify the horrible things you have done. As well, you should think that if you continue to do such things, you will only experience greater suffering in the future. Therefore, in addition to purifying past negative karma, you must also avoid creating actions motivated by ignorance, attachment, and anger. If you purify the nonvirtuous actions you created in the past and refrain from creating them again, you can avoid the suffering result. The main factor that determines the kind of karma created by your actions is your motivation. It is up to you whether that motivation is positive or negative.

Although I was talking before about the negativity of breaking precepts, you should not feel that by taking precepts you have somehow imprisoned yourself. It's exactly the opposite. Precepts make you free. Some people feel a sense of loss after they have taken precepts. They feel a heavy weight upon their shoulders. If you understand precepts correctly, you will feel happy when you have taken them, because you know that you are well on your way to a blissful destination.

If your mind is limited, you will probably feel guilty or depressed when you break a precept. Say, for example, you have taken the eight Mahayana precepts for a day. During the morning ceremony you generated bodhichitta and the enthusiastic determination to keep the vows perfectly for the benefit of all sentient beings. But that evening somebody offers you a piece of chocolate. Unconsciously, out of habit, you eat it. Then you panic: "Oh my god! This morning I promised not to eat after midday, and now I've broken my vow. It's completely gone!" Many people react like this, but what's gone? There's no such thing as "completely gone." You kept the precept perfectly from the time you took it until you inadvertently broke it. You didn't break it intentionally. None of that positive energy has been lost.

Instead of beating up on yourself when you break a precept, you should rejoice: "Unbelievable! I really meant not to eat, but my old habits snuck up and cheated me when I wasn't looking." Feel happy about the time you kept the precept purely, and be happy to learn how your negative mind works. In this way your experience becomes wisdom. Taking precepts increases your awareness: it helps you understand karma at its deepest levels by bringing to your notice the subtle way in which it expresses itself. If you didn't take precepts, you would remain unaware of your negativities and would never know that they were there in your subconscious.

Without understanding this, you will never be really happy. You might take precepts but later regret it. "Oh, I made a mistake. I didn't realize it until I got back home to the West, but that Kopan lama must have hypnotized me!" Anyway, I'm joking, but some people might think along those lines. It is well worth taking precepts, even though you might break them occasionally. If you check up wisely, you will realize that you are really fortunate to take precepts. You don't break them on purpose, but you see how your old habits push you to break them unconsciously. That's a very useful revelation. That's how you develop your wisdom.

11 ~ An Initiation into Heruka Vajrasattva

THE BASIC QUALIFICATION for undertaking a tantric practice, such as the purifying yoga method of Heruka Vajrasattva, is a clear understanding of the three principal aspects of the path to enlightenment: renunciation, bodhichitta, and right view, shunyata. I'm sure you have a reasonable understanding of these, but day by day, year by year, you should be constantly striving to deepen it.

There are also many aspects to purification, such as making prostrations, reciting texts, and practicing the yoga methods of other deities. But the Heruka Vajrasattva method is perhaps the most powerful of all. This is just what we need. And while the Geluk tradition of Mahayana Buddhism stresses the great importance of purification, we need more than that. We have to integrate other activities—such as studying the teachings on the graduated path to enlightenment and helping others—into our practice of the purifying meditations of the yoga method. Some people seem to think that it's enough to practice only these meditations, but they're wrong. We have to take the middle way of balanced activities.

Old students who have done the three-month Vajrasattva retreat know just how profound a method of purification it is. New students will find out. It's not easy, but simply trying to face up to and overcome the difficulties is extremely worthwhile.

Now, as well as giving you a retreat commitment with this initiation, I'm going to add another condition. Based on my own experience of observing my students over a period of years, I have come to the conclusion that group retreats are much better for you than individual ones. In a way, that should be obvious. We all have a certain degree of knowledge-wisdom—don't think that knowledge is the exclusive domain of Tibetan lamas. Within each of us, certain aspects of it are better developed than others, so when we come together as a group, our collective wisdom forms a deep pool that we all can share.

For example, one day you might be feeling strong, but I'm overwhelmed by delusion. I can come to you and say, "Look, I'm freaking out here...what should I do?" You have the answer. This is what we mean by Sangha. You're having a hard time, you express your feelings to a Dharma brother or sister, and that person gives you wisdom, strength, and a solution to your problem. That's why I'm adding the condition of group retreat. I hope you understand. I'm not on a power trip: "This is *my* initiation; you have to do it my way." No! I just want this experience to be as beneficial for you as possible.

When we do Dharma things, we should do them professionally, with understanding. The Vajrasattva retreat has been structured to be of maximum benefit to the human mind, so you should do it properly. But having said that, I want to stress that you can retreat only to the best of your ability. In my commentary and retreat instructions, I'm a little bit strict, and it's true that strict is better. But if you can't practice exactly as I suggest, you shouldn't just give up altogether. You can't always do what you want to do, because you're subject to your own limitations. You have to accept yourself as you are and take it from there. Encourage yourself: "Well, it was a bit difficult today. I couldn't do the visualizations exactly as Lama recommended. But still, I got the main things right; I didn't break any sessions and did them as best I could. It was just that my concentration was a bit off."

I know that my Western students want to do things 100 percent as I say, and that's a beautiful quality. It's good to do anything perfectly. But you have to be reasonable. When you encounter difficulties, accept them. Sixty percent is better than nothing, better than running around the world like a wild animal with a confused mind. Think: "I may not be perfect, but I'm still better off trying to do the mantra as well as I can and giving energy to my Dharma brothers and sisters."

And if you can't do the meditations as explained, generate compassion instead. Remember the compassion that you feel for yourself when you're having a difficult time, and transfer that compassion to all mother sentient beings. Crying with compassion for others while reciting the Vajrasattva mantra is okay. It's certainly a lot better than just sitting there thinking, "I'm bad, I'm bad, I'm bad." Meditating with bodhichitta while reciting the Vajrasattva mantra is fine. As long as part of your mind is watching with mindful awareness that your mantra recitation is correct, you can generate compassion for others instead of doing the more complicated visualizations. I want new people to be clean-clear that this kind of skillful technique— directing whatever energy arises into the right channel—is permissible.

So, people who have done the retreat can take the initiation without having to do the retreat again. For new people, there's no consideration; you have to do the retreat. But when you do it, despite what I've been saying, I don't want you just to take it easy, mixing a little samsara with your nirvana. That doesn't work. Your retreat should be as pure a liberation, nirvana trip as you can make it. Our tendency is to mix things up—not this time, okay?

One thing that will make your retreat easier is being strongly dedicated to doing it well. If you're a bit wishy-washy about doing it—"maybe I should; maybe I shouldn't"—or if your mind is agitated, or you have a lot of expectations, then you can really freak out. You'll always feel like you're missing something: "Why am I sitting here? If I were in Melbourne I'd be having a good time. Why should I stay here?" This kind of question will arise. I would like you to be very single-minded about doing retreat—clean-clear and dedicated. Then you'll be comfortable: just sitting on your meditation cushion will be a blissful experience. And should superstitious thoughts bother you, remember the techniques for dealing with them, such as the vase-breathing meditation explained in the commentary. Practice that, and when your mind is calm again, return to what you were doing.

I'd also like to add a point about mantra recitation to what I've already said in the main commentary, although perhaps I shouldn't state this publicly in case you start rationalizing. However, if after a couple of months' retreat you find you have very good single-pointed concentration, and you know from experience exactly how many mantras you recite in a session, you can recite the mantra silently, without using your rosary. But before you do this, be sure you have reached that level of development, and don't let your rationalizing mind cheat you.

Old students who have already done the retreat and completed their mantra commitment but would like to retreat again can do so alone, without joining a group. They can also practice mental recitation or even concentration without any recitation at all. After you have gone through the sadhana and become Vajrasattva, you concentrate on the blue seed syllable HUM at your heart and focus on that alone. You can work up to it by doing verbal recitation, then go deeper and deeper to mental recitation, and finally don't even do that but just concentrate single-pointedly on the seed syllable HUM. This can be very useful.

Now, before I give the initiation, I'm going to do a ritual to purify hindrances. These are subtle, formless manifestations of ego energy that prevent us from receiving the initiation perfectly and must be dispelled before we proceed. We transform this energy into some kind of wrathful form, and visualize Lama

Heruka Vajrasattva chasing it away, beyond this solar system, from where it can never return. So, while I do the ritual, you meditate like that.

THE HERUKA VAJRASATTVA INITIATION

[Lama Yeshe gave the initiation stage-by-stage in the following, unique way: first he explained the visualization to be done by the disciples; then he recited the text in English while the students did the visualization just explained; finally he recited the text in Tibetan. What follows below is the explanation, published in order to give readers an idea of the initiation process. Technically, this is not a full initiation (wang) *but is instead what is usually called "permission to practice"* (jenang).]

The essence of Heruka Vajrasattva is the collected pure energy of all enlightened beings. This energy manifests as the white, blissful, radiant body of the deity. So when you take the initiation, instead of seeing the lama as a confused, ordinary person, transform him into the translucent appearance of the deity.

Then, according to tradition, you must ask him three times to confer the empowerment upon you. This is because we don't allow people the presumption of saying, "Hey! I've got a perfect, powerful, and very speedy method of attaining enlightenment. Come here, and I'll give it to you." Before they can receive an initiation, students have to be properly qualified and must request it most sincerely. So repeat three times after me: "Lama Vajrasattva, please give me the divine initiation of Vajrasattva."

Then you have to generate the enlightened attitude of bodhichitta. This is to ensure that your taking the initiation does not become a selfish power trip but instead an action dedicated to the enlightenment of all sentient beings. However, today you are not taking the full bodhisattva ordination of sixty-four vows but simply generating the strong motivation to use the yoga method for the sole purpose of benefiting others and not for any personal, temporal pleasure. With the divine, dedicated thought of reaching the highest destination—the everlasting, blissful realization of enlightenment—repeat three times after me: "The only reason I want to take this initiation is so that I can practice the yoga method in order to attain the everlasting, peaceful state of enlightenment for the benefit of other sentient beings."

Now remember, you receive the actual initiation only if your mind communicates, or meets together, with that of Lama Heruka Vajrasattva in the same space, or at the same level of consciousness. To generate that experience, it is very important that your concentration remain strong throughout the entire initiation.

From the seed syllable HUM at Lama Heruka Vajrasattva's heart, much powerful white radiant light comes into your heart, its electric energy magnetically burning your ego's conception, your image, of your entire physical nervous system, transforming it into white radiant light. This light dissolves and condenses, becoming smaller and smaller until it completely disappears into empty space. Concentrate on that emptiness.

Suddenly, in that empty space, a precious lotus flower appears. On the lotus flower appears a moon disc. At the center of the moon disc appears a radiant white vajra—the essence of your consciousness. Radiant white light emanates from the moon disc and vajra, embracing all of space. The all-embracing radiant light returns to sink into the vajra, the essence of your consciousness. The absorption of the light into the vajra acts as the cooperative cause for your consciousness to transform into the translucent, rainbow body of Heruka Vajrasattva—no flesh, no blood, no bone.

Your right hand holds a vajra, and your left hand holds a bell, signifying your complete realization of method and wisdom. You are embraced by the divine female, Nyema Karmo, whose translucent holy body is also made of radiant white light and whose realizations are equal to yours, energizing within you the transcendental, blissful experience of the fully awakened mind.

You, Heruka Vajrasattva, are adorned with a radiant white OM at your crown chakra, a radiant red AH at your throat chakra, and a radiant blue HUM at your heart chakra.

From the white seed syllable OM and the Heruka Vajrasattva mantra that surrounds it at Lama Heruka Vajrasattva's crown chakra, powerful radiant white light emanates, pervading universal space and invoking all the supreme beings' pure energy, which transforms into blissful, radiant white light and sinks into the crown chakra of you, Heruka Vajrasattva. Like a powerful, rushing waterfall, this energy enters your Heruka Vajrasattva body, filling your nervous system with blissful, radiant white light, especially your crown chakra. That blissful experience purifies countless lives' accumulated impurities of body.

From the red seed syllable AH and the Heruka Vajrasattva mantra that surrounds it at Lama Heruka Vajrasattva's throat chakra, powerful radiant red light emanates, pervading universal space and invoking all the supreme beings' divine speech, which transforms into blissful, radiant red light and sinks into the throat chakra of you, Heruka Vajrasattva. Your Heruka Vajrasattva nervous system is completely filled with blissful, radiant red light, especially your throat chakra. That blissful experience purifies countless lives' accumulated impurities of speech.

From the blue seed syllable HUM and the Heruka Vajrasattva mantra that surrounds it at Lama Heruka Vajrasattva's heart chakra, powerful radiant blue light emanates, pervading universal space and invoking all the supreme beings' divine, transcendental wisdom, which transforms into blissful, radiant blue light and sinks into the heart chakra of you, Heruka Vajrasattva. Your Heruka Vajrasattva nervous system is completely filled with blissful, radiant blue light, especially your heart chakra. That blissful experience purifies countless lives' accumulated impurities of mind.

Now, simultaneously, from Lama Heruka Vajrasattva's crown chakra, comes blissful, radiant white light, which enters the crown chakra of you, Heruka Vajrasattva; from Lama Heruka Vajrasattva's throat chakra comes blissful, radiant red light, which enters your throat chakra; from Lama Heruka Vajrasattva's heart chakra comes blissful, radiant blue light, which enters your heart chakra. Through this, you and Lama Heruka Vajrasattva are indestructibly unified.

A duplicate mantra emanates from the mantra at Lama Heruka Vajrasattva's heart, leaves through his mouth and enters the mouth of you, Heruka Vajrasattva, and sinks into your heart. This happens three times. The first time it encircles the seed syllable HUM at your heart; the second time it dissolves into the original mantra there, increasing its power and strength; the third time it dissolves into it, making it indestructible, now and forever.

Visualize the mantra as a rosary of electrical energy. The mantra is like fire. Fire has the property of automatically burning anything that it touches. Similarly, the mantra's electrical wisdom energy automatically burns all the impurities of negative energy. Repeat the mantra after me three times. After the third, think that the blessings of Lama Heruka Vajrasattva have made it indestructible.

Now, from Lama Heruka Vajrasattva, a duplicate Heruka Vajrasattva emanates, coming to the crown of your head, descending through your sushumna, and entering your heart. Your body, speech, and mind are completely unified with Heruka Vajrasattva's divine body, speech, and mind.

Here, Tibetan lamas have a method to help those whose concentration is not strong. We touch the crown of your head with this torma that has the painting of the deity on top of it. As you file past and I touch you with it, concentrate strongly that Heruka Vajrasattva comes down your sushumna into your heart, and that the body, speech, and mind of you, Heruka Vajrasattva, are completely, nondualistically unified with the divine body, speech, and mind of Heruka Vajrasattva.[19]

Now the initiation has finished. As you repeat the dedication prayers after me, make a heartfelt request for your group retreat to be as successful as possible.

ை

You can see from your experience of this initiation that for the person whose concentration is very good, the process itself can be an enlightening experience. This highlights the difference between the Vajrayana and the Hinayana and Paramitayana schools of Buddhism. There, the emphasis is upon avoiding the kind of enjoyments that we grasp at; in tantra, we have the powerful wisdom and method to transform this ordinary energy into the blissful path to enlightenment.

This principle is not entirely dissimilar from the way modern scientific technology employs the earth's resources in an attempt to improve people's standard of living. Of course, the shortcomings of this approach are now becoming evident, with even politicians decrying the depletion of these resources and the pollution of our environment—something that can never happen through Dharma practice. When we take energy and, through skillful wisdom and method, transform it into the blissful path to enlightenment, no negative vibration can result.

It is most important that during your retreat you strongly maintain the transcendental experience that your entire consciousness has been transformed into the blissful, radiant white light body of Heruka Vajrasattva. You must really believe this. The psychological benefit of this is that you remove all thoughts of, "I am Thubten Yeshe; therefore, I'm hungry. I am Thubten

Yeshe; therefore, I'm thirsty. I am Thubten Yeshe; therefore, I need beautiful objects." This eradicates your entire ego projection. It's incredible—the Mahayana has fantastically powerful methods of overcoming all your ego's vibrations. This is an extremely important part of your retreat.

Now, when I say that you should strongly believe that you are Vajrasattva, I don't mean that you should think that your physical body has changed. I know the kind of Western, pseudoscientific argument you're going to make: "My body is made of flesh and bone. How can I transform it into light?" Well, you can indeed say that, but I'm going to reply that besides your physical body, you have a psychic body, the body of your subtle consciousness. It is your subtle conscious body that transforms into the white, radiant, translucent, rainbow-light body of the deity, and you generate divine pride on that.

Divine pride is very important. Let me tell you why. Normally, we think, "I'm negative. I'm *this;* therefore, I'm negative." Do you know what I mean? I'm talking about the fact that you feel guilty, even when you're not. Even though you're not a religious person, you still feel guilty. Don't think that only religious people feel guilt. I've had enough experience with Westerners to know that they always feel guilty about something or other, even nonreligious Westerners. Perhaps you think, "Oh, I only feel guilty because I'm trying to be a Buddhist. If I give up Dharma, I won't feel guilty any more." That's not the way to get rid of guilt. Even nonreligious people feel guilt.

The way to abandon feelings of guilt and low self-esteem, such as "I'm bad; I'm negative," is to generate divine pride and thereby transform all your negative thoughts into blissful wisdom energy. With this technique you can deal with any situation that arises: take that energy and transform it into divine white radiant light and emanate as the deity. That's why I said "strongly" before—you have to really believe that you are Heruka Vajrasattva instead of "I'm Thubten Yeshe, born in Tibet, having this mother, that father, escaped...refugee...hungry." You have to overcome your ego trip. Whenever the mundane thought "I am" arises, mundane body, speech, and mind manifest immediately. The moment you generate divine pride and experience transcendental transformation, you eliminate all ordinary conceptions. And while it is essential to do this during your meditation sessions, of course, it is also necessary during the breaks. Instead of coming down when the session finishes, going to lunch, and allowing old habits to arise, looking at each other with lust or anger, maintain the energy of divine pride.

You can see how such method and wisdom can help you control your deluded energy. And you can see this through your own experience, not just my words. If I tell you too much about how tantra contains all these incredible methods, you'll just think, "Oh, he's so arrogant. He's just boasting about the power Tibetan lamas are supposed to have." It'll be too much for you. But if you check up for yourselves, you'll taste the benefits. And before you retreat, study the commentary well. Read it sentence by sentence, stopping to check and meditate on each one. If you are clean-clear about whatever you do, you'll be free of doubt and agitation and feel very comfortable. That is both important and necessary for your retreat to be successful.

If you start to experience difficulties during retreat, don't think, "I'm bad; I'm not a good retreater." Instead, simply ask yourself, "Why is my retreat not going well?" You have the answer: "It's because of my incredible delusions. And I'm not the only one. All my poor mother sentient beings are in this situation." Cherish others instead of yourself, and feel much compassion for all universal sentient beings. Instead of crying neurotically when you're having problems during a session, a perfect technique is to transform the energy of the mantra into compassion. Of course, emotional tears are not necessarily bad; crying can also be a blissful experience.

For example, the first time people discover shunyata, they're incredibly shaken and can completely space out. Inside, they experience a blissful shaking sensation; psychologically, they are transported way into space and then suddenly brought down. They almost don't know what's going on. Philosophically, this appears to be the very antithesis of the shunyata wisdom experience, which is supposed to be totally divorced from emotion. But the experience of an individual who actually discovers shunyata for the first time can be completely different. A close disciple of Lama Tsongkhapa, who initially experienced emptiness during a teaching on it, thought he'd disappeared and grabbed at his lapel. Lama Tsongkhapa laughed, and said, "My disciple so-and-so has just found himself on his shirt!" He went on to explain that that's how the experience is supposed to be. So crying is not necessarily bad.

When difficulties arise, remember the reason: "All sentient beings, including myself, are in this situation. We are all objects of compassion." If you realize compassion during your retreat, what more could you ask? That's perfect. After retreat your actions will be imbued with loving kindness. It's possible. But be skillful, too; learn to relax during retreat, and be skillful in the way you relax. I don't mean that you should just lie about.

After retreat, do the simple fire puja of Dorje Khadro, which I explain briefly in the next chapter. There are many kinds of complex fire pujas in the Tibetan tradition, but this one is fine for us. You can even do it in everyday life, whenever you feel psychologically unwell, heavy, or impure. Just make a fire and do the Dorje Khadro puja with much meditation. It's like tumo meditation—it burns all your impurities.

Q: At the end of the sadhana, we meditate on ourselves as Heruka Vajrasattva. How do we concentrate on this?

A: This kind of concentration is very profound—much more profound than concentration on an external object, which, because it's easier, is what we usually do. Sometimes people experience heart pain or a rapid heartbeat when they do this meditation. This will happen if you are not relaxed or if you don't recognize the object of concentration as being in the nature of consciousness. When you are meditating on yourself as Vajrasattva and concentrating on the HUM at your heart, if you think of your body as physical, your heart may start to hurt; this is because your thinking is too concrete. It is extremely important to recognize your body as formless, as a psychic body. If I'm sitting here meditating and try to put a physical HUM where my heart is, there's be no room for it. The space is occupied. But if it's all in the nature of consciousness, anything is possible. Therefore, it is necessary to visualize the HUM as blissful, transcendental, and in the nature of consciousness.

Ordinarily, a deluded, grasping man might look at a beautiful woman and feel some kind of samsaric bliss. Similarly, the blue HUM at Vajrasattva's heart is a blissful, or bliss-generating, object. Whenever you visualize it, you feel blissful. This is an important point. As a result, you will have good single-pointed concentration. Why? Because the object of concentration itself—in this case the blue HUM—gives you a blissful experience. When you have a blissful experience, you feel satisfied; the hole in your psychological stomach is filled. When your psychological stomach is satisfied, you don't feel lonely or dissatisfied. When you are lonely, you are dissatisfied.

Monks and nuns often feel lonely…well, we all feel lonely. It's true. We have to know these things. It's necessary—this is Dharma. Perhaps you think I'm talking about dirty things, but we have to understand the dirty things in our lives in order to know what to clean. So why do we feel lonely and dissatisfied? Because we're looking for satisfaction—no blissful experiences, so our psychological stomachs are hungry. I'm sure you understand what I mean.

12 ~ A Brief Commentary on the Vajrasattva Sadhana

Tibetan Buddhism considers the Vajrasattva practice very important. We call this teaching *Gel-kyen dik-drip jong-wa dor-je sem-päi tri*.

Gel-kyen means hindrance; *dik* means negativity, some kind of immoral action; and *drip* means obscuration. The difference between these last two is a little technical, but both are hindrances. For an action to become a negativity, there has to be a negative motivation, such as one of the three poisonous minds of ignorance, attachment, and hatred. An obscuration is not necessarily created with negative motivation. For example, the dull, sleepy, sluggish mind that stops you from developing single-pointed concentration is an obscuration, but there's not necessarily any negative motivation behind it. There are many levels of good and bad within the mind. Therefore, when we say that the Vajrasattva meditation is very powerful in eliminating negativities, we don't mean only immoral negative actions but any kind of hindrance.

For example, some of us take precepts. We make a vow before the Three Jewels of refuge—Buddha, Dharma, and Sangha—to do or not to do certain actions. When we make these vows, we are enthusiastically determined and quite confident that we shall be able to keep them purely. But then circumstances change, our internal wall crumbles, and we break a precept. Never mind; we can purify such breaks.

On the other hand, sometimes Western students come to me feeling very guilty, thinking that they have broken one vow or another, but when I ask them exactly how they broke the vow, I find that they have not broken it at all. They have a kind of concrete understanding, "I should never do this," when usually it is not the action itself that breaks the vow but the attitude, or motivation, behind it. Thus, even though whatever you did might appear to be contrary to your vows, if your motivation was not negative, you did not necessarily break it.

The most important thing for you to know is that no matter what sort of negative symptoms you have, all can be purified by the yoga method of

Heruka Vajrasattva. Buddhism, especially tantra, asserts that you can purify any negativity whatsoever.

When we think about certain heavy negativities, it seems as if they are somehow permanent, unchangeable, impossible to purify. This idea of self-existent negativity is most dangerous. Fundamentally, all positive and negative phenomena are interdependent and changeable in nature. Certain Hindu philosophies hold that objects of the five senses are composed of permanent, unchangeable, self-existent atoms. Western scientists used to believe that too; some still may. Those are wrong conceptions.

It is important for you to know that we ourselves and all other phenomena, such as sense objects or qualities of positivity and negativity, are interdependent and changeable. Especially in the context of purification, you should be aware that symptoms of negativity, like desire, or anger, or whatever else you can think of, never stay the same. For example, you enter a certain environment, and all of a sudden your mind changes; you start shaking. That demonstrates the impermanent character of these emotions. They come, and they go. And not only can you solve the problems of negativity temporarily, but you can also eradicate them completely and forever.

I believe that people who practice purification are brave: "I can face and overcome any problem, any difficulty." Don't think that they are practicing purification because they're miserable. Many followers of Western religions accept the philosophy of permanent sin, and therefore they feel guilty. You have to avoid the heavy attitude thinking that it's impossible to overcome negativity. From the tantric point of view, the practitioner of purification is brave: "I can do it. Even though I've made mistakes, I am sure there's a solution to my problems." That's the right attitude; you are not afraid to admit your negativities. "Yes, that was negative; that was my uncontrolled mind." You accept it, but you don't feel hopeless. "I can change my mind. Anyway, it has been changing constantly ever since I was born. Now I can change it for the better." It is very important to know this—very important.

Now, besides bravely seeing the *possibility* of purifying any hindrance, you should also understand that you can purify the imprints that negative actions have left on your consciousness. In Tibetan, we call these *pak-cha*. Over countless lifetimes you have repeatedly created negative action after negative action, each of which has left an imprint on your mind. Even though an action may have finished, its imprint is still there and will cause you to do that action again. With the right wisdom, all negative imprints can be completely purified.

Where do hindrances come from? From the unskillful, polluted, dark, dualistic, egotistic mind. The way to overcome them is to practice the Heruka Vajrasattva yoga method again and again. This builds up, or reinforces, the transcendental, pure energy within you so that you come to see things non-dualistically, in their true nature of emptiness, or shunyata. According to tantra, when you see things more realistically, they no longer appear concrete but blissful. When an object becomes blissful, it becomes a deity; it appears in divine form.

Sometimes we see each other as ugly, don't we? Ugly things irritate us. That's the problem. When we see things more realistically—for instance, the deeper nature of other human beings—we are transformed. Happiness and bliss are energized within us. As a result, we see the qualities of the deity within other human beings. What are these qualities? Wisdom and compassion. What is a deity? Fully developed wisdom and compassion, the qualities of enlightenment. This applies to any deity whatsoever.

THE SADHANA

Taking refuge and generating bodhichitta

We take refuge in Buddha, Dharma, and Sangha, the Sangha of the three Buddhist vehicles. That means you can no longer say, "I'm a Mahayanist; I don't take refuge in Hinayana arhats." We take refuge in Sangha without differentiation. We also take refuge in both dakas and dakinis. You can't say, "I'll take refuge in males, but not in females." We take refuge in all bodhisat tvas. And you particularly take refuge in the person *(lop-pön)* who gave you the empowerment of Heruka Vajrasattva.

The principal object of refuge is standing two-armed Heruka, holding a vajra and bell, embracing his consort Vajravarahi. It might be too difficult for you to visualize the aspect with all the arms and legs. They are surrounded by all the figures mentioned in the main commentary, who fill all of space. These melt into light and dissolve into Heruka, who then sinks into you. You become Heruka. Concentrate on that for as long as you can.[20]

When you generate bodhichitta by thinking, "I must become Heruka...," you can send radiant light into the ten directions, purifying all sentient beings in the six realms and transforming them into Heruka. All these Herukas then sink into you. That is one technique for actualizing bodhichitta.

The actual yoga method

When doing the Heruka Vajrasattva yoga method, you can visualize yourself as Heruka, or Vajrapani, or whomever else is your favorite deity. But then the question might arise, "If I am Heruka, what need is there to purify?" Of course, if you really are Heruka you certainly don't need any purification. Here, when you transform yourself into the divine aspect of Heruka, even if you have very good concentration, your dualistic mind will be lurking somewhere in the depths of your consciousness, just waiting to jump out and confuse you.

This reminds me of a story about a Yamantaka practitioner in Tibet. As you know, Yamantaka has all these hands, each one holding something or other. One day this monk was visualizing himself in that aspect, and he must have been quite convinced, because when his lama tried to give him something, he said, "Sorry, my hands are full." So his lama replied, "Well, just use your regular, impure hands instead."

Even if you can visualize yourself as Heruka with complete conviction, not an ordinary thought in mind, you still need purification. Not just because Buddha says so, but because your dualistic mind is still there. Therefore, even if you manifest as Heruka, you can still practice the Heruka Vajrasattva method. When you do, however, you simply maintain divine appearance without emphasizing divine pride.

Visualize Heruka Vajrasattva above your crown, at whatever height is comfortable for you. However, he shouldn't be miles above you—a hand's breadth, or something like that is enough. His body is not like our material, physical bodies but is a rainbow body: clear and transparent, a psychic body. He is completely unified with his consort. She symbolizes enlightened wisdom; he, enlightened method.

Light radiates from his heart into the ten directions, invoking all the buddhas and bodhisattvas. This white radiant light is the energy of divine, enlightened wisdom, the pure knowledge-wisdom that understands the deepest nature of totality. That is the pure mind. The impure mind is just the opposite. It is narrow; it lacks skillful wisdom and produces impure actions.

The white radiant light of supreme wisdom-energy that is invoked sinks into Heruka Vajrasattva's heart, goes down his sushumna to his secret chakra, into Dorje Nyema's secret chakra, and fills her sushumna, too. Their bodies are filled with blissful white radiant light. From the mantra at the heart of each deity, blissful white kundalini energy rushes down their central channels, through their secret chakras and into your crown chakra. It is very powerful, like a waterfall. In this yän-de visualization, white light rushes down your sushumna pushing out through your secret chakra all negative energy and impurities in the aspect of pigs, chickens, snakes, and so forth. These and other animals, like scorpions, monkeys, and cows, symbolize all the different sorts of negativity within your nervous system. All are completely flushed out. Your dissatisfaction and loneliness are also purified, as are any other disturbing negative symptoms that you can think of.

You can also do män-de visualization at this point. Here, you visualize all your internal garbage floating up on the surface of the blissful kundalini energy as it fills your body from bottom to top. This garbage leaves your body through your nose, eyes, mouth, and ears, and also bubbles out your crown chakra.

Then you can do the third meditation, or pung-de, visualizing brilliant radiant light. It beams down from Vajrasattva's heart, through his secret chakra and then through your crown, and purifies your entire nervous system. These are the three visualizations to do while you are reciting the mantra.

At the end, Heruka Vajrasattva sinks through your sushumna into your heart. Your body, speech, and mind are unified with his divine body, speech, and mind. You become Heruka Vajrasattva. From your divine heart much light radiates through the six samsaric realms, purifying all sentient beings and transforming them all into the aspect of Heruka Vajrasattva. All these Heruka Vajrasattvas then sink into you.

This is important. We are always involved with other people and often have heavy karma with each other. We get angry with others; we get strongly attached to others. Most of our problems are with other people. We are so strongly connected that we go through our entire lives constantly bumping into each other.

When you do the above meditation, you transform yourself, and you also transform all objects. Thus, for you there are neither objects of craving desire nor objects of hatred, so you remain healthy. The Vajrayana places great emphasis on the transformation of objects so that rather than energizing the three poisons of ignorance, attachment, and anger within you, they energize bliss instead.

You also emit from your divine Heruka Vajrasattva heart countless manifestations of Heruka Vajrasattva and whatever else you consider attractive and desirable—beautiful men, beautiful women, or any other beautiful object of the senses—as offerings to the supreme beings in the ten directions. Visualize that this offering gives great bliss to those buddhas and bodhisattvas.

In fact, the essential meaning of the word "offering" is that which energizes transcendental bliss in whomever receives it. That is a proper offering. If you give something that causes suffering, it's not an offering. Since the Buddhist connotation of offering is that which brings happiness, you can see that most of the time our gifts don't work that way; even though we mean well, our presents often make people miserable.

So much for the essential points of the sadhana. You now have to understand the actual purpose of the transformation we are practicing here. If someone asks you why you are practicing this yoga method, you might reply, "To purify myself." Well, that's basically okay, but the real answer should be, "I want to understand the true nature of all existence; I want to understand reality." That's the real purpose of the Heruka Vajrasattva yoga method. It shows you what is reality and what is not; it helps you realize shunyata, nonduality, and stops you from continuing under the influence of the concrete conceptions of your ego.

The more you understand the fundamental nature of all existence, the greater the bliss you experience. The greater the bliss you experience, the closer you are to attaining the beautiful form of the deity. That is the main point.

Many Westerners think that it must be painful to understand samsara the way it's explained in Buddhism: "Buddhism says that life is suffering; that means there's no way out!" It seems that Buddhist philosophy and meditation were created for the express purpose of making people miserable! That's a completely wrong attitude; they don't understand what they really need.

What I'm saying is that the whole purpose of practicing Heruka Vajrasattva is to realize nonduality—the fundamental reality of yourself and all other phenomena. That realization is an extremely blissful experience. Once you've experienced that bliss, you can see the beauty of the deity in every other person and stop putting negative projections onto others.

Tantric philosophy teaches that whoever practices tantra must see other sentient beings as deities. That's the *philosophy*. Those who have realized the fundamental nature, the nonduality, of other human beings have the transcendental experience of seeing the enlightened qualities of the deity in others. Such practitioners have no room for negative thoughts.

Those are the main points; I hope it's enough. Are there any questions?

QUESTIONS AND ANSWERS

Q: We are supposed to see others as Heruka Vajrasattva, but what happens when we see someone doing something negative?

A: You mean, should you try to stop them? Well, remember the story about the monk who was visualizing himself as Yamantaka? It's similar. If you see someone doing something wrong, you can say, "Hey, what's going on?" The thing is, however, that you still have to see Heruka Vajrasattva somewhere within him. It's just that he's forgotten who he really is and is acting under the influence of his chicken or snake mind. So you can say, "Excuse me, your chicken is showing!" Something like that!

My experience is that it's difficult to visualize women as, say, the male deities Vajrasattva or Vajrapani. But I try to see that somewhere within the atmosphere of the female body is the crystal, clean-clear psychic body of Vajrasattva or Vajrapani. You can understand that. Each of us does have Vajrasattva quality, Vajrapani quality within us, so we can visualize the divine body co-existing with us.

Q: Sometimes when I meditate I see a kind of blue light in front of me. Is it real or imaginary, and what does it mean?

A: It depends a bit on how you feel when you see it—whether you feel relaxed or irritated. But it's not necessarily just a mental projection. Sometimes when your mind has developed in a certain way, you can see light physically, with your eye sense. I think it's very good if someone has this kind of natural vision of light. Normally, when we meditate we don't see any light at all; only darkness. If I see green or blue light, even in my imagination, I feel happy. Blue light is somehow related to infinity; seeing blue light suggests a mind that's very expansive, not narrow.

Q: How big should you visualize Vajrasattva?

A: It varies with the person. Some people like to visualize him big, others small. He shouldn't be too big; most people tend to favor something similar to their own proportions. Also, he should not be heavy or physical, and he shouldn't touch your head. You don't have to force the visualization, either. He simply manifests in the space above your head, appearing spontaneously. Out of Heruka Vajrasattva's divine omnipresent wisdom his energy appears without effort, like a reflection in a mirror. If you don't have some under-standing of shunyata, then he seems really heavy: "Oh, Vajrasattva is too heavy for me. This retreat's too heavy, and he's too heavy!" That shows you don't really understand the wisdom of nonduality.

Anyway, visualize Vajrasattva as whatever size feels comfortable but clean-clear, crystal, like a rainbow, so that just looking at him energizes a clean, blissful kundalini experience. Sometimes these experiences can feel like an orgasm, but they are not physical reactions. If you are meditating with intensive awareness, there's no problem, but if you don't have some understanding of nonduality, then things become too physical and that can be dangerous.

Q: Please would you say something about the quality of Heruka Vajrasattva.
A: Heruka Vajrasattva is the fully developed pure wisdom of the three time buddhas and bodhisattvas manifesting in a pure emanation of white radiant light. Therefore, his essence is nondual wisdom. Whenever you practice the yoga method, his divine form is demonstrating reality for you. He is the eternally blissful state of pure wisdom.

Q: What does Heruka mean, and how is Heruka Vajrasattva different from other Vajrasattvas?
A: Literally, "Heruka" means drinking blood, but it symbolizes experiencing eternal bliss. Bliss has the quality of the totally developed unity of male-female energy. Dorje Nyema holds a kapala containing what seems to be blood. That symbolizes her giving eternal blissful energy. When you practice Heruka Vajrasattva, you drink the blood of the emotion of the experience of eternal bliss. Red signifies emotion. As human beings we need to express emotion to each other. Some people are completely unemotional—they are just like wood. That's no good. Even if you are an enlightened being or in deep samadhi, you can still show emotion; it's just that you don't get involved in emotionally suffocating situations.

Heruka Vajrasattva has a kind of unique energy and emphasizes the development of wisdom. There are four classes of tantra; Heruka Vajrasattva is from the highest yoga, or highest, class.

Q: When visualizing the two deities in union, do you visualize yourself as the male, the female, or both conjoined?
A: Whatever feels comfortable for you is good. As I said before, sometimes women find it difficult to visualize themselves as male deities and vice versa. But we all have male and female energy within us. Sometimes it gets unbal-

anced. Some men are too feminine, others, too masculine. The same goes for women. We have to develop the totality of the male-female energy that lies within each of us.

Also, when you look at Vajrasattva in union with his consort Dorje Nyema, you cannot say that one is higher and the other is lower. They are both at the same level, totally unified in nature. If it's easier for you, you can visualize yourself as Yum Dorje Nyema Karmo, with the Heruka Vajrasattva mantra at your heart. But no matter how you visualize the deity, the key is to visualize with intensive awareness of the fundamental nature of nonduality. If you do not, there's a danger that your visualization will become physical and will energize sense desire. The purpose of this practice is to eliminate desire.

Q: How far above your head can you visualize the deity? I find it easier to get a waterfall effect with the purifying energy when it's higher than the usual few fingers' breadth.
A: If it's easier, you can make it a little bit higher. Then, a tube of rainbow light emanates from his heart and connects with your crown chakra, and the blissful kundalini energy rushes down that.

Q: How can we use the Vajrasattva meditation to deal with feelings of guilt that might come up during the day?
A: Whenever you feel guilt arising, transform it into Heruka Vajrasattva. From head to toe, you are Heruka Vajrasattva. Also, besides the psychological effects of negative emotions, there are subtle physical effects that energize dissatisfaction. When you feel the energy of guilt within you, transform its subtle physical aspect into the Heruka Vajrasattva mantra. In that way it becomes the solution to your problems.

We need such active solutions to the negative habits that plague us. Knowing intellectually that they are negative is not enough to stop them. Here, we are acting in a practical way, building a defense against them instead of just dreaming. This is integrating Dharma with your daily life.

RETREAT

When you retreat, you shouldn't push yourself too much. Sometimes retreat can feel quite heavy; three months can seem like an eternity. Also, Westerners often don't know how to retreat. I have given the technical details elsewhere, but as far as your attitude is concerned, you should think that the pleasure of retreat is like that of a nightclub. You're gaining blissful wisdom—enjoy yourself!

Take it easy. Make a schedule. If a session is difficult, not coming together, the techniques are difficult to master, the vase breathing too hard to do, take a break. Go outside. People feel, "Oh, retreat. I should be strict; I should be mean; I should struggle; I should give myself a hard time." It's not like that. Don't push.

You should keep yourself clean; wash regularly. And eat nutritious food. Don't try to be this big ascetic. Tibetan Buddhism teaches you to use all your energy—wealth, beauty, whatever—to bring yourself closer to enlightenment. That's what life is for.

The reason I mention all this is that Western people seem to think that retreat means not eating good food, not eating chocolate. That's stupid. Eat well—you're working for enlightenment. Don't treat yourself like a cow. Encourage yourself. I have to tell you that retreats have been the most pleasurable experiences of my life. I really enjoy them. I'm not hard line. Last time, at Tushita in Dharamsala, I had a hammock! In the breaks I'd go out and lie in it. The students used to gather round and look at me: "That's the way to retreat?" They couldn't believe it!

Retreats are for enjoyment, but not in the confused, samsaric sense of the word. There is something healthy to be gained; some satisfaction, some integration. Don't make your retreats unnecessarily difficult.

FIRE PUJA

When you have finished your retreat, you should do the Dorje Khadro fire puja. This is very useful. It's a bit like tumo meditation.

You visualize at your heart a black seed syllable that draws into you all the sickness, disease, and other negative symptoms of yourself and all other sentient beings. At your navel chakra there's a fire. Wind energy comes up from your feet and fans the blaze until it's roaring like a furnace. The fire gets stronger and stronger and explodes up your sushumna, pushing all the negative energy from the black seed syllable at your heart out through your nostrils into the mouth of the deity. That is the basic meditation technique.

The actual fire burning in front of you activates your mind so that the meditation becomes more intensive and realistic, and that helps you to realize shunyata. This is the main point of the Dorje Khadro fire puja. There's no commitment to do this after the Vajrasattva retreat, but if you could do

110,000 or 115,000 Dorje Khadro mantras it would be very powerful and beneficial.

Do four meditation sessions a day. Before breakfast, you should do a Vajrasattva retreat session, but since you've already finished your mantra commitment, use the session for contemplation instead. By reciting all those mantras in retreat, you have already built up within you a certain essential energy—the "nuclear energy" of the mantra. So now, simply contemplate.

After breakfast, make the fire and do a two-hour Dorje Khadro session. Then have lunch, and after that have a rest, and study some Dharma books. In the late afternoon do another two-hour session of fire puja. Finally, in the evening, do another session of single-pointed concentration, again without verbal recitation of the Vajrasattva mantra.

Actually, you can do the Dorje Khadro fire puja any time you feel bothered, hassled, irritated, or uncomfortable. You don't have to be in retreat. Morning, afternoon, or night—It's very powerful, very useful. It can stop those feelings right there. This comes from Lama Tsongkhapa's experience; it was one of his favorite meditations. When you do it, you're getting a real taste of his practice. It's like gold, a real golden Dharma.

Sometimes we need to do these active meditations. Visualize Dorje Khadro, a manifestation of Guhyasamaja, with his huge gaping mouth open, like a powerful black hole, sucking everything into it. All negative energy disappears into it forever.

13 ~ Vajrasattva Practice and Highest Yoga Tantra

B EFORE YOU CAN PRACTICE the completion stage of highest yoga tantra, among other things, such as guru yoga, you must practice the Vajrasattva yoga method. The Panchen Lama said that in order to understand the reality of your mind, you have to do intensive purification and collect a vast amount of merit. Both are important.

Take, for example, our own experience. We are very enthusiastic and really want from the bottom of our hearts to enjoy deep meditation, but no matter how hard we try, we always encounter mental garbage, distractions, and the sluggish, sleepy mind. Without control, millions of concepts, negative thoughts, and superstitions gallop through our minds. That means something's missing. And what is that? Purification. We need a lot of purification.

You can't blame the practices you've been doing: "I've been meditating for two years, and I still haven't achieved single-pointed concentration. What's the point of meditating?" You can't say that. Every day your superstitious mind takes you on an unbelievable trip. In one night it can take you around the whole world. Every trip leaves deep karmic imprints in your mind. It takes a long time to eradicate these. So you shouldn't be arrogant: "I'm not particularly negative. I'm pretty pure. I've never killed anyone; I don't lie; my parents take care of me, so I don't have to fight and cheat for food and clothing. I don't need purification." That's just an ego trip.

Impurity comes from the mind as well as the body. Check out the trips that your mind has been on from the time you were born until now. It's unbelievable. If you look at those experiences in the light of the twelve links of dependent arising, you'll practically drown in the ocean of superstition. That's why we need a great deal of purification.

For example, it would be pretty hard to grow fine, delicate lettuce here in Dharamsala. The soil here is very rocky, and the weeds are out of control. The ground would need a lot of work. Similarly, our minds need a lot of purification to eradicate the gross superstitions that prevent our fine, most subtle consciousness from functioning.

Also, sometimes we might think we're very capable of doing something, but deep inside, a subconscious voice keeps saying, "I'm incapable, I'm incapable; I'm not good at anything. I'll never be liberated, never be enlightened, never be Vajrayogini." Inside, that kind of stuff is going on all the time. Within your subconscious, a million chickens are clucking, "Not possible, not possible"; a million snakes are hissing, "Not possible, not possible"; a million pigs are grunting, "Not possible, not possible." Your subconscious mind is deeply contaminated by billions of delusions like these.

You'd be surprised at how pervasive this contamination is. You truly believe at the intellectual level that "I can do it," but deeply concealed, the billion voices of the pig-snake-chicken "can't-do" mentality keep telling you that you can't.

It's a psychological thing. You might accept something intellectually— "I want to become Vajrayogini"—but simultaneously that voice keeps saying, "No, you don't." There is acceptance and rejection at the same time. You can't understand it. You get really confused: "Do I want it, or don't I? Do I want an apple or not?" You're not sure, not sure, not sure.

That's the dualistic mind. We always talk about the dualistic mind—that's it; that's how it works. The dualistic mind is always comparing two things. You want to achieve deep concentration and discover eternal liberation but at the same time you resist, you reject it. The human mind is very funny.

So you can see from the practical point of view that you do, in fact, need purification, because when you meditate there are so many hindrances. That is the logic, and it is based on your own experience. You definitely need purification. You can't say, "I'm meditating, that's enough." It's never enough. There's a clear difference between meditation and purification. As Mañjushri told Lama Je Tsongkhapa, "Meditation is not enough. You also have to purify the hindrances and accumulate great merit. It is very important that these things be done simultaneously."

Now you can see why Mañjushri advised Lama Je Tsongkhapa in this way: "Don't just meditate all the time. Do some purification, too." That also shows that Lama Je Tsongkhapa liked to meditate a lot. Many Western scholars think that Lama Je Tsongkhapa was just an intellectual—some sort of Tibetan Buddhist professor, not a meditator. But then Mañjushri told him, "You are doing too much meditation. That's not enough. You also have to do purification and accumulate more merit." Lama Je Tsongkhapa was an unbelievable yogi. You cannot imagine. Even as a ten-year-old boy he was a great meditator. And when he was doing Mañjushri meditation in retreat, a figure of Mañjushri appeared spontaneously on the wall of his cave. I think you can still see that in Tibet.

Purification is very important. It is the only way to get rid of those billions of subconscious animals that keep telling you, "Not possible, not possible."

There's another slightly different psychological symptom, too: "It's not possible to purify, not possible to improve yourself, not possible to eradicate your dissatisfaction, not possible to release your attachment and desire." Does this sound funny? Check it out. At one level you want to do these things, but when you try, there's a voice deep down saying, "Hey, come on. It's not possible." That's what we call Mara, and he's there all the time.

This is why we don't have strong energy to purify ourselves, why we are not really convinced that we can overcome our grasping Western karma and gravitational attachment to sense pleasures. Go deep into your unconscious mind and you'll see what I'm talking about. Intellectually we know we can get enlightened, but deep down there's the hindrance that just keeps on saying, "No."

The point is this: the voice that tells you it's not possible to purify your negative karma also results from a lack of purification. That's the main point. In Buddhism we talk a lot about purification. We're talking about purifying the mind, not the body; purifying negative attitudes, negative psychological expressions. That's why it is extremely important to be totally convinced that you can purify any negativity whatsoever, any negativity you can think of. For example, Hitler exterminated millions of people. Even the murder of so many people can be completely purified, leaving not the slightest trace of negativity.

In Nagarjuna's *Letter to a Friend,* he tells the true story of Lord Buddha's brother, who had incredibly strong desire, more than all of ours put together. Still, he was able to purify that and become an arhat. Then there was Angulimala, who followed the wrong guru and was told that he would not gain realizations until he had killed a thousand people. Believing this, he started killing people and had killed 999 when the Buddha appeared and showed him how wrong it was. Even he was able to purify his negativities and become an arhat. Finally, there was King Ajatashatru, who lived at the time of Lord Buddha. He committed one of the five inexpiable sins by imprisoning his father, who died in jail. Even this extremely negative karma could be purified, and he too became an arhat.[21]

Therefore, through these examples, you should understand that any negative karma that you have created in this life has been made by your pathetic, weak, illogical, grasping negative mind. The inner nuclear missile of your powerful, transcendental, simultaneously born great wisdom can definitely purify it all. You should be thoroughly convinced of this, not "Maybe it can, maybe it can't." Think instead, "It is 100 percent certain that any negativity I have created by body, speech, or mind can be completely purified." This brave, understanding mind is very, very useful. Without it you will never succeed in meditation, because those billions of animals in your subconscious will be telling you, "No, no, no, no, no, no, no...."

If you recite the Vajrasattva mantra twenty-one times every night, it stops the otherwise exponential proliferation of negative actions created during that day. Without purification, one day's negative energy will have doubled by the next, redoubled by the day after that, and so on. The tantric texts also explain that if you recite the mantra properly one hundred thousand times, you can completely purify all negativities whatsoever, even broken root tantric vows. There is no negativity that cannot be purified by this method. It's very powerful.

Also, as I've explained before, there are various aspects of Vajrasattva: kriya, charya, yoga, and highest yoga. The latter also includes the Guhyasamaja and Yamantaka aspects, which, as His Holiness Song Rinpoche said, emphasize physical purification, purification of the body. Heruka Vajrasattva focuses more on mental purification. That's why it is such a powerful method. Not only for Tibetans. It is possible that some practices that are suitable for Tibetans might not suit Westerners, but this is not one of them. I've been doing some anthropological experiments on my Western students, and so far I think that their Vajrasattva practice has been pretty successful. After retreat their brain is something else! I wasn't expecting such a big change. For some reason, practicing Heruka Vajrasattva transforms them into quite different human beings. I'm glad that Westerners find this practice so suitable and helpful.

The actual practice of Vajrasattva is quite simple. First, as I stressed before, you have to be aware of your negativities. You may not seem to have anything gross or anything that you're even aware of, but you certainly will have a lot of stuff deep down in your subconscious. When you practice the Vajrasattva meditation, you have to purify all these things. You also have to have strong confidence that you're capable of being purified, the strong belief that purification is possible, and the powerful determination never to repeat those negative actions ever again. The latter is one of the four opponent powers, which I have explained in the main commentary. Using those powers is the right way to purify.

The meditation itself is simple. I'll run through it very briefly. A few fingers' breadth above the crown of your head is a lotus and moon seat, upon which is a white vajra with the syllable HUM at its center. Light radiates in all directions purifying all mother sentient beings' environments and wrong conceptions; it then returns, unifying with and transforming the vajra into the radiant white body of Heruka Vajrasattva. Lama Je Pabongka describes different shades of white for the various aspects of Vajrasattva's body. The body itself is clear like crystal, the lotus at his heart is milky in color, the mantra around its edge is silver. Everything is still white, but differentiated slightly in order to help you visualize.

He has one face and two arms and holds a vajra in his right hand and a bell in his left. He embraces his consort, Dorje Nyema, who holds a curved knife in her right hand and a kapala full of blissful energy in her left. Then blissful white kundalini energy gushes down from their hearts, through their sushumnas to where they are joined at the lower chakra, through the lotus and moon seat, through your crown chakra, and down your sushumna, purifying all the conscious and unconscious negativities we were talking about before. And to do this, we use three different meditation techniques—män-de, yän-de, and pung-de—which I have described in detail elsewhere.

The great yogi Lama Je Pabongka further said that if you are doing completion stage practice, you can do an additional visualization that will help you with it. When the blissful kundalini energy rushes down your sushumna, it energizes the four types of bliss—bliss, great bliss, extraordinary bliss, and extremely great bliss—as it passes through your crown, throat, heart, and navel chakras, respectively.

Also, when you think about negativity, don't just think physically, but purify mental weaknesses as well, such as sadness, loneliness, and so forth. Other benefits of the blissful energy pouring down your sushumna are that it helps you to open all your chakras and to develop tumo meditation and great bliss. So now you see that you can practice the Vajrasattva meditation at the simple level of the generation stage or the more advanced level of the completion stage.

Because the Vajrasattva practice allows you to overcome any sort of negativity, you become very courageous and liberated. You feel confident that anything is possible, that you can conquer any difficulty. That aspect is very important. It gives you great inspiration. The weak mind keeps saying, "Not possible, not possible, I can't do it, I can't do it, I can't decide, I can't decide." Some people can't even decide whether or not to go to the bathroom. What do you think of them? They need Vajrasattva meditation! It's true, unbelievable. I don't understand some people's minds. They can't decide about anything. My goodness. When I see people like that, I feel maybe I'm not so bad after all!

Purification is very useful. It gives you great satisfaction and flexibility of mind. You know you can do something. You can go into darkness; you can go into light; you can even go underground! You become confident in your ability to do anything.

I really hope that all my students will do at least one hundred thousand Vajrasattva mantras before they die. I truly believe that after doing a Vajrasattva retreat they cannot be reborn in the hell realms. No way! They can make a decision: "After the Vajrasattva retreat there's no way I can be reborn in a miserable realm. I don't care whether I live or die." You get some sort of insurance. Vajrasattva retreat is insurance against being reborn in the lower realms. We need such insurance. Now I'm becoming an insurance salesman! That's terrible, isn't it! Still, I need your help to make my insurance company successful.

Whether we are believers or nonbelievers, we do need some confidence. We're all impermanent. We don't know when we're going to die. We have all these shortcomings. But if you have indestructible insurance, who worries about death? Death is natural; worrying about it is a waste of time. Instead of feeling upset that your body is not as beautiful as it once was, look forward to being reborn with a better one. Anyway, I'm joking. My point is, however, that you need some kind of self-confidence, "I'm definitely going to die, but at least I'm guaranteed of not being reborn in the lower realms." There is such a guarantee, because there definitely exists a level of mind that you can reach, from which you cannot descend to a lower rebirth.

For those who cannot do the long mantra as a daily practice, His Holiness Song Rinpoche said that you can recite the short one: OM VAJRASATTVA HUM twenty-one times, before you go to sleep at night. It only takes a minute or two; anybody can do that.

Now, I want to make sure you understand clean-clear that you don't have to have killed, stolen, or beaten people up to need Vajrasattva purification. There's a deeper reason than just wanting to purify what people commonly refer to as negativity. What is negativity? Most people will interpret it as doing bad things to other people. Americans always say, "We didn't do bad things; we always help other people." That's a joke! They're fooling themselves. Even if you have devoted your entire life to helping others, the weak mind is still there. That's why you need purification.

One thing I have observed is that someone who has done very bad things is also capable of tremendous good. This may not be a fact, it's just something I've observed. Some people are almost numb. Neither their positive nor their negative actions have any strength; all their actions are like water. People like that tend to think, "I haven't done anything bad, I'm always careful. I don't need purification." They might be careful, but it's out of self-pity and concern for their own well-being. That doesn't mean they do not need purification.

Take Milarepa, for example. After his father died, the villagers confiscated his mother's property, so she sent Milarepa to a black magician to learn the craft so that later they could take revenge. One night all the villagers came together at somebody's house for a party. With his black magic Milarepa made the roof collapse, killing them all. You can see how he had built up a tremendous force of negative energy. He studied for years and then watched and waited for the right opportunity with only the negative motivation of killing all those people in mind. But later he was able to generate even more powerful positive energy, purify all this negativity, and reach enlightenment in that lifetime. In contrast, some people are ineffective either positively or negatively, completely wishy-washy.

Human potential is incredible. You can do such positive things. Jesus was unbelievably powerful. People thought he was crazy. Shakyamuni Buddha, too. He had enormous wealth and power, but he gave it all up, escaped from samsara, and became enlightened. People thought he was stupid: "If he'd remained as king, he could have done so much for others, but he went into the jungle to live like an animal. He's ridiculous." Humans have tremendous power and potential and can purify vast amounts of negativity.

If you want to practice the completion stage of tantra, you should first do one hundred thousand Vajrasattva mantras. Purification is important, because freedom from the dualistic mind *is* enlightenment. We talk about enlightened realizations, buddhahood. That's freedom from the dualistic mind. Purification eradicates the dualistic mind.

When Atisha was making the long overland trip from India to Tibet more than a thousand years ago, he kept stopping the caravan and jumping down to do purification at the side of the road. Whenever he noticed the slightest negative thought or concept, he would purify it then and there. That shows he was a great yogi, a great bodhisattva. That shows he understood karma. We don't understand karma; we just let it go. But he understood how negative karma multiplies in the mind, and so he made a point of purifying it right away.

It depends on how sensitive you are. If you are sensitive, you notice the effect of even the slightest negative karma. If you are immersed in an ocean of negative karma, you don't feel it. The heavy blanket of negativity is always there.

Once there was a great lama who was so pure that he always had a vision of light in front of him. One day a Tibetan family invited him to do a puja at their house. But the money they had used to buy the food and tea they offered him had come from the sale of prajñaparamita texts, books on the perfection of wisdom. As you know, money from the sale of holy objects like books and statues should not be used to buy temporal needs.

When the lama got home that night he noticed that his vision of light had disappeared. That was because he had eaten impure food that day. If you are sensitive and your karma is light, you notice the effects of negativity quickly and easily, the result comes soon. Our karma must be very heavy, because whatever we do, we don't notice it. Therefore, observing karma is very important.

When we talk about taking care of the various vows we have taken—the five precepts, our vows as monks and nuns, our bodhisattva vows—it all has to do with karma. We don't take these ordinations to become prisoners. Therefore, purification is very, very useful.

14 ~ The Qualities of Vajrasattva
Are Already within Us

WHY DOES THE TIBETAN BUDDHIST TRADITION contain the practice of Vajrasattva?

Everybody would like to be as happy as possible and totally satisfied. We would all like our minds to be clean-clear, controlled, and stable, instead of up and down as they usually are. We would all like to have good concentration, the ability to place our mind on whatever object we choose and have it remain there.

Unfortunately, every day of our lives we are overwhelmed and thrown off balance by the eighty superstitions, or in common Buddhist terms, the three poisonous minds of ignorance, attachment, and hatred. Therefore, we find it hard to be happy. Forget about liberation or enlightenment; we don't even know how to be happy people leading happy lives.

Within us, there is something missing. We are not well balanced; our internal energies are unequal, so our minds are up and down, fluctuating from one extreme to the other. We *are* extreme. We may seem normal from the point of view of the general public, from the New York or Paris point of view, but if you check a little deeper, you will see that we are a little crazy. So, what to do?

We need purification. First, we need to realize, or recognize, our own experiences. Even though they are our own, we are unfamiliar with most of them. To help us understand our own experiences, we need a great deal of purification, and in the Tibetan tradition, the Vajrasattva yoga practice is considered to be one of the most powerful methods of purification.

Who is Heruka Vajrasattva? We consider him to be a manifestation of the unity of fully developed male and female energy, the complete purity of the state of enlightenment. Out of their great compassion and limitless love, the buddhas and bodhisattvas have manifested their collected purity in the archetypal image of Vajrasattva so that we can identify ourselves with him.

We have to understand that the qualities of Vajrasattva are already within us. But our realizations, method, and wisdom are limited. They have to be developed through identification with the limitless, pure energy of the archetype. Instead of thinking of ourselves as limited, hopeless sentient beings, we have to recognize our incredible potential. We can free ourselves from the confusion of uncontrolled concepts. We can develop our consciousness to the limitless states of universal compassion, universal love, universal wisdom, universal freedom. The Vajrasattva practice can lead us beyond ego, beyond grasping, and beyond the dualistic mind. That's what the Vajrasattva practice is about.

Why do we identify with the deity? The deity is the manifestation of the qualities of supreme method and wisdom, so when we unify ourselves with that limitless archetype, we are identifying with those qualities. This leaves no room for our usual limited concepts. Most of you probably know all this, so I don't have to go into detail.

I hope now that you understand why you need to practice the Vajrasattva method. You have to feel that it is very close to you, somehow real, something you can do. That is important. It gives you the courage, space, and freedom you need to cut the limitations that make your life difficult. You know that you can handle, go beyond, be free from those difficulties. That is very important.

Through the experience of purification you can discover that although you might have created a lot of negativity, you are basically a pure person. You might have beaten other sentient beings, your mother, your father; you might hate your friends; you might even want to kill people. We do have negativities. We all live in the sense world. Our egos are in conflict, and we deal with each other with impure energy. The important thing is to overcome all these problems by realizing that since we have made things difficult for ourselves, since we have created our own complications, it is up to us to free ourselves from them. But it is not enough to realize this in a merely intellectual way. We have to gain deep understanding through practice. That way we can really feel that although we have difficulties, we can do something to liberate ourselves from them.

Personally, I feel it is very important that each of us realize and accept that we ourselves are responsible for all negative attitudes and actions. We, not God or Buddha, created the world's problems. Buddhism does not believe that God created misery. Misery is the creation of the negative, egotistic mind. We have to understand that. If we smash the negative, egotistic mind, we can overcome all problems.

Therefore, we can't blame others for our problems. We created them ourselves. We've created our industrialized society; we've created the Californian life; we've created the New York life; we've created the Paris life. God didn't create them, we did. We've made everything so expensive! A couple of years ago I went shopping in Paris. I couldn't believe how expensive it was. I didn't buy anything. I've been shopping in Ulverston, in Barcelona, where I bought lots of stuff, but I didn't buy anything in Paris. It's all our own doing.

It is very important to recognize how we've created all our own problems. Just understanding this is so important. We've created these problems because we've not been handling our body, speech, and mind correctly. The result has been problems for ourselves, problems for others. We have confused ourselves and others for centuries, millennia, countless lives. It has been this way, it is this way, and it will continue to be this way unless we renounce this cycle of suffering. When you are miserable, you make others miserable. When you are happy, you make others happy.

You have to feel incredulous when you realize the endlessness of all this confusion, and make a strong determination to clear it up: "If I truly love others, if I really have compassion for others, I must improve myself. I must better my behavior, my speech, and my thinking. Without doing so there's no way I can help others. I'm only dreaming if while saying that I want to help others, I merely perpetuate the disastrous actions of my uncontrolled body, speech, and mind."

That's the attitude you need if you want to help others in the best way you can. You're always around other people, aren't you? Even if you go off into the Himalayas, you'll be with people. If you go to where there are no people and try to make friends with the tigers, you'll get eaten up and disappear! So you have to stay around people. We always talk about love. We need love; other sentient beings need love. But our attitudes are childish, and such attitudes make others childish. We need to grow up. Look at what's happening here, even as I speak. With my limited mind, I tell you, "Blah, blah, blah." You take that limited thinking away with you, pass it on to others, and the whole cycle continues to spin. That's the nature of samsara.

However, I am always very happy when people want to practice purification. I truly believe that if religious people really want to practice Dharma, or meditation, the most important thing they can do is to improve their attitude, their actions, and their speech. That is done through the sincere practice of purification.

Most people, especially Westerners, think that they are already pure, that they don't need purification: "I'm pure, I don't have any problems." This is my experience. Many Westerners have come to our Kopan meditation courses, where we teach basic lamrim, the four noble truths, suffering, and so forth. They tell me straight out, "What are you talking about? You're always going on about problems. I don't have any problems, I'm happy. I've got plenty of money. Why do you keep telling me I'm miserable?" This is the Western mentality. People think that if they've got money, they're happy. From the Buddhist point of view, they're wrong. We think your dollars only make you more miserable.

I'm not saying that only Westerners think like that. Many Asians also think that they're problem-free. But they have problems—they just don't recognize them. They recognize others' problems, but not their own. That's how we are. We see the problems of the people we're with, but we don't see our own. We think we're pure. Such are the limitations of the samsaric mind.

That's why I feel happy when people recognize that they need purification, that there is something they can do to improve their lives. I consider that some kind of realization. You recognize that since your own mind created the negative experiences you have, your own mind can counteract them. This is the main point. Don't think, "I created my own karma. I deserve to suffer in hell." This is completely wrong.

Of course, most of us carry negativities. Our minds are out of control. But we haven't killed people; we haven't killed our parents, or an arhat, or a buddha, so I still think we're lucky. Remember Milarepa. He killed all those people with black magic. Even so, I don't regard him as a criminal, a bad person. On the contrary, I think he's a great person; he set us a good example. He did incredibly negative things, realized black magic was bad, gave it up, practiced pure Dharma, and became completely liberated. Compared to him, we are lucky. We've never killed anybody. But we still have negativities; our minds are still out of control. Yet, we can overcome these problems by practicing the profound methods of tantric yoga.

I feel inspired by Milarepa's attitude. It makes us want to do something, to act. That inspiration itself is liberating. Otherwise we feel, "I'm completely incapable. I'm the most hopeless person in the world. I can't do anything about my motivation or my actions. I'll never be able to change." That's wrong. We can change in any way we like. That's the beauty of the human mind.

Now, before I give this highest yoga initiation, I want to remind you that anyone who takes it is making a commitment to retreat on Heruka Vajrasattva for three months. If you have already done this retreat, you don't have to do it again, but if you have retreated on only an aspect of Vajrasattva from one of the lower tantras, you will still have to do the three-month retreat on Heruka Vajrasattva.

However, if you are going back to the West and will have to work, you can do the one hundred thousand mantras as a daily commitment, instead of in retreat, as long as you use the same seat until you've finished, as I have explained elsewhere.[22] I'm sympathetic to that need.

You know, the mantra itself has incredible power. You begin at the level that you're on, but each time you say the mantra, each retreat session, you start to improve. Slowly, slowly, the mantra elevates you. Even though you might not have deep concentration, just trying to visualize and repeating the mantra has what I would dare to call a miraculous effect on you. Without your even trying, the mantra touches your deep subconscious and purifies you. There is nothing at all worldly, contaminated, or evil about the mantra; it has an inherent power to elevate that automatically burns up your impure, garbage energy. That's the great beauty of mantra. You don't have to be a great meditator to benefit from it. Mantra can automatically elevate you from your ordinary way of thinking and speak to you in a place beyond heavy worldly concepts. That gives you the space to see things more clearly, and that is good enough.

Mantra is also a kind of secret language. Normally, we communicate on a very low level. When we argue with each other, we're on a low energy plane. Our quarrels are very worldly. Mantra takes you away from the things that usually drive you crazy, from the things in which you are normally involved. It sort of hypnotizes you into communicating with higher levels of mind by blocking normal, conventional, low level communication. That's another way in which mantra is very helpful. Of course, mere words can never explain the true nature of mantra.

Another thing: we don't consider Vajrasattva and the mantra to be two separate things. The Vajrasattva mantra is Vajrasattva; Vajrasattva is the Vajrasattva mantra. Buddhism is set up for us to transform our ordinary body, speech, and mind into those of an enlightened being. By emanating as the deity, we transform our body; by reciting the mantra, we transform our speech; and by generating bodhichitta and the wisdom of shunyata, we transform our mind.

Vajrasattva is not simply for purification. The visualization you do is a process to help you generate wisdom and compassion and to experience something akin to what you would experience in completion stage practice. You visualize Vajrasattva above the crown of your head in union with his consort.

From their heart chakras, blissful white kundalini energy rushes all the way down their sushumnas and comes out where they are joined at their secret chakras. It continues down through the lotus and moon seat, through your crown chakra and down your sushumna, and you practice the various purifying meditation techniques. You then unify and identify with Vajrasattva. You experience enlightened energy. This is not just a purification practice.

Some people think visualization is a bit funny; that when you visualize you are just making something up. I think it is a most powerful method; a powerful method to break your ordinary concepts, your preconceptions. I cannot just tell you, "You are wrong, you are wrong. Your way of thinking is wrong; you are so deluded." Those are just words. You have to experience for yourself, "How deluded I am, how I project things." You have to see for yourself how different projections make you feel and affect your view of reality. Vajrasattva introduces you to the way you think, the way you interpret the reality of yourself and your world. That's what visualization shows you. The visualization of Vajrasattva is a teaching on shunyata.

I can listen to teachings on shunyata twenty-four hours a day, seven days a week, for a year, "Shunyata, shunyata, shunyata, ego is bad, wrong view…," listening, listening, somebody is up there teaching me. But in the end, I'll still be full of concepts and thoughts. In just the shortest time, Vajrasattva visualization can completely shut down your mental chatter, giving you the space to work out what you see. I really believe that this is a much stronger way to introduce you to shunyata, with your own experience, your own language, your own mind, and your own thinking. I'm probably wrong, but that's what I believe. Really, this is most powerful.

Basically, I'm a skeptic. I don't believe things easily. I didn't expect that Vajrasattva meditation would do much for the Western mind. I just observed what was happening. So far, I think that Vajrasattva retreat has been an unprecedented success among my Western students. Their minds have definitely changed for the better. Without retreat, their minds would not have changed. It takes a strong retreat to change Westerners' minds. Then something really happens. The evidence of this experience has convinced me that the Vajrasattva practice really works for Westerners.

15 ~ Action Is Everything

WE HAVE TO ACT, not just philosophize. Philosophical concepts may be able to correct wrong ideas, erroneous ways of thought, and mistaken beliefs, but intellectual correction is not enough. Along with that we need a powerful force to channel our minds into the correct, divine philosophy of the middle way.

For example, Lord Buddha taught that we should avoid extremes and follow the middle way, because going to extremes and avoiding everything would make us sick. He said that we should adjust our lives both relatively and absolutely. But these statements are still views, ideas, and opinions, aren't they? Our lives should be more active than that. When you get your hands dirty, touch the earth, plant seeds, and water the ground, green plants manifest organically. Vajrasattva practice is a lot like that.

The Vajrasattva meditation is not complicated; it's very simple and easy to understand. It's not something that takes a lot of intellectual thought. You just do it, just act. That is what we need. Transformation never comes without action. No matter how much you study and learn, how much information you collect, it is action that really helps you integrate your life. The Tibetan Buddhist tradition contains a wide range of preliminary practices *(ngöndro)*. Vajrasattva is one of these. Even though it is very simple and practical, it is one of the most powerful methods of purification we have.

At first I was very skeptical that a method that worked for Easterners would also work for Westerners, but I have now seen hundreds of Westerners retreat on Vajrasattva with great success and great improvement in their minds. This experience has both amazed and satisfied me, and there is no doubt that it is highly worthwhile.

Buddhism always emphasizes meditation, mindfulness, awareness, method, and wisdom. Every word of the teachings points you in the direction of insight. The Vajrasattva yoga method is a very simple means of showing you who you are. It reveals your shortcomings and your strengths and is especially helpful in ripping off the heavy blanket of wrong conceptions that prevents you from seeing the reality of yourself. Even if you find it difficult to meditate or have poor concentration, this practice can give you inner satisfaction and a real taste of Buddhadharma. Therefore, it is very useful.

Normally, our motivation is at a very low level, and our actions are quite mundane. Sometimes I feel as though we're dealing with the hell realm in our human relationships. Well, that may be a bit of an exaggeration, but what I mean is that we don't use our human intelligence enough. Vajrasattva meditation brings you up from those lower levels of mind to a higher, more human plane of consciousness. You just have to do it, that's all.

Furthermore, the practice is structured so that while you are working with and meditating on the sadhana at a conscious level, positive energy from your subconscious mind is being activated and drawn upon to enhance your practice. This is one of the psychological features of tantra and one of the reasons that it is so powerful. Tantra liberates you by working at both the conscious and subconscious levels to lead your mind into the gradual path to enlightenment.

Most of us are limited when it comes to recognizing both the male and female aspects of our being. Vajrasattva meditation demonstrates the magnificent blissful unified energy within us. We need this. We feel lonely because we are unaware of the totality of the inner human environment. And as long as we follow our monkey minds, we'll remain unaware of it and continue to feel lonely. Vajrasattva shows you what it's like to be a complete person, an emanation of totality. This is very helpful.

The Vajrasattva mantra is especially powerful. I call it "miraculous television"! On regular television you see incredible things, don't you? All sorts of samsaric things can manifest on your screen. Similarly, mantra is like divine television. By simply reciting the mantra, you bring the three principal aspects of the path—renunciation, bodhichitta, and right view—into your stream of consciousness. Divine pride and clarity also enter. Mantra is very powerful because it gives you access to levels of consciousness that are far beyond the ordinary, mundane, lower levels on which you usually operate.

Intellectually oriented people find it difficult to transform themselves because they think that the way to perfection is through their intellect: "This is knowledge; this is the liberator; intellect is everything." Intellect is not everything—action is everything. For example, if a simple person who doesn't have great intellectual learning gets into a jet plane, he still gets to wherever he wants to go. Similarly, if someone who has not studied Dharma extensively climbs aboard the jet of the Vajrasattva yoga method, he or she can be carried to transformation without having to worry about accumulating intellectual knowledge.

Our problem is that we are too intellectual. We say, "This is no good; I don't want that; I want the other." That's how we choose, and that's our problem. Our intellect causes most of our dissatisfaction. We have taken so many intellectual trips in our life, yet we are still dissatisfied. You can see this most clearly in the West.

The nuclear essence of tantra is that the human being is the deity. The human being *is* the god; the human being *is* the deity. I have to emphasize this. We have the qualities of the deity within us. You always think that the deity is something rarefied and inaccessible, but through tantra you can touch the deity, recognize yourself as the deity. That's why it is very powerful.

Buddhism teaches that the basic human problem is the ridiculous thought that we are hopeless. This way of identifying ourselves damages our human quality. Therefore, we need to discover the divinity within us, the divine qualities that are already there. Buddhism is really so realistic, so scientific, so down-to-earth, so clean-clear: human beings *do* have a pure nature and divine inner qualities, so they should recognize and unify with them. And according to Lord Buddha, the way to recognize our divine qualities is not simply to *know* that they are there, but to act, to act. The way to act is to practice tantra. Tantra is not about words; the essence of tantra is action.

Of course, I'm not a great meditator; nor have I had much experience. I'm somewhat narrow and out of touch with reality. Nevertheless, I have done mantra retreats and, miraculously, have experienced to a certain extent things that I have never experienced when not in retreat. I have discovered new dimensions to life, a new reality. Mantra has the power to take you into a new dimension, a new space. That is what tantra and mantra can do.

Sometimes these new experiences can shock you because they are so different from your normal reality. On the other hand, you can experience clean-clear visions that are very real for you. Anyway, I'm not going to try to explain all this. I just want to say that is extremely worthwhile for you to act. Action is simple and direct. I'm telling you all this because many would-be practitioners get confused by the many teachings and practices they find in Buddhism. They don't know what to do, what practices are for them. Consequently, they don't do anything properly. If you can concentrate on certain meditation practices and be very focused when you do them, I can guarantee that you will change for the better.

Therefore, when I give the Vajrasattva initiation, I don't make you commit to doing the practice or reciting the mantra every day of your life, but I do ask most of you to do a three-month group retreat. The only purpose of making a retreat commitment is to ensure that you have some experience, that you are not just spiritually grasping but are doing something to elevate yourself. People who have already done the retreat have already gained the experience and don't necessarily have to do it again.

I understand that life in the West does not always allow you to go off for a three-month retreat, so I sometimes make an exception. If you don't have time to do the strict retreat, you can practice at home for an hour a day until you have recited the required number of mantras. You should try to finish within two to three years.

The main condition here is that you sit in the same seat. Usually our minds are fickle; we can't focus intensively and are completely distracted, constantly looking for something new, something different. This is an unhealthy attitude. You lose penetrative insight; you lose intensive awareness. It's not that a constantly changing environment drives you crazy, but it does spoil your meditation. A stable situation promotes simplicity, clarity, insight, and intensive awareness. If we were beyond conditioning, it would be all right, but our minds are at a lower level, where conditions affect us. Everything affects us: stars, poisonous plants, snakes, human beings, colors. Consciously or unconsciously, we are affected. To overcome this tendency, we meditate in the same place.

However, I think I have to make another compromise here to accommodate a lifestyle such as that in America, where people move around a lot. Make a small meditation box that will fit into your car. Then when you move house, you can take your seat with you. The continuity of daily practice is very important, so please don't break it—wherever you go, take your meditation box with you.

Continuity is really important. We have all had moments of sensitive, intensive awareness where we could almost hear the flowers breathe; perfect, blissful, satisfied experiences where we have never wanted to look at anything else. But what we have lacked is that state of total satisfaction; our intensive awareness has been interrupted. We are always on, off, on, off, up, down, and that's the problem. In fact, the Tibetan word for tantra, *gyü,* means continuity, and continuity is very important if you want to stay happy. If you reach a certain state of happiness and satisfaction, you want to maintain it, don't you? You don't want to fill your consciousness with disasters. This is so simple, so logical. We *can* be logical at times. The problem is that when we are off, we are illogical, and it is only when we are on that logic prevails. It is important to maintain the continuity of happy conditions without allowing misery to interrupt. Continuous practice is therefore very important.

Retreat is very special. The literal meaning of the Tibetan word for retreat, *tsam,* is isolation. But isolation from what—reality? Well, we're already isolated from that. We need to isolate ourselves from mentally or externally confused situations, any circumstances that tend to make us unclear. If you can avoid all that for the duration of your retreat, transformation will come of itself, without your even having to worry about it. And as I said before, if you can't isolate yourself in strict retreat, the continuity of daily practice is very important. If one day you are busy and can't manage your usual session, do half an hour. If that's too much, do twenty minutes, or ten, or even five. There has to some continuity. Your stream of consciousness is like a highway, so keep the energy flowing along it.

Buddha manifests in the radiant white form of Vajrasattva. Why does Buddha manifest in different ways? Because different sentient beings have different needs, and Buddha himself said that he would manifest in various forms in accordance with those needs. We believe that he can appear as Krishna, as Jesus, as a woman, as tea, as a criminal—in whatever form will benefit each sentient being, to fulfill whatever needs we have.

In order to dispel the darkness of ignorance, Lord Buddha manifests the totality of his pure energy in a radiant white body. You can see for yourself that when you are confused and negative, your mind gets very dark. The blissful radiant white emanation of Vajrasattva purifies that darkness.

When you practice the Vajrasattva meditation you should not feel discouraged, "Oh, I can't do it perfectly." What is perfect? You have to build up to perfection from the level you're on. You build your dream home on an empty piece of land; here you build up perfect energy from the emptiness of shunyata. Just do your best according to your own ability and don't expect too much. Lord Buddha doesn't expect everyone to be at the same level. We might all be doing Vajrasattva meditation, using the same words, the same method, but each of us has his own understanding, her own conscious realm. Buddhism understands that. So don't worry about trying to be the same as your neighbor. Just take it easy, keep yourself clean-clear, and do what you can. That's good enough.

When you take the Vajrasattva initiation you should have a strong motivation and no doubts. Motivation is the nuclear essence of liberation. The right attitude will set you free. When you take the initiation, you should not be seeking the short-term pleasures of beach and ice-cream. You should instead have the strong intention to make your life as beneficial as possible for others. This is the most important factor in taking the Vajrasattva initiation. And I think that you already have that motivation. Don't think, "Oh, that doesn't sound like me." You can definitely purify all negativities of your ordinary body, speech, and mind and thereby discover the vajra body, speech, and mind.

[Lama Yeshe gives the initiation.]

Now the initiation has nearly finished. According to Tibetan tradition, at this point the lama touches each disciple's crown with the torma that represents the deity, as I have explained on an earlier occasion. I think this may have been a Tibetan innovation and not something that came down from ancient times. Lamas are very kind and not so busy, so they try to put all their energy into the Dharma path. They make tormas, transform them into the deity through meditation, and then place them on the disciples' heads to ensure they experience Vajrasattva descending to their hearts. I'm not going to do this today. I've got nothing against the practice, but we're in the West, and I think Vajrasattva is already in your heart, so it's not necessary.

You can see that the Vajrasattva practice is very simple, but if you find it difficult to visualize the deity above the crown of your head, you can visualize Vajrasattva at your brow chakra. If this is still too hard, instead of visualizing him in the usual form of the deity, you can visualize at your brow chakra a white OM on a moon disc surrounded by the mantra standing counterclockwise around its edge. As you concentrate on the OM and the mantra, blissful energy emanates from them and fills your entire nervous system, forcing out all the garbage of your impurities, especially those of your body.

You should be able to feel your impurities. If you can't, it may well mean that you have already achieved a certain degree of purity. "Pure" and "impure" are not simply dependent upon your belief, not necessarily just religious ideas. In your mind there is a kind of substantial psychological entity that depends upon your conventional mode of thought. This is what determines purity and impurity, and you should be able to detect it.

Similarly, at your throat chakra there is a red AH on a moon disc, surrounded by the mantra, and at your heart, a blue HUM on a moon disc, surrounded by the mantra. When you recite the mantra, blissful energy emanates as before and purifies your negativities of speech and mind, respectively. So, instead of just sitting there feeling lonely, miserable, and incapable of doing the meditation with the complete visualization, you can practice this simplified form. It works; it really opens you up.

The main commentary will tell you most of what you need to know to do the Vajrasattva retreat. If you study it, you will see how worthwhile and effective for your mind retreat really can be. Retreat is not a joke. All of us need to make the time and space to elevate our minds. If we don't do this for ourselves, how will we ever develop our human potential? Also, students who have completed the retreat can help explain the commentary to you.

After your retreat it is good for you to do the Dorje Khadro fire puja, although this is not a commitment. Some people feel upset that they did not do the retreat as well as they might have, that they didn't recite the mantra properly, or something like that. The fire puja burns all those doubts away, leaving you clean-clear and satisfied with what you did.

Let me emphasize again the benefit of short sessions. Do your practice intensively and well and you'll enjoy it; you'll leave your meditation seat wanting to come back. It somehow retains the energy of your positive mental vibrations. This helps to make your retreat easy.

I think it is wonderful that you people want to practice purification. There is so much impure energy around the planet these days, so much contamination of various sorts. It is rare that anyone even knows about purification, let alone thinks about practicing it. You are so brave. I am very pleased that you want to purify your miserable energy and have a happy life. Also, purifying yourselves properly benefits mankind. That's all we can do. I feel blissful that you are serious in wanting to purify yourself, that you are not hypocritical, and that we are not wasting our time. I would even go so far as to say that even if you are not going to act, just wanting to purify yourself is enough for me. You touch my heart. Thank you so much!

PART 4
Heruka Vajrasattva Tsok

16 ~ What Is Tsok?

Tsok MEANS GATHERING. We gather together the things that we're offering, and we gather together to do the practice. This is the Tibetan connotation of tsok. Gathering together with other practitioners and concentrating our minds into the same space gives us great inspiration. It's much better than just doing a puja alone in our own rooms. In my college at Sera, we compare group puja to a straw broom. You can't sweep much floor with just one straw, but when many straws are gathered together to make a broom, you can quickly clean an entire assembly hall. Though distinguished practitioners such as Milarepa successfully practiced alone, we're not ready for that yet. It's good that we come together to develop single-pointedness of mind. One hundred people's minds all meeting at the same place become very powerful.

In the Tibetan tradition tsok is a most profound method of purification and way of gaining realizations. When you recite the text in English you can see how many subjects are included in the practice. The *Guru Puja,* for example, covers the entire path to enlightenment from beginning to end. Even if you're not making any obvious progress in your daily meditations on the lamrim, some realization may come into your mind because of the conducive atmosphere you've created during puja. Many people have gained realizations during puja simply because of the atmosphere.

You might have done a particular puja one hundred times before, but somehow you have never quite reached the right spot. Normally, we push ourselves to achieve, but nothing happens because we've not made the space to allow for something to happen. By gathering together to offer tsok we're creating space. When the right space opens, zoom!—realizations come as if magnetically attracted. This is true. To grow, we need the right atmosphere.

In the philosophical explanation of Buddhism, we talk about karma: "Create good karma, and you'll get this or that good result." I'm simply saying this a little differently, that to get the results you want, you have to create the right atmosphere. If you build a greenhouse, flowers will grow, protected from the elements. It's the same thing with our baby minds. We need to protect them and create the proper environment in which they can develop. Our gathering together for puja and giving each other energy is the kind of protection our minds require.

In the Tibetan tradition of Mahayana Buddhism we're always talking about the benefits we derive from all mother sentient beings. Take this Darjeeling tea we drink. Think of how many people were involved in its production: the growers, the pickers, the sorters, the packagers, the shippers, the shopkeepers, our own cooks…finally, we get to drink it here. You know from your lamrim studies that, directly or indirectly, every sentient being has helped you get that cup of tea. And not just that cup of tea. All our happiness, from the lowest samsaric pleasure to the eternal bliss of liberation and enlightenment, comes from each of us to the other.

Thus, to gain realizations we need to create the right atmosphere. We do this by gathering together and directing our minds to the same place. The power of this practice brings understanding. We're an international gathering, and each of us has developed in our own unique way. Despite our differences, our minds can still meet at the same place, and we can communicate with each other. I really think it's wonderful. Even parents may have difficulty communicating with their children, but here we are, from different countries all over the world, communicating with each other, heart to heart.

Another connotation of tsok is "party"—a party at which we share simultaneously born great wisdom and bliss. Now *that's* a party!

17~ Heruka Vajrasattva Tsok: The First Commentary

WHEN I WAS SELECTING a title for this tsok offering, I had many names to choose from, but somehow I thought "An Antidote to the Vajra Hells" was the most suitable. Many of my students have done the Heruka Vajrasattva retreat, an extremely powerful way to purify all one's negative energy. Therefore, when I was asked if we could offer tsok under the bodhi tree here in Bodhgaya,[23] I thought it appropriate to write a short tsok offering to Heruka Vajrasattva.

We call this offering a banquet because it is like a great blissful party to which we invite from the ten directions the buddhas, bodhisattvas, dakas, dakinis, and any other pure manifestations we would like to be there.

THE OFFERING INGREDIENTS

Any kind of food and drink can be offered as tsok. You don't have to offer Tibetan-style tormas made of tsampa—they didn't do that during Nagarjuna's time in ancient India. You can offer carrots, chocolate, milk shakes, or even black foods, such as onions, garlic, and radish—anything you like—whatever is clean and available where you live. If you are an exceptionally strong tantric practitioner you can even offer unclean things, such as excrement, but since we are not that advanced, it is better for us to make clean offerings.

THE MERIT FIELD

First verse. Since this is a tantric practice, before we actually offer the tsok, we have to transform our ordinary view of the environment and all the beings in it. Visualize yourself, the other people offering the tsok together with you, the offering ingredients—in fact, everything—as manifestations of the totally unified great bliss and wisdom of nonduality. Then, in the space in front of you, the Vajrasattva mandala appears from nondual bliss and emptiness, with Heruka Vajrasattva and his consort at its center.

Following its natural tendency, our narrow mind will visualize this mandala as small and crowded, but it is not. The mandala occupies all of space and is filled with infinite objects of offering, whose nature is blissful nectar and transcendental wisdom. You should transform your offering—whether a single orange or a table overflowing with food—into infinite offerings filling space: billions of oranges, apples, and so forth. Sometimes I visualize and offer a cosmic Western supermarket—a much better offering than some limited, third-world vegetable market! Your offering should be limitless. Even if you are offering only one object, infinite objects of the five senses, all in the nature of bliss, emanate from it.

Second verse. We usually perceive ourselves and others as very ordinary. When, for example, we gather to offer tsok, we may see ourselves as hopeless, pathetic individuals surrounded by other hopeless, pathetic individuals, all striving earnestly to make some kind of offering. From the tantric point of view, offerings made like that don't work. That is not the way to offer tsok. You should feel that all those around you are your dear friends—even those with whom you might be fighting at present—and see each of them as a Vajrasattva of radiant white light. You can do it. One of the great beauties of being human is that you can change your mind at any time. It is flexible, and you can develop the skill of changing bad situations into good ones.

Thus, in the sphere of great nondual bliss all beings appear as male and female deities—dakas and dakinis. Their appearance is like an illusion—something created by a magician. Have you ever been in a busy place and watched people of various nationalities, shapes, and sizes pass by and felt as if it were a dream or an illusion? When offering this tsok, you should transform all beings into the aspect of Vajrasattva and regard your entire visualization as illusory. The way we see each other is already illusory, even though we think we are so solid and real.

Some of the dakas and dakinis we visualize are extremely peaceful and blissful in appearance; others are in the aspect of granting spiritual realizations. Some manifest power and others, great wrath. They all seem to be dancing. You should also see yourselves as dancing wherever you go. In a way, whenever you go to the movies, to a restaurant, back home, you are dancing. When offering tsok, you should visualize the dakas and dakinis as very active and alive—really doing things to benefit all mother sentient beings—not as dull, inactive, or dead. They manifest in all these different ways for the benefit of all sentient beings, embodying fully developed and totally unified method and wisdom.

All tsok gatherings are based on transformation. In the *Guru Puja,* for example, you first generate nondual, transcendental great bliss and wisdom, and then everything—all actions, the offering ingredients, yourselves, the guru to whom you are making the offering—arises from that. At these times you should not see any living beings as invalids, cripples, hungry ghosts, or as other suffering creatures. Everything should look transcendental and evoke great bliss. Therefore it is best that you visualize all beings as Vajrasattvas. It is really excellent if, during the offering, you can control your mind and prevent ordinary, garbage-like concepts from arising. Usually such thoughts fully occupy our minds, causing us much confusion and making us more deluded than ever. How wonderful if for just one hour your mind gave no space for self-pity to arise.

BLESSING THE INNER OFFERINGS

(OM KHANDA ROHI…) Here we bless the offering ingredients. The deity Khandarohi has one face and four arms and, if possible, should be visualized dispelling interfering spirits. It does not matter if you cannot make this visualization, but you should at least sprinkle some inner offering nectar on the offering ingredients and feel that all negative, miserly spirits have been driven away. "Spirits" are not only the outer hindrances but are also any negative energy within you that pollutes your offering. This energy, too, is purified.

(OM SVABHAVA…) This is called the shunyata mantra. Recognizing the shunyata, or emptiness of inherent existence, of the offering ingredients is a very powerful way of purifying ordinary conceptions and negative energy. This recognition is essential to a proper tsok offering.

The seed syllable OM symbolizes the divine vajra body, which is unified with the divine vajra speech and mind. SVABHAVA means natural, not artificial; SHUDDHA (and SHUDDHO) mean pure; SARVA means all; DHARMA means existent phenomena; and HAM means I am, which should be felt with divine pride. These Sanskrit words contain a profound explanation of the pure, fundamental nature of human beings and all other phenomena. The mantra means that, in the absolute sense, all existent phenomena, including you, are inherently pure.

You have to understand your real nature. Most of the time you are unnatural. With intelligence your ego produces anger and desire; this is the wrong sort of intelligence. Your ego creates an artificial image of yourself, and you present this false image of yourself to others. As long as you are under the control of your ego, you are not natural. You have to listen to and touch your fundamental, true nature; if you can do this, you will touch purity. Thus the usual human self-projections—"I am hopeless; I am impure; I am bad; I cannot do anything; I cannot help myself"—are completely false and exactly opposite to what the shunyata mantra is saying.

Your nature is not what your negative projections would lead you to believe. Buddha explains that it is mistaken to think that you are truly evil or sinful; your fundamental nature is pure. The artificial cloud that your ego produces is not your true nature but a fabrication dreamed up by your ego. Therefore, be natural.

In shunyata meditation you listen to your inner self, go beyond artificial thoughts, become tranquil and peaceful, and touch the fundamental reality of your being. Thus shunyata meditation slices through all the concepts that make you miserable, especially those that lead you to believe that you are somehow permanent and inherently self-existent. If these wrong beliefs are merely suppressed, the symptoms they produce will keep recurring. You might be able to control one kind of suffering, but another will arise in its place.

Whether or not you recite the shunyata mantra, it is imperative to see that the self-image maintained by your self-pity does not exist. I could explain this in deep philosophical terms, but I prefer to keep it simple. Think back to the "I am this" you were holding a year ago and compare it with your current self-conception. Has the "I" that you feel changed at all or not? Careful analysis will reveal that although some things have changed, you feel that the "I" of today is identical with the "I" of a year ago. You can see how wrong, both relatively and absolutely, this feeling is.

All phenomena are changing from moment to moment—there is no way for our "I" to remain unchanged. When you realize how your ego-grasping ignorance has been clinging to its nonsensical self-identity, believing, for example, that the you of ten years ago is still here today, you will laugh at how deluded you have been. Buddha always taught that we are deluded, holding nonsensical, hallucinatory conceptions. Even if you have been meditating for twenty or thirty years, if your meditation has not begun to shake your ego and destroy your delusions, then you have not been meditating properly. The more extreme your ego's self-identity, the more solid your ego appears, and the more tightly you hang on to it. When you shake your ego to its foundations you create an earthquake that causes the Mount Meru of your samsaric mandala to crumble.

Buddha's teaching on universal reality is profound. It shows humans the best way to be healthy; it breaks all concepts, shatters all illusions. Buddha even said that if you become attached to a fixed conception of *him,* you will be trapped. Spiritual seekers of today, under the control of their egos, grasp at their self-existent gurus, saying, "I love you; you are a wonderful guru. Do you love me? You should." Buddha would have rejected such disciples. He did not want anybody to grasp at either himself or his teachings. You should not grasp at samsaric phenomena; you should not grasp at Dharma. There is nothing to which you should become attached. That is Lord Buddha's prescription for perfect health.

These days many gurus seem to be attached to their disciples and want their disciples to be attached to them. This is completely wrong. It is most unhealthy for disciples to be attached to their teacher or their path. Buddha wants you to be healthy, forever happy, and free from attachment to all concepts and doctrines. Therefore you have to recognize as false all concepts of "me" that you are holding right now and break them down. In the gloom of this ignorance you are deceived by the seductive dance of the objects of the five senses. But when you recognize the way your ego cheats you, it will no longer be able to do so. If you really understand this, you will understand shunyata.

The profound shunyata mantra tells you that the true nature of all phenomena is one. But your ego divides, separates, and categorizes everything so that you can never be close to anything. Even after a lifetime together, husbands and wives are not really close; they don't understand each other because their egos have kept them apart.

The mantra states that in reality all existent phenomena are one and "HAM," "so am I." You are pure, one with all existence; therefore, generate divine pride. When you experience shunyata, you become one with all phenomena, inseparable, like milk poured into milk. When you realize shunyata, your dualistic mind vanishes. It is dualistic because it divides everything into two—for example, "me" and "you." When you realize your own ultimate nature and mine, there will be no distinction between us.

The social ramifications of the dualistic mind are numerous. For example, people in the world protest racism and stage political demonstrations against it, sometimes getting killed in the process. From the Buddhist point of view, racism will continue to exist as long as the dualistic mind exists. Until you discover ultimate reality and the unity of existence, all talk of abolishing racism is just a joke. Buddha gave the perfect, practical method of integration, which we all can experience in our daily lives. The great beauty of being human is that we can transcend the relative world and experience the absolute.

All becomes empty... The skull cup we visualize here is not small like the ones we use in pujas. It should be huge—the bigger the better. It contains the five meats and the five nectars. You are in the aspect of Vajrasattva. From the HUM at your heart a beam of light shines into the skull cup, heating its contents and melting them into a vast ocean of inexhaustible, blissful nectar.

Whenever you offer tsok, recognize the blissful nature of whatever you offer. For example, oranges might appear as oranges, but in essence they are blissful nectar. And the deity to whom you are offering the tsok—in this case Vajrasattva—does not just munch it up like we do but extracts the essence of the tsok, great bliss, through a thin straw of light that he sends out from his tongue. You too should recognize all the offerings, and indeed all your everyday food and drink, as being in the nature of great bliss.

Then, saying the mantra OM AH HUM HA HO HRI three times, you bless the tsok.

This pure offering... Reciting this verse helps your mind avoid energizing superstition.

VERSE ONE

Here we offer the tsok with a request to develop within us the simultaneously born great bliss and wisdom, the unique tantric path to enlightenment.

Recite the Heruka Vajrasattva mantra once after each verse. If you recite it clearly, evenly, and at the right speed, you will purify millions of lives' negativity. Sometimes you may feel so heavy with nonvirtue that you cannot move; you feel as if you are drowning in a vast ocean of negativity. And once you have decided that you feel heavy, you feel heavy! Buddhist psychology contends that if you believe you are negative, you will become negative. If I project that you are hopeless, to me you will appear hopeless. We should not think like that. We have powerful methods of purifying even the most serious downfalls—for example, broken root vows of tantra. It is the experience of many great yogis that the Vajrasattva practice can purify all negative energy; there is no negativity that Vajrasattva meditation cannot purify. It is very important for you to understand this. You already have a very low opinion of yourself; your encounter with religion should not make it worse. You should of course recognize your shortcomings, but at the same time you should always remember your potential to become a buddha.

Verse two

How do we make our precious human rebirth useless? By clinging to the pleasures of the objects of the five senses. Why do we do this? Because our sense consciousnesses hallucinate. We have to purify their impure, dualistic vision. We are too concerned about the welfare of just this life. For example, look what happens when you go to India for a Dharma festival. You are full of good intentions, but when you arrive, you get upset because there's no good food, tea, or coffee. Of course, you have to make sure your body remains healthy, but even when it is, the lack of amenities disturbs you. You say you want to be liberated, enlightened, and compassionate, but in reality, your mind is completely obsessed with your own pathetic, ego-determined pleasures. Such exaggerated concern for the happiness of this life alone must be eliminated; it only makes your understanding of reality progressively narrower. There is more to strive for than this life's happiness.

Students put a great deal of effort into studying so they will do well on their examinations and get a good job. They may enjoy certain diversionary pleasures while doing so, but these are secondary to their main purpose. They do not allow the small pleasures to prevent them from attaining their overarching goals. In the same way, you who seek the highest goal of everlasting satisfaction should be strongly dedicated and prepared to sacrifice the comfort of this life for it. Without sacrificing attachment to samsaric pleasures, you cannot gain liberation. When you make the decision to attain liberation and realize that it will involve making sacrifices, you will experience a kind of bliss whenever you encounter obstacles. All ego conflicts and suffering come from the poison of clinging to the ordinary concepts and appearances of this life. When we offer the tsok with this verse, we request blessings to enable us to abandon such clinging.

Verse three

This verse illustrates how you create bad karma and add to your delusions. Improper attention, whose nature is superstition, produces more superstition. Acting under its influence you create bad karma. It covers your mind like a heavy blanket and, along with the demon of the impure, dualistic view, must be purified.

Here we request blessings to develop perfect renunciation of samsara in our hearts. To achieve true renunciation it is not enough to have strong aversion to samsara. You have to investigate how improper attention generates superstition and thus fuels samsara. Dualistic, improper attention has to be purified, before renunciation can be developed.

Some monks and nuns seem to think that they became arhats the moment they were ordained. You can't become an arhat in a day. Some laypeople also seem to think that monks and nuns should be arhats, criticizing them when they do something wrong: "Oh, look at those monks; they're no better than me." It is easy to criticize the Sangha. You can even criticize the Buddha: "He was so selfish, going off alone to meditate for six years." I don't believe that the renunciation of monks and nuns is necessarily better than that of laypeople, but at least monks and nuns have recognized what they need to do to overcome their samsaric difficulties and are trying to develop renunciation. They may not be arhats, but they are doing the best they can.

As you know from studying the middle-level teachings on the graduated path to enlightenment, where it explains the causes of samsara and how to get rid of them, it is difficult to achieve perfect renunciation. We have difficulty renouncing samsara because our superstitions cause us to create more and more karma, and as a result, our blanket of obscurations gets thicker and thicker. Therefore, we pray to Guru Vajrasattva to help us purify all this.

Verse four

You also know from the sutra teachings that the dualistic mind of self-cherishing is the foundation of all suffering; it is the principal evil. We make this offering to purify self-cherishing and to generate the most perfect bodhichitta in our hearts.

Verse five

All phenomena are labeled—given names—by superstition, and as a result, they exist. But our superstitious minds are not content to leave it at that. For example, when you see a beautiful object, you try to make its beauty concrete, self-existent, special. You don't allow it to exist as merely a projection of your superstitious mind. This is dualistic vision and has to be purified.

Thus we make this offering with the request that we might realize *mahamudra,* the great seal of emptiness.

VERSE SIX

In life, as soon as I consider other people to be ordinary and bothersome, my problems start. I begin to disrespect and belittle them. All this arises from the ordinary concepts of my superstitious mind. According to tantric philosophy, there are eighty superstitions, some are gross and others are subtle, but all of them have to be purified. We also have to purify impure dualistic vision, which is like a hurricane that crashes planes and destroys houses. Thus we offer the nectar tsok, whose nature is that of the wisdom of the five dhyani buddhas, to Guru Vajrasattva, requesting the blessings of the four actual initiations.

Why are we asking for more initiations when we have already received so many? Actually it's not certain whether we've really received any initiations. It is difficult to receive a real initiation; it is not something you simply receive from a lama. In my opinion—and I hope this does not sound too extreme— in an initiation, the disciple is more important than the guru.

Although I say it is very difficult to receive the four actual initiations, I do not mean that you have necessarily received nothing. The initiation you receive is determined by your level of understanding. In a gathering of two hundred people, no two have the same experience. Although the lama gives all four initiations, it is likely that nobody receives them all. Some people might feel that they have received nothing and will compare their experience with those of their friends. However this is something you have to judge for yourself; no one else can tell you what you have received. Just realize that is extremely rare for someone to really receive the four initiations.

Also, the degree to which you receive an initiation depends upon the deity concerned and the conditions under which the ceremony is performed. You have a strong karmic connection with some deities and a weaker one with others. Conditions affect your experience in the relative initiation, not the absolute. Therefore, your experiences will vary.

The main thing is for you to raise your mind above the ordinary, concrete concepts of everyday life. If you can do this, you are doing well. Most people never put themselves in a situation where they can meditate or be sensitive and aware. If attending an initiation gives you the chance to do so, you should take full advantage of that situation. You are not looking for some extraordinary experience; in the modern world, it is enough simply to try to experience tranquillity, bliss, and transcendence.

Some people say, "I have received this initiation and you haven't." I don't agree with that kind of arrogance. Who can say who has received what initiation? Only the individual concerned can tell what initiation has been received. You cannot determine this for others. That is why I usually allow any sincere person to come to an initiation. I cannot tell whether others' minds are high or low; I cannot tell whether the initiation will be helpful for them or not. Be careful. Even though you might arrogantly believe you have received this or that initiation, you need to check up. You might have been present when the initiation was given, but that does not mean you received anything.

If you go to an initiation with the right attitude and an open mind, I am sure that you will receive an extraordinary vibration. That is enough. You do not have to be super-intellectual and ask, "Why do we do this? How does it work? What are all those Tibetan things for? I'm not going to take the initiation until I understand everything." That's nonsense.

VERSE SEVEN

Consciously and unconsciously we break our vows and commitments, pushed by a force like a raging thunderstorm. We find it extremely difficult to control ourselves. I think, in a way, people who believe themselves to be very pure and holy may be more negative than those who recognize how impure they are. The former never make an effort to purify themselves with prostrations or retreats, while the latter practice diligently to purify their minds. The negativities, the broken vows and commitments, the feeling of being impure, and the result, the hallucinated vision of the Vajra Hells, are all dualistic and must be purified. We offer the tsok with a request for blessings to perceive only purity.

OFFERING TO THE VAJRA MASTER

The "circle of pure offerings" in the title is called a circle because both male and female deities gather to offer the tsok. When the deities are only male or only female, we do not refer to the tsok as a circle. According to tantra their combined presence makes the offering far more powerful. The next line says that the nectar we offer is free of the dualistic appearance of subject and object.

The vajra master replies. Each time you taste the tsok it goes to your navel chakra, causing an inconceivably blissful explosion of tumo energy within your central channel.

Offering the remaining tsok

The protectors to whom we offer this are the external, internal, and secret protectors. We ask them to help us practice Dharma in order to benefit others in as many different ways as possible.

18~ Heruka Vajrasattva Tsok: The Second Commentary

I WROTE THE SHORT TEXT, *A Banquet of the Greatly Blissful Circle of Pure Offerings: An Antidote to the Vajra Hells,* because I thought that we needed a powerful method of purifying our negativities and that this would be a good way to do so. Even though it's very short, this text covers the entire graduated path, from renunciation to the tantric experience of enlightenment.

In texts like the *Guru Puja,* the offering section comes first and the review of the graduated path to enlightenment follows at the end. Here I have tried to include the graduated path subjects in the tsok offering verses. Each verse contains some lamrim subject because I thought this was a more direct means of communicating what our lives lack, what ruins them, and how we can improve them. We begin with guru yoga, then move on to the precious human rebirth, impermanence and death, renunciation, bodhichitta, shunyata, and tantra.

Also, Western Dharma students do a lot of pujas—the *Guru Puja,* Tara puja, *jorchö,* and so forth—so I thought I'd write a new one in case they were getting bored with the others! Moreover, since the regular pujas are rather long, and in today's world we're always short of time, I kept this puja brief. It's easy to do and quick. Anyway, it's a product of my own fantasies.

Now, what do I mean by *vajra hells? Vajra* can be relative or absolute; here I am referring to the relative vajra, as in vajra and bell, the tantric implements we use. The word means indestructible, diamond-like. Diamonds are stronger than most other materials, so it is hard to destroy a diamond. That's the connotation of vajra. Is it possible that there could be an indestructible realm of misery? Well, that's a bit of poetic license, a slight exaggeration; there's no such thing as an unchangeable, permanent phenomenon. For most of us depression lasts only a few hours, but there are people who remain depressed for their entire lives. When you've been miserable for a long, long time you might feel that your misery is endless. That's a vajra-hell-like experience. Vajra hell is just an expression; you should not take it literally.

THE MERIT FIELD

Normally when we make offerings, we visualize the object to whom we are making the offering—in this practice the object of offering is Guru Vajrasattva. We also visualize and meditate on the Vajrasattva mandala, where Guru Vajrasattva resides.

The first two lines of this verse are talking about the quality of the visualization that you make. It is a transformation of light. *De* means bliss, and *tong* means the universal reality of shunyata; *nyi-su me-päi* means without dualistic entity. The Vajrasattva mandala manifests from an appearance that has those qualities. This is actually quite profound. Old students may understand it, but new, mushroom students will probably find it a bit dreamlike, a kind of spacey new concept.

Fundamentally we all have limited understandings of our natures and the nature of the world in which we live. Furthermore, we lay an exaggerated projection on top of our already limited view of reality. We do not penetrate the heart of reality; we don't even touch the reality of the ground on which we stand. This is the human problem. We have no insight into either our inner or our outer reality.

We always say that we want to improve the quality of our lives—to have happy, joyful, profound, and meaningful lives. We use all kinds of words to describe the perfect life we'd like to have. To lead a perfect life you have to understand how you see your own nature and the nature of external phenomena. Whether or not you can do that will determine whether or not your life will be happy.

A mandala is a vision of a complete world in which you recognize the nature of reality without any artificial projection, without hallucinating. Once you see that, you have more flexibility in your decisions; you have choices. Maintaining preconceived ideas and the dualistic notion of self-existence makes your life impossible. When you visualize a mandala, you see everything—yourself and your environment—in the nature of bliss; you touch the fundamental reality of all existence. With that sort of recognition, or comprehension, you can eliminate depression and other miseries and enjoy your life.

The question might arise: "How can you say that everything is blissful? Some things are just miserable, so how can you say they can be transformed into blissful objects?"

When you touch the fundamental nature, the ultimate reality, of any phenomenon whatsoever, there is pleasure. Everything that exists is capable of eliciting pleasure in your mind. But you are narrow. Your mind has neurotic obsessions such as, "I only like things that are purple." For you, only purple things are beautiful. This sort of neurotic, dualistic, unrealistic way of thinking only gets you into trouble. But we do it all the time, don't we?

Check what your mind considers to be beautiful. True beauty is everywhere. California is not the only place where there's pleasure and an attractive environment. Every place has a beauty of its own. An object's ability to give bliss is independent of the object itself. From the scientific point of view, every object has a sort of common reality, a shared fundamental nature. This true nature is what is really beautiful; this is what really gives you satisfaction.

The way we interpret the beauty of an object—by its shape, color, and so forth—is too relative, too conventional. Such beauty is like a yo-yo: this morning I see a particular object as beautiful; this evening it looks ugly. I myself go up and down. That's the main trouble. We need to have a broad view of what constitutes a blissful object.

According to the philosophy and psychology of tantra, if you comprehend the fundamental nature of all existence, everything manifests as a blissful object. Without that wisdom, objects alone cannot make you blissful. Human experience shows this to be true. When you are having a painful, miserable time, nothing you see makes you happy. If I show you something beautiful when you feel terrible, does it make you happy? No. There's no magnetic energy. Normally, subject and object sort of magnetize each other to produce an atmosphere of pleasure or pain. The qualities of life do not come from outside but from your own degree of satisfaction. If you have richness within you, everything external will satisfy.

A happy, satisfied family life comes from people's minds, not from their material possessions. Rich families in America are not necessarily more happy than poor families. However if you are born into this society, it is hard to see that possessions don't bring happiness because the whole society is built on the connection between wealth and satisfaction. However this attitude is the complete opposite of the truth.

I'm not taking a shot at America just because I'm a foreigner. When I come to America, I don't have any particular agenda; I just look and see what's going on. Perhaps I'm critical because I'm not involved in the American way of life; if I were, I probably wouldn't notice the things that I see. True satisfaction comes from within yourself. This does not mean that you have to give up your American pleasures; whether they become pleasurable for you depends on your mind. American pleasures can make you miserable. If that happens it is your own fault, not that of American society.

The Buddhist attitude is, "I am responsible for the quality of my life. I am responsible for my own satisfaction." You cannot blame your father or your mother, your husband or your wife. That sort of blame is endless. It is illogical, and incapable of solving problems. Materialism and capitalism breed wrong ideas. From the Buddhist point of view, wrong ideas are the main cause of suffering.

What is a fundamentally wrong idea? Thoughts like "My pleasure and success depend upon other people," or "A higher standard of living and more material possessions will bring me satisfaction," or "Material objects are all I need to be happy" are fundamentally wrong ideas. If you know how to think, it won't matter whether your standard of living is high or low—you will know how to enjoy yourself. That is the most important thing.

Visualize that in front of the Vajrasattva mandala, all of space is filled by magnificent objects of the five senses, greatly blissful objects of [Samantabhadra's] offerings, as it says in the fourth line of the first verse. In Buddhist practice, offerings are made not only to buddhas and other holy beings but also to all sentient beings. You should recognize the divinity within other people—their potential for enlightenment, or buddha-potential. In tantra we transform all beings into greatly joyful and magnificently appearing dakas and dakinis. In the blissful space of nonduality, all sentient beings manifest as dakas and dakinis in various aspects: joyful, peaceful, powerful, wrathful—a whole variety of different but totally unified manifestations. We see them as the embodiment of unified method and wisdom, not as hungry ghosts or other emanations of misery. If you visualize miserable-looking objects, you'll feel miserable yourself.

Therefore it is important to transform the nature of the object you visualize into great bliss and to recognize its fundamental reality, eliminating all dualistic concepts. You can visualize and offer any sense object whatsoever. Most of us are psychologically hung up by miserly and limited thoughts, but when we practice this tsok offering, we should visualize limitless objects of the senses, as beautiful, blissful, and inexhaustible as possible, and offer them to all—buddhas and sentient beings—without discrimination. We need this kind of training.

Usually we give things only to the people we like and don't give anything to those we dislike. That's the Western way. In the East the prevalence of beggars helps keep us oriented toward giving to strangers. Rich people come along and give away thousands of rupees to the poor. They're not the rich people's friends; it's just that the environment encourages this sort of thing. So we *do* have some good things in the East! Some people think the third world has nothing at all to offer: "They haven't even got the brains to get rich and be happy."

Of course, the United States has poor people, too. There are many hungry people rummaging through others' garbage all the time, eating stuff that has been thrown out. You can see all this on television and in the big cities. The rich don't give to the poor, not because they can't afford to but because they don't like them. They just let them go hungry. I'm not talking politics or religion here; that's just how it is. This attitude is very bad. The selfish mind gives to those it likes and not to those it doesn't, irrespective of other people's needs. Our own need is the most important thing; after taking care of that, we give. That's samsara.

We should train our minds in generous and impartial giving. But giving doesn't mean just handing over cash or material goods. Don't think, "I am poor. How can I give?" Real giving is having a giving attitude. Not giving is the selfish attitude of "I don't want to give." Offering tsok is excellent training in overcoming such attitudes: all sentient beings are guests at your offering party, and you make extensive offerings to them all. It is essential to train our minds in this way if we want to be successful in both our Dharma practice and life itself.

BLESSING THE INNER OFFERINGS

Remember that the way to offer anything is to recognize the fundamental nature, or mode of existence, of whatever it is you are offering. This applies to the actual offerings you have placed on your altar and to the magnificent offerings you visualize filling all of space.

The vast subject of inner offering has been explained elsewhere, so my explanation here will be brief.[24] Say you are offering a bowl of tea. Visualize in the space above the bowl the letters OM, AH, and HUM, beginning with OM at the bottom and moving up. Radiant white light emanates from the OM throughout the ten directions of space, magnetically attracting the supreme qualities of the body of all enlightened beings, who have great wisdom, great love and compassion, and extremely joyful lives. These qualities return to the OM in the form of light and sink into it. The OM melts into blissful energy and dissolves into the tea.

Red light radiates from the AH invoking the pure speech of the supreme beings of the ten directions. This returns and sinks into the AH, which melts into blissful light energy and also dissolves into the tea. Similarly blue light radiates from the HUM, invoking the divine wisdom, love, and compassion of the supreme beings of the ten directions. These enlightened qualities return to the HUM in the form of light. The HUM too dissolves into the tea.

You can bless anything you eat or drink in this way. When you eat and drink things you have put such concentrated thought into, the energy communicates and agrees with your nervous system. There is harmony between your physical nervous system and your consciousness.

In the West we don't communicate with the things we eat or drink. Substances coming into your nervous system can be very destructive; they may even cause cancer. This is what happens when you are unaware or ignorant of what you eat and drink. You might find it hard to believe, but the human body is not like rock or concrete; it is as organic as a flower. When you over-fertilize a flower, what happens? It burns out. Organic things need balance. I really believe that in the West, there is not only a breakdown of human relationships, but there is also a breakdown of the relationship between people, the food they eat, and the environment.

Perhaps I don't know what I'm talking about. You probably think that a mushroom monk like me must be dreaming when he tries to describe life in America. Well, I'm joking a little, but I do feel that people in modern industrialized nations have very little appreciation for the importance of the nature of their food and drink. They just gobble up whatever's put in front of them. This can shock your body; your nervous system can't cope and will cry out in protest. You must pay attention to the organic nature of your body. Be conscious of what you eat and drink. With insight you can develop a communicative relationship with the things that nourish you.

With the offerings, the objects of the five senses should be recognized as the five wisdoms in the appropriate colors and in their true nature of blissful nonduality. They energize great bliss and satisfaction within you. Recognizing this is very helpful for developing great bliss.

PRESENTING THE OFFERINGS AND RECITING THE MANTRA

Next you make a request to the guru to whom you are offering this tsok. The blissful nectar in this verse, which you can also think of as perfect energy, is fundamental to the attainment of all realizations. It is the yogis' and yoginis' pure vision, which is beyond the view of ordinary beings. The offering is made for the guru to enjoy with this nonsuperstitious, greatly blissful wisdom. It's important to note the implications of this practice. When we enjoy sense pleasures, we are full of superstition, or wrong conceptions. When higher beings enjoy pleasures, they do not react to them with superstition.

What do I mean by superstition? It is like this: I see, for example, a flower, and gradually, I develop a relationship with it. I touch the flower, grasp at its color. I think how wonderful, how kind and generous it is; it gives me great pleasure—nothing else gives me such pleasure. The flower becomes my best friend. This attribution of fine qualities to the flower is superstition. I'm superimposing upon the relationship many qualities that are not actually there.

This puts great pressure on the relationship; as soon as you start ascribing qualities to the flower, you are putting pressure on the relationship. Each time you see the flower as wonderful, beautiful, and gorgeous, you bind yourself tighter and tighter. The whole thing becomes a fantasy; it is too superficial, unrealistic. Tension builds up, and instead of being loose and relaxed, you are tied in knots. That is superstition. Building fantasy relationships with people and objects in that way can only lead to trouble.

Buddhas and bodhisattvas, on the other hand, enjoy pleasures in a far more reasonable way. They don't have our superficial, conventional, exaggerated way of relating to them. They are realistic; they touch the fundamental nature of reality. Their pleasures are more stable and subdued, bringing great love and peace. That's why the last line of this verse asks Guru Vajrasattva to enjoy the supreme nectar with greatly blissful, nonsuperstitious wisdom.

So you can see now that superstition is the mind that misleads you by exaggerating the qualities of objects, by seeing things that are not really there. Superstition is unrealistic and makes your life a fantasy. But if you clearly understand your relationship with others, just as it is, there will not be too much tension between you. If you can overcome superstition, then you will always be happy. That's why we have meditations to eliminate superstition: to make you healthy and to bring clean-clear awareness. Then you will not be polluted or deluded.

Any relationship, be it pleasurable or miserable, is impermanent, transitory. We ourselves are transitory, so our relationships must be transitory too. We have to accept this. It is especially important for Americans to understand the nature of relationships. Relationships between men and women, between friends, between whomever, are changing all the time. At the same time, the people in the relationships are miserable. It is change that causes misery; I hope you understand this. Everything changes, so of course your friendships will change. If you understand that relationships are transitory by nature, you won't feel any pressure, and you'll have the space to communicate, to let go. You'll see how changing relationships make you unhappy. But don't think that it is the changing object that makes you miserable. No! It is your unreasonable communication within the relationship that is the source of confusion.

When your closest companion dies, you cry and feel terribly depressed. You may even remain depressed for a long time. That is not useful. Death is death; death is natural; death is okay. You should accept it. Of course, I'm only talking intellectually here.

Enjoyment without superstition is very difficult. Buddhism says that you should have great enjoyment and a blissful life. Superstition prevents this experience. Superstition prevents you from touching fundamental reality.

Verse one

In space is the rainbow body of Vajrasattva. This is in the nature of your spiritual guide, your deity, the dakas and dakinis, and your Dharma protector. In this verse we ask Vajrasattva to purify our hallucinatory, superstitious delusion that Vajrasattva is not of the essence of the guru, the deity, the dakas and dakinis, and the protector. *Trül-nang* here means hallucinating, deluded. We have to purify this hallucination. Offering all magnificent sense objects to Guru Vajrasattva, we request blessings, or inspiration, that simultaneously born, great blissful wisdom will grow in our hearts.

While making the offering, meditate on purifying the hallucinatory, dualistic thought that does not recognize the unity of those holy objects but sees them as separate. Then recite the Vajrasattva mantra using one of the three usual meditation techniques for purifying negativities. This eradicates all superstition and negative appearances in general, and the hallucinatory, dualistic vision mentioned in this verse in particular.

This practice is very powerful because you meditate while making the offerings, saying the prayer, and reciting the mantra. This has a profound impact on your mind. You will realize that you are hallucinating when you do not recognize the unity of Vajrasattva, your guru, your deity, the dakas and dakinis, and your Dharma protector. They are of the one nature, but you see them as two. That is a hallucination, an appearance projected by your dualistic concepts. That is what you have to purify."

Verse two

Our human lives are precious and meaningful, but we ruin them and render them useless through the contamination of our five sense consciousnesses' craving for and grasping at pleasurable objects. We ask Vajrasattva to purify the hallucinatory, dualistic appearance that causes us to cling to sense objects, and we make offerings with a request for blessings and inspiration to abandon clinging to the worldly pleasures of this life.

I thought it important to describe how we ruin our perfect lives. At the moment, there is nothing physically wrong with us, and even when we are sick, we can usually still accomplish things with our body, speech, and mind. However we spend most of our time in useless activities, doing things that have no value. What makes our human life meaningless? What destroys it? The perceptions of our five senses are the main problem. There's no bright, powerful wisdom behind them, yet they dominate and control our lives.

Blindly, we follow our sense perceptions. They tell us, "Ice cream is fantastic!" So we eat ice cream in order to find satisfaction. Then what happens? Most people who eat a lot of ice cream are miserable. They get fat and think that other people don't like them. It's probably not even true that people don't like them, but we make up fantasies like that.

Our five sense consciousnesses crave and grasp at pleasurable sense objects. They ruin our lives by making us shallow. We don't serve others, and our lives become meaningless, devoid of satisfaction, and unhappy. The cause of all this misery is our preoccupation with the sensory pleasures of this life. This obsession has to be purified.

For example we've all had good meditation experiences, but they were just flashes, like lightning; they didn't last. You have some great experiences in retreat, but when you get back home, your old habits surface, and your meditation experiences vanish. I have no doubt that you have had meditation experiences, but why do you fall back into misery when you stop meditating? Why does your precious human life become meaningless when you're not meditating? Why do you fall back into the same old garbage? Because you fail to understand that this world's pleasurable phenomena are illusory. As long as you think they are real, you will continue to ruin your life.

You think things are real because you can touch them with your hands: you may feel something, but it's not reality. They are mere mental projections, but we build a fantasy relationship with them. Take this flower, for example. I close my eyes and grasp it, hang on to it; I won't let it go. If I left it alone, it would stay nice, but as I get more and more attached to it, I destroy it. Our relationships don't have to be like that. We can see and enjoy the flower while simultaneously recognizing it as a fantasy, an optical illusion. It does not really exist as it appears to our eyes; our sight is completely deluded. From the Buddhist point of view you should have no confidence in what your sense perceptions tell you; no confidence that things really exist as they appear to your senses.

How do you eliminate your sense perceptions' craving for and grasping at sense pleasures? By recognizing the objects that appear to your senses as hallucinations. You should realize that you're hallucinating, whether you have taken drugs or not. You do not understand what appears to your senses. Thinking that the fantasy is real poisons your sense perception and ruins your life. That's the point. You should not base your life decisions on what your eyes tell you, what your physical sense perceptions tell you.

It's the same thing with people who come to a Dharma center for a meditation course. While they are there, they feel that they are getting something worthwhile and gaining some control over their lives, but when they get back home, they lose it all. Why is that? Why is it that when you are meditating at a center, you feel that you are gaining something, that you are on the path to liberation, but after only one night back in your regular environment, your mind completely changes? Check that out. I think it means that you don't actually understand Dharma.

When you come to a center for a meditation course, you have some sort of fantasy about the environment, and you grasp at it as real. When you leave this environment, its reality disappears and is replaced by that of your new location. Thus, the valuable things you gained at the center vanish, and you end up with the misery and unhappiness of your old habits. What you don't understand is that no matter where you are—at the Dharma center, downtown, or back home—whatever you perceive is illusory, a projection of your own mind.

If you can realize—really understand—that the Dharma center environment is illusory, and with intensive, conscious awareness keep this recognition with you wherever you go, your experiences will be very different from what they normally are. Whether you are in the big city, at the beach, or in the Himalayas, you can maintain the same energy, stay in the same space.

Buddhism is very realistic in its description of human nature. I'm sure you've all heard that you shouldn't be judgmental, discriminating between good and bad, and so forth. Normally we'll say, "Oh, nirvana! Fantastic!" and grasp at it, or "Yeekh, samsara is terrible!" and try to push it out of our mind. We say, "My guru is fantastic, Dharma is so fantastic!" and "That person is so awful." All these judgments are based on our own superstitious mind's interpretation of our own deluded perceptions. We have to recognize that.

It is not enough to be convinced of all this intellectually, either. It has to be experienced. Actually, you have already had enough experience—enough to break your heart! So Buddhism is dealing with life, with experience, and that's the way it shows you how to be healthy, how to have a healthy mind. Brief meditation experiences at Dharma centers are not enough. You have to maintain continuous awareness of the right view, wherever you are.

This verse, then, is talking about how we render our lives useless. Most of us would like our lives to be useful for ourselves and others. We all look for satisfaction. What makes our lives meaningless and unsatisfactory is the mind that grasps at the pleasures of the senses and at their concrete, permanent appearance. We must completely abandon both these faults. If we want our lives to be happy and satisfied, we must be determined to eliminate these faults forever. In order to do this, we need to understand clean-clear that the way sense pleasures appear is illusory. Nothing is permanent and unchangeable.

As long as your hallucinating mind keeps exaggerating the good qualities of a pleasurable object, there is no way that you will ever be really satisfied. Therefore, Buddhism emphasizes understanding pleasures as they are, by knowing the quality of their being. Then you have space; this makes you less neurotic. When you have pleasure, it's okay; you recognize it as illusory. When you don't have pleasure, that's okay, too. It is only your concrete concepts' grasping at the pleasure that makes you confused, dissatisfied, and emotionally disturbed.

Keeping in mind the meaning of this verse, recite the Vajrasattva mantra. At the same time, do the three usual meditation techniques to purify your concrete concepts, hallucinated appearances, any impure energy associated with your physical nervous system, and the ignorance that is the foundation of all these problems. Deep within your psyche you might feel that it's impossible to purify all your shortcomings, sense desires, and selfish attitudes. "How can I ever get rid of all that?" Even though intellectually you might accept that purification works or that the Buddhist teachings are correct, deep inside you have doubts. Practice of the Vajrasattva meditation can eradicate all those afflicted doubts by revealing the possibility of completely eliminating all negative energy and giving you the great inspiration to do so.

Verse three

"...Please bless me to generate immaculate renunciation." Our lives begin in misery, and throughout their duration we add more and more confusion. Delusion is the cause of all this karma. With delusion we create the karma that leads us repeatedly into misery and confusion. We get caught in an almost indestructible trap of neurotic concepts and emotions. In the verse this is explained as *tsül-min yi-je,* which means that you are imagining something that has nothing to do with the objects you perceive, neither relatively nor absolutely. The deluded mind may occasionally be mixed with a little relative truth, but most appearances are completely deceptive. What you see is only your imagination.

On the basis of that imagination, you begin to develop hallucinatory, concrete ideas, an ego-grasping mind, and dualistic concepts. You build an unreal fantasy of the object in your imagination, your concrete conceptions harden, and then you decide that this is good or that is bad. You hold on intensely to what you call good and build it up further. You make determinations, and in that way you build your own doctrine, your own world, your own Mount Meru. Then it becomes very difficult for someone to tell you that your world is a fantasy; your attachment to it is too strong. From the beginning all these fantasies are just your own experiences, but for you they are reality. From the Buddhist point of view all sentient beings are trapped by their egotistic, solid, dualistic concepts that are rooted in fantasy. That is how we get caught in the net of samsara.

Each time you recite the prayer, you have to think quite precisely about your own state of being, your own life situation. "How deluded I am; how I deceive myself dualistically! Everything I do in my life is superficial. Whether I'm dealing with my work or my friends, it is always with superstition, completely removed from reality. I always build up an unrealistic fantasy of any sense object I perceive. That is how I trap myself in samsara." With this strong understanding, recite the mantra with the three purifying meditation techniques. Your purification will become very powerful.

The reason that the purification becomes so powerful is that you single out the real obstacle preventing you from discovering reality. Just to recognize this is some kind of realization; even this is very difficult to do. As soon as you recognize the actual troublemaker, you naturally begin to change. Many times our purification is complete nonsense because we don't exactly know what our problem is. When you have a clean-clear understanding of your problem, you can do your purifying meditation properly, and it becomes very strong. You become more realistic, more sincere. Sincerity is an important part of religion and comes from understanding your own life situation, how your own samsara has developed and how you attain nirvana. Then you become serious about your practice, and your appreciation of the Buddhadharma grows.

By recognizing your problems and knowing how to practice purification, you ask blessings to develop pure renunciation. You have to develop pure renunciation, whether you are a monk or a layperson, a Buddhist or a non-Buddhist.

What does it mean to renounce the world? Renouncing means becoming more reasonable through knowing the characteristic nature of pleasure and of the objects of pleasure. From the Buddhist point of view, everybody in the world needs renunciation. Without it, there is too much suffering; people become crazy, broken-hearted, and emotionally disturbed. Take Shakyamuni Buddha, for example. He left his kingdom and went into the jungle. We call that renunciation, yet he had the sun, the trees, and the earth all around him, and although he had left his wife and family behind, perhaps he had other pleasures there. Since we dedicate our lives to pursuing pleasure, it is important to know precisely what renunciation means.

Before Shakyamuni Buddha renounced the royal life, he had seen various manifestations of suffering: old age, sickness, and death. He realized that there was no reason to cling to the reputation of being king or to the pleasures of marriage. He was flexible. He saw that he was okay with these things but that he'd be just as okay without them. He knew he could live in the jungle and be as happy and healthy as he was in the palace. Flexibility is the key—you are all right if you get pleasure, and you are all right if you don't. In this way, you become very easygoing. Renunciation does not mean that you have to give up ice cream, but rather that if you get ice cream, you enjoy it in a reasonable way, and if you don't get ice cream, you are still all right. If you get the chance to enjoy something, then enjoy it with dignity and a refined, or transcendent, attitude. Enjoy that pleasure as it is instead of with delusion, superstition, and fantasy. When you discover the "as it is" of things, everything gives you pleasure. That's true. I really believe it. When you touch reality, you find and appreciate beauty everywhere and get pleasure from whatever object you encounter.

When we are ruled by fantasy, we become very particular and put limits on beauty. When you have a narrow definition of beauty, a limited conception of pleasure, you exaggerate the beauty of the objects that give you pleasure and build up an inventory of "favorite things." You are not open to the true nature of things; you are closed, become confused, and suffer.

Look at the ads on television. They show you only objects of obsession. They never show you flowers, for example. Why not? Check it out—it's human psychology. Those advertisers know how our minds work. Beauty is everywhere. It is very important to touch reality and place a reasonable value on each object. Value it for its unique beauty, its own proportion of energy, its own relative reality, and its own absolute reality. Understanding these notions will allow you to become flexible with pleasurable objects.

You can see from this why Buddhism is considered to be a realistic religion, philosophy, or doctrine—whatever you want to call it. Who can reject or disagree with the fact that your misery, confusion, and dissatisfaction come from your own deluded mind? Obstacles are within you; superstition, fantasy, concepts, and imagination are within you; those factors are the cause of all your suffering and confusion. This is a very simple, observable thing.

Many people are afraid of Buddhism. "Oh, in Buddhism you have to renounce the world. The Buddha gave up his wife and child and went into the jungle. He was irresponsible—a bad example for society." That's a complete misunderstanding. Renunciation doesn't mean just tossing something out. For instance, your body is always with you. From the abhidharma point of view, even Guru Shakyamuni's body was samsaric.

Milarepa, for example, gave up everything, including his teacher, and went off into the mountains. We say he renounced samsara, but he still had to take his body with him. His body was samsaric, and the nettles he ate to sustain it were samsaric. But he was easygoing, so he had no problem. Meanwhile, we're all neurotically grasping at sensory pleasures. The most important thing is that we understand the nature of sensory pleasures, both the object itself and our experience of it. Be reasonable.

Even in the Theravada Vinaya it is explained that whether or not a monk or nun has broken a vow depends primarily on the mind, not on the object or the external action. All four components of an action—the motivation, object, action, and completion—must be present for the breaking of the vow to be complete. The key component is the motivation, how much you are grasping.

Proper renunciation requires that you understand the nature of reality. Without understanding reality, there's no way you can develop renunciation, but once you understand it, renunciation comes naturally. Simply willing renunciation doesn't work. True renunciation means discovering a new, basic reality.

The logic for all this is in the lamrim: there's no reason to crave sensory pleasures because they're so small, so transitory, so impermanent. You only deceive yourself when you crave and cling to objects as permanent. In the lamrim, you deal with reality, and reality speaks to you. That understanding helps release the pressure created by your grasping mind. I'm only talking theoretically, but if, in your everyday life, you analyze how your imagination builds up fantasies, how these fantasies become concrete, and how this leads to deluded action, you will see the evolution of samsara in your own experience.

Maybe you're confused by the process of the Vajrasattva practice. On the one hand, we're asking Vajrasattva for the realization of renunciation, and on the other, we're offering him blissful sense objects. If you ask people what their particular interests are, everybody will tell you something different. Some people like music, some art, others astronomy. In my opinion, each person should enjoy everything. Everybody should appreciate forms, colors, tastes, smells, and sounds; every sense object has the ability to give pleasure. Therefore, it is good for you to offer all objects of the five senses to Vajrasattva, using your imagination as much as you can.

When you make your offering as extensive and beautiful as possible, you awaken the totality of your own mind to appreciate pleasure. We are so limited. Our minds cannot embrace the totality of pleasure. I do believe that within us we have the potential to experience complete pleasure, complete happiness, but we have to awaken it. You simply have to discover the total pleasure and satisfaction that are already within you.

Don't complain, "I have such little pleasure. Everybody around me is miserable. I am miserable too." That is ridiculous. Look around the world. There are so many different conditions, so many poor countries, so many people. Yet everybody finds some beauty, some pleasure, some purpose in life. Check it out. This is human experience, an empirical fact, not just religious dogma. In my opinion even if you are depressed or upset, no matter where you are, pleasurable objects are always at hand. Try just to discover relative beauty; don't limit your mind by deciding that one person, one little thing is the most beautiful of all.

Tantra talks about absolute beauty. Absolute beauty is shunyata, and tantra identifies it as female. This is simply an expression. What you should try to understand is that beauty is limitless. Try to discover the totality of both relative and absolute beauty. Then true renunciation will come. Is this clear? Renunciation and offering all sense objects transformed into bliss go hand in hand. That is my message.

Sometimes renunciation means that you literally *do* have to give some things up. If you live in a big city or are trapped in an unsettling situation, it may be hard to find space. In that case it is better to leave the situation until your confused mind has had a chance to clear itself. You are not leaving because you are renounced but because you are overloaded, overwhelmed, and without space to sort out the mess. When you leave such a situation for a while, you can look at it objectively and see more clearly what to do. If you stay, day by day the confusion will build until it completely suffocates you. There's no way that wisdom can grow while you are smothered by the demon of dualistic conceptions. Therefore, it is important to go away for a while, but be skillful when you do.

Real renunciation comes from understanding; escape is not the same as renunciation. We already do this; when trouble comes, we go somewhere else. That's our style. We have vacations to get away from daily problems; that's not true renunciation. On the other hand, many Buddhist meditators have done the same thing, going to secluded places to escape from samsaric situations. It depends upon how you manage your life, how you cope with normal situations.

Remember the story of Lama Je Tsongkhapa? He studied and taught for years and had thousands of disciples. One day he selected eight bodhisattva-disciples and took them to a mountain retreat where they remained isolated for a long time. It wasn't that he had to worry about samsara—he was already renounced—but through his actions he was telling us something: if you want to shift from your present level of consciousness to a higher one, you need a long period of peaceful tranquillity to practice intensive awareness.

I recommend that my students spend at least ten days in retreat every year, renouncing all their worldly relationships for a period of strong meditation. Cutting off completely for ten days is not too much, but it will give you a taste of renunciation. If you don't experience the peace and tranquillity of at least this level of renunciation, it will have no reality for you, and you won't be convinced of its benefits; renunciation will be just something else that you've heard of.

Experience of the teachings is the most important thing. That's how you find solutions to your problems. Our problems—as mentioned in this verse—are so deeply rooted in our unconscious that it takes tremendous energy to eradicate them. It's certainly not a short, one-time job.

Verse four

Here we request inspiration to develop immaculate bodhichitta. *Bodhi* means totality; *chitta* means heart. *Totality-heart* implies that at present our hearts are narrow, not fully developed. What we have to change is the feeling that we are more dear than others. We have to get rid of this in order to open our hearts completely.

Why are we bored, lonely, and lazy? Because we don't totally open our hearts to others. If you have the strength to open your heart to others, you will eliminate laziness, selfishness, and loneliness. Actually you become lonely when you are inactive. If you are busy, you don't have time to get lonely. Basically, boredom and loneliness come from a selfish attitude, concern for yourself alone. There is no way to get everlasting satisfaction unless you change your attitude from one of holding yourself dear to one where you open your heart and dedicate yourself to others. If you can do this, you are guaranteed satisfaction and will never be lazy.

The selfish mind is more painful than a knife in your heart. Selfishness kills you; it destroys your life. All the political troubles in the world today come from selfish attitudes. Regardless of the object of your selfishness—your own reputation, your own nation, the planet's resources, money—the selfish attitude is the main troublemaker. We kill each other because of self-cherishing thoughts, holding ourselves dear and not worrying about the welfare of others. All bad relationships—between husband and wife, guru and disciple—come from the selfish attitude. When you think about it, you can see that every problem on earth comes from being concerned for oneself instead of for others. Selfishness is painful, really painful. If you want to be free of selfishness, open your heart by developing universal concern for others, bringing all sentient beings into your heart as much as you possibly can. That is the antidote to the pain in your heart. I truly believe that this is the way to liberation.

We are always concerned that we won't be liberated. We don't want to be unhappy or emotionally disturbed; we want good relationships; we worry about our own welfare. We constantly talk about these things. The most practical way to liberate ourselves from pain and emotion is to dedicate ourselves to others as much as we can. This automatically eliminates self-cherishing thoughts and the pain of selfishness. If you can't dedicate yourself to others, just equating yourself with them will stop the pain in your heart. Think, "I want to be as happy as possible; I don't want the slightest unhappiness. Others are the same. Irrespective of race, skin color, or anything else, in this we are the same. Therefore, I should not make myself uncomfortable by discriminating."

Trying to develop this attitude is easier than trying to develop indestructible meditation. It is powerful, easy to understand intellectually, and you already have a certain degree of this dedicated attitude within you. You just have to increase it. Also, meditators can become hypersensitive and full of anger. They don't want any distractions and can be quite selfish. Somebody makes a little noise, and they get upset: "You destroyed my meditation!" A practice that you can understand philosophically, psychologically, and scientifically can be a lot easier for you. The moment you dedicate yourself to others, you have space—the space not to get angry when somebody else abuses you.

I think most people do have a good heart and some dedication to others, but many of them are not meditators. That's why I feel that the dedicated attitude is so simple, so logical. It brings an entirely different kind of satisfaction from what you normally experience and eliminates all kinds of negative thoughts. If you can adopt it, you'll be able to say that your dedicated attitude is your meditation, your life; your practice of awareness will be to eliminate your selfish attitude and dedicate yourself to others. Living your life for the benefit of others is wonderful and practical. It may not make you famous, but it is enough to simply do it in your own way. My parents used to disagree over how to help others. My mother was a very practical person, so whenever an opportunity to help others arose, she took it. My father would tell her that she needed to be selective about whom she helped. Her logic was, as she would tell my father, "Suppose you are traveling in some far off place and have nothing to eat and no place to stay. You ask people for help but they tell you that you are not worthy of charity. How would you feel? No matter who comes to you, I think you should just serve them." In a way they were both right, but my mother was more practical.

I don't need to go into the details of how to meditate on bodhichitta because it's all in the lamrim teachings. Just remember that all the difficulties in the world—power struggles, the pursuit of wealth, hunger, fighting—come from cherishing oneself above all others. This is the problem, has always been the problem, and will continue to be the problem. Therefore dedicate yourself to others as much as you possibly can. This is the only way you'll be happy—nothing else can truly satisfy you. You don't need to be wealthy to dedicate yourself to others. Even if you have nothing, you can still dedicate your life that way.

I hope you are clear about all this. This verse refers to the door that leads to all misery and confusion, which is self-cherishing, and to the demon of dualistic conception, which is the mind that puts yourself first and others second. We offer transcendental, blissful sense objects to Guru Vajrasattva with a request to purify our dualistic concepts and appearances and to bless us to generate immaculate bodhichitta, the essence of the bodhisattva path.

VERSE FIVE

This verse deals with shunyata, the great seal of emptiness *(mahamudra)*. Historically, seals were used as signs of official approval; a seal represented real authority. "Seal of emptiness" might look a bit strange to you; you might think that an empty seal is ineffective or means nothing. From the Buddhist point of view, the state of nonduality is supreme. What does it hold? It embraces every existent phenomenon, without exception; nonduality pervades all existence, both relative and absolute.

We all look different: he, she, you, me, that, this. The person who understands nonduality sees the unity that lies beneath our different appearances. When we look at each other, we all seem so real, discrete, unconnected. The person who has realized emptiness not only sees us individually, but also as a whole, as if we were droplets in a cloud of steam. That is the seal. It holds the totality of absolute nature, just as it is. With a prayer for the understanding of the great seal to grow within us, we offer Guru Vajrasattva the blissful experience of the objects of the five senses.

All phenomena exist merely as images of mental speculation. You create an appearance and then label it, to give words to that reality. Tok-pä par-zhak means produced or projected by superstition. All things exist merely by imputation of name. There is not the slightest trace of self-existence in any phenomenon. Whatever you consider beautiful, ugly, wonderful, tasty, or aromatic is simply a projection of your superstitious mind.

This is the reason advertising is so effective. Products are presented as excellent, successful, and certain to make us happy; ads make us believe that a particular product is worthwhile. As a result we grasp at what we see as a self-existent object. First, it is nothing; then, the advertisers visualize, imagine, and fantasize; finally, they decide how to present it. Of course, the object does have its own relative and absolute function, but we grasp at it as self-existent. We're not aware of the evolution of superstitious projections. Our responsibility is to realize that whatever they advertise is a dualistic projection of the superstitious mind; absolute happiness cannot be achieved through such objects. That sort of understanding helps to relieve the pressure of your conceptualizing, grasping, egotistic mind. You need to think about it deeply and, in the light of that reflection, examine your everyday life so that you can gain some experience of how it works. You cannot understand it through just the words.

To summarize, all existence is merely labeled, given value by superstition. This contaminated, foul-smelling *(dri-ma ngän-päi),* dualistic hallucination has to be purified.

Each verse of this practice covers a different subject. You need to think about each one very deeply and intensively to know clearly what you should extinguish and what you should accomplish. From this understanding you will develop the strong motivation to purify the faults mentioned in the verse. Then you recite the Vajrasattva mantra with the three different meditation techniques. If you can practice like this, your purification will be logically based and, therefore, very sincere and extremely powerful.

Now, instead of my talking, let's do a short meditation. Contemplate that two hundred years ago, none of the mentally labeled objects that we find today in supermarkets existed. Then people started conceptualizing them, and superstitious fantasies grew. They produced Coca-Cola and all the other things in the supermarket that we know so well. All these things have been labeled, or produced, by the mind of superstition. From their own side, these objects have no trace of duality or self-existence. As long as you want to see things dualistically, the dual appearance is there. When you see totality, dualistic appearances vanish. You and I are one nondual totality. Be aware of totality; feel totality. Totality has no idea of good or bad, beautiful or ugly. Meditate on totality with focused awareness.

ᘉᓍ

Buddhism believes that all human beings have the ability to understand their true nature and that developing that understanding is the most important thing we can do. All the problems, confusion, and dissatisfaction we experience are the result of not having developed this understanding, and until we do, we will never be free from bondage. The main human problem is failing to understand our own reality.

Therefore, all the teachings of the Buddha, regardless of which you choose, are directed at helping us realize both the conventional nature of our lives and universal totality, or shunyata. Both are of great importance.

This fifth verse refers to the Buddhist scientific theory of reality, describing first of all the conventional—relative or interdependent—way in which our body and mind exist. As our obscured mind perceives these conventional existences, it tries to identify the reality of what it sees, to comprehend the reality of our own existence, others' existence, universal existence, the existence of all phenomena. What do we end up doing? We *name* perceived objects in an attempt to give them reality.

That's what *tok-pä par-zhak* means: something is there—a nectarine, for example—and we try to identify its reality. We give it the name "nectarine" to represent the reality we identify. In fact, the true reality of the nectarine is just the collection of its constantly moving parts: the right elements have gathered, the fruit has developed organically, and it's somehow edible. Apart from this superficial interdependence and moment-to-moment transformation of the elements of the nectarine, you can't add further dimensions to its existence; to do so is to exaggerate, or overestimate, its qualities.

When we understand the cooperative, interdependent mode of existence of the nectarine, its transitory energy, its color and vibration, and the relationship between ourselves and the nectarine, we will begin to understand its universal reality—or at least we will soon have the potential to do so. The first thing we have to realize—and this is important—is the way the conventional I, or self, exists and how it operates. If you investigate this, you will find that it exists simply because the mind applies a temporary label to a bubble-like collection of parts: the combination of the name and the bubble constitutes the object's conventional reality. Apart from that, there is no absolute conventional reality: it is merely conventional.

Whenever you see a beautiful body, remember that it is simply an interdependent conglomeration of vibrations named by the mind. If you can understand conventional reality in this way, you will eliminate your habitual exaggeration and reduction of the relative truth. This is Buddhism's middle way, the way to eliminate confusion and become healthy. This is the door to satisfaction. From the Buddhist point of view if you don't understand the true nature of conventional reality, you are only dreaming if you talk about comprehending absolute truth; you can't do it.

Buddhist philosophy, psychology, and doctrine all deal with human reality: How do we eradicate all our problems? In other words, how do we become enlightened or, in philosophical terms, unify with the totality of being, as taught in the completion stage of tantra?

Lately I've developed a taste for nectarines. The other day Åge, one of my students, took me nectarine shopping, and we agreed that we should pick out only the good ones. So, we both selected some. Last night Åge and I were eating nectarines, and one of his was rotten inside. He said, "I picked this one; I thought it was okay, but it's rotten." He admitted it himself without my saying anything! I'm telling this story because it's a good example of what we do. We pick something up, touch it, look at it closely, and finally declare, "Ah, here's a good one." But by the time we get home, it's rotten. Now, the question is—we've labeled a particular substance "nectarine"—but what is the reality of that substance? Is a rotten nectarine a nectarine?

Calling something a nectarine is supposed to somehow touch its reality, but from the Buddhist point of view that is very superficial. The superficial mind labels something a nectarine, and a nectarine comes into existence. But in our delusion, we hear the word "nectarine" and a concrete nectarine enters our perception. But there's no such thing as a concrete, inherently existent, independent, or permanent nectarine. Fundamentally, the relationship between the name "nectarine" and the reality of the nectarine is for us the product of ignorance, developed through our not having touched the nectarine's reality.

Instead of thinking of a nectarine as a nectarine, try calling it "John"! Give it a human name! We have a fixed idea about the name John. If I ask you why he's called John, what qualities does he have to warrant being called John, what are you going to say? Your answer will be very superficial; it won't even cover his beard! It might just cover a tiny part of his reality, but even that's doubtful.

Buddhism warns against jumping to fixed conclusions, "You *are* John; I know you are." Instead, look at the history of that projection, why he was given that name. Then you can see how untrue the reality of "John" is. Names are given to things and people in very contrived ways and have little to do with the reality of the named objects. Look at the history of conventional existences and you'll see why Buddhism says *tok-pä par-zhak;* the superficial, superstitious mind makes a certain projection, gives a name, and behold, a functioning human being. That's all it takes to make us function. We are so sure we know what we are. How can we be so certain when we choose rotten nectarines believing them to be good ones?

From the Buddhist point of view, human existence is the most sophisticated and profound form of life—much harder to know than a nectarine. It is hard to understand who we are, what we are, and the true nature of both our relative and absolute modes of existence. But it is most worthwhile to develop this understanding. Lord Buddha himself said, "I tell some disciples that things truly exist and others that things do not truly exist. I explain things differently according to the situation. It might look like I'm contradicting myself, but whatever I teach is to lead those particular disciples to a better understanding of reality." Everything Lord Buddha taught was to help us discover the two levels of truth: our relative and absolute modes of existence. All his teachings were given for this purpose.

How do we stop delusion? First, recognize that the deluded mind is, in fact, deluded, and that its concepts are false. Recognizing delusions for what they are is the only way to break them down. You have to take responsibility for your own mind, analyze it, and check it out thoroughly in order to eliminate your confusion. There is no permanent, concrete existence out there waiting for us.

A favorite example of mine is the linear accelerator. Scientists take millions of photographs of a particle accelerating through the same space under completely controlled conditions, trying to get identical photographs, but every one turns out different. Why? Because they are filming an impermanent, relative phenomenon subject to conditions, so it doesn't matter how many pictures they take. Our minds are so coarse that we can't see even the conventional movement of the process of change. This example shows how deluded our conceptions and sense perceptions really are.

In my opinion, just thinking about how your body exists, or about how your friend exists, is one of the best kinds of meditation. It makes you scared; instead of grasping at your friend you're afraid of him. You can even see him as a skeleton. That's the best way to eliminate your neurosis, grasping, and egocentricity. Most people misunderstand the meaning of meditation; they think it's something that makes you numb. Meditation should help you overcome the distractions of the polluted, hallucinating mind and bring it closer to reality. Lama Je Tsongkhapa said there were two kinds of meditation: analytical and single-pointed. It's possible that we're all meditating right now. Though we're intellectualizing, our minds have entered some kind of spiritual zone.

All the prayers in the text keep mentioning duality: duality this, duality that. Our mind is constantly dealing with conventional phenomena, so we are always in conflict. As our mind operates on the basis of conventional phenomena, consciously and unconsciously, there are always at least two things in conflict. Our mind is always comparing one thing with another. All this is duality in action. Nothing can exist for us unless we're comparing two things.

But don't think that only the good-bad dichotomy is dualistic. Good itself can be dualistic: what you think of as good is usually just a fantasy. All the phenomena that you consider good and bad function dualistically because they are all relative. Even when you experience pleasure, it's dualistic, because it is limited. Your pleasure is limited because you function within the framework of duality. If you dismantle this framework, you will experience limitless joy.

Verse six

The subject of this verse is tantra. I'm going to assume that, from your previous tantric studies, you know what the gross and subtle bodies and minds are.[25]

One of our biggest human problems is that we have a limited conception of ourselves. In other words, we put ourselves down. We have a low opinion of ourselves and a low opinion of others. We think "He did this, therefore, he is bad"; "I did this, therefore, I am bad." We constantly see ourselves in a very ugly light; we project ourselves in an ordinary way. These are the problems that tantra can solve.

Ta-mäl nang-zhen means ordinary vision, ordinary projection, or the generation of ordinary concepts. The way we appear to this ordinary mind and our very ordinary conceptions of ourselves are dangerous. They give rise to a limited, self-pitying image. All this prevents us from developing our human potential, from generating great love and great wisdom, and from growing the totality of wisdom and love. If you project yourself as a limited, self-pitying entity, your belief will cause you to become one. You will manifest like that. Tantra is the antidote to such ordinary, self-pitying ego conceptions.

To eliminate all this, you manifest in the present time the archetypal image of the deity, which gives you a self-image with divine qualities and a pure nature. This reflects your true mode of existence. Thus, you eliminate the totally deluded, nonsensical, self-pitying image that your ego projects.

You need strong penetrative insight and intensive awareness to convince yourself that you have the perfect qualities of a buddha or deity. Tantric practice is based on visualizing yourself as a deity and concentrating on that with divine pride, so you have to completely identify yourself in this way.

The tantric method of eliminating the gross mind brings out the function of the subtle, unconscious mind by using techniques like tumo or vase meditation. These techniques are designed to energize the fundamental consciousness that resides within the unconscious—to make it function at the conscious level. The gross mind has to be eliminated, because it is so deluded that it prevents you from touching reality. That is why you have to meditate.

Nyi-dzin lung-shuk drak-pöi. The gross, dualistic mind is like a tornado because it shakes and disturbs your life. Our lives have been captured by the dualistic, superstitious mind. So my dualistic, superstitious mind brings me to California, then pushes me to Europe, then to Asia. It always leads me here and there, driving me like a tornado. Maybe I'm exaggerating; check it out for yourselves. The superstitious mind is very powerful; it makes all your life decisions for you.

Perhaps I can put this another way—I can say that your original mind is asleep; your fundamental mind is sleeping. It's as if it is closed for business and not taking any responsibility for your life. Who is taking that responsibility? That joker, your superficial mind, has taken over and is making all your life decisions. But if you can make yourself tranquil and peaceful, calm and clear, through practicing tantra, you can get your original mind to function. When it enters your central channel, you are automatically in contact with your own universal reality. We call that the clear-light experience, or the vision of totality.

Why do we pray to attain the four actual initiations? Receiving initiations has more to do with your own level of development than with the qualities of the guru. You don't receive an initiation just because the guru is special—in fact, it's the other way around. You receive initiation because of your own qualities. Due to your mind's capacity to attain higher states, during an initiation it can somehow meet, or merge with, the guru's mind, such that you both experience the same thing. That sort of experience can really be called receiving an initiation.

If you merely happen to be in a place where an initiation is being given, you receive something, of course, but probably not the real thing. *Nge-dön* means "that which can truly be defined as an initiation." Is that what you received? Did you experience the true nature of the relative initiation? It all depends upon your level of mind.

In ancient times, when highly qualified gurus gave initiations, some of their disciples would receive realizations instantly! Those sound like Western realizations—like instant coffee! But really, we know from history that the moment those highly qualified gurus gave the initiation, the mature disciple was magnetically opened, as if struck by a nuclear missile. The initiation would go straight into the disciple's heart, and he would be totally transformed. It's good to know these things. Usually it's like what we're doing here: I sit in front of you talking nonsense; you don't touch reality while I talk, and as soon as I go, you forget everything I said. Compared to the ancients, we're very poor quality practitioners. Perhaps I shouldn't say that about you, but it's certainly true for me.

People interpret the experiences of others very unrealistically. Let me give you an example. Say I've explained a certain practice and later a student comes to me and reports having had a particular experience. I reply, "I don't believe you. You're just a mushroom student; you haven't studied Buddhist philosophy for twenty years. How can you claim to have had that experience?" Of course I'm free to believe that his experience has no basis in reality and that without academic study one cannot touch reality, but I'd be wrong. You can never tell what someone else's level of consciousness is.

For a start, there is more than one life. We bring to our present life the experiences of countless previous lives. How can I pass judgment on someone else: "You haven't studied doctrine for a long time; you're a non-Buddhist from an irreligious country; you can't possibly have had an experience like that." I don't know what's going on in that person's mind. How can I deny his experiences? Yet we deny other people's experiences, others' reality, all the time. That's not right; be careful. You should not put others down.

All human experiences are transitory, momentary, impermanent, and not inherently existent. What you receive during an initiation depends entirely upon your own level of development. However don't start thinking, "I've been to a hundred initiations—maybe I haven't received anything. It's all been a complete waste of time." That's not true. You must have received something—how much simply depends upon your own level of mind. The four great initiations have different stages; there are degrees of readiness for an initiation. There is no question that good things have happened, but the real question is, did you receive the *actual* initiation?

Be reasonable and accept your own physical and mental qualities: "I'm all right. My face is not so horrible that I can't show it in my local supermarket. I've nothing to worry about." If you have a bad opinion of yourself, it's not a true picture, and you will only make your life difficult. As soon as you start accepting yourself as you are, you begin to transform. In a reasonable way, bring your good qualities to mind and try to develop a positive attitude toward life. With this as your foundation you will be more successful, more positive, and more realistic. This will lead to spiritual growth. It's a very practical way to be.

VERSE SEVEN

We have so many negative imprints on our consciousness. We create them day by day, week by week, month by month. Why? Because our minds are uncontrolled. The more uncontrolled our minds and habits, the more we hallucinate and become deluded. The more we hallucinate, the greater the dark shadow of ignorance in our minds. The greater the dark shadow, the less the wisdom. Then fear and tension tend to arise, because everything is unclear. We are in the dark; our surroundings are murky. Neurotically, we project all our doubt, fear, unease, and anxiety into the darkness: "Maybe this is happening; maybe that is happening." We live in a world of fantasy, where fantasized reactions are the only reality, and this is how we end up in the vajra hells—a self-created hallucination of a dark prison. That, actually, is what the hells and the other miserable realms are.

There is no miserable place waiting for you, sitting and waiting like Alaska—waiting to turn you into ice cream. But whatever you call it—hell or the suffering realms—it is something that you enter by creating a world of neurotic fantasy and believing it to be real. It sounds simple, but that's exactly what happens.

So when you touch the really deep, deep, neurotic, hallucinated, deluded dark shadows, it is difficult to be calm and difficult to return from or go beyond that space. You can analyze this and see for yourself that it's true. Many depressed people can be seen on American TV explaining how they've been depressed for so many years. You see, I don't need to go to some laboratory to do research; my TV set tells me exactly what's going on in your minds! Hell, or whatever you call it, has to do with your own mind and your own interpretation of reality. Whatever you interpret as reality will manifest to you as reality.

Therefore, in this verse we pray for the infinite pure land to appear: *Dak-pa rap-jam ba-zhik char-war shok!* Psychologically, how does this work? If you have a completely positive attitude about yourself and touch the pure nature of your fundamental reality, your negative projections disappear, and the world improves. Your environment becomes positive, more beautiful, and attractive. So instead of projecting a dangerous world beset by pollution, radiation, and poisoned resources, you project an incredibly beautiful land-scape of trees and water and gentle human beings all helping one another, which gives you great pleasure. If you can interpret the world in that way, it really will become a pure land for you.

So, the actual pure land depends a lot on your own mind. If your mind is happy, clean-clear, and in touch with fundamental reality, then the true nature of the pure land appears around you. When you have the pure vision in this life, you are guaranteed that it will continue in the next. That's how karma works. The reverse, of course, is also true. If you are miserable, think-ing ill of yourself and others and always emitting negative vibrations, the karmic impact of this experience guarantees that you will be reborn in a miserable place. Such a result is no more than the karmic impact of your own experience.

OFFERING TO THE VAJRA MASTER

With the next verse, the tsok is offered to the vajra teacher. It asks him to listen and to please enjoy the blissful nectar that is free from the confusion of dualistic concepts, which is offered by the courageous males and females—the dakas and dakinis.

Tantra understands that at the fundamental core of human existence lies inseparably united male and female energy. Practicing the path, we recognize the simultaneous existence of these energies. When we become enlightened, we manifest as Vajradhara, the total union of male and female. It is very important to know this.

In the perfect tantric gathering, men and women come to make offer-ings together. *Tsok-kyi khor-lo* means circle of offerings. It's called a circle because of the sense of unity or completeness of energies when men and women make offerings together. The totality of the experience is beneficial for each other's minds.

We usually enjoy things with a dualistic mind, but through tantra it is possible for us to enjoy sense objects nondualistically.

In the next verse, the teacher replies, saying something like, "Oh, great blissful wisdom, the great collection of tumo heat energy; the experience is beyond words or concepts. Enjoy that great bliss forever." I don't need to say any more about this.

OFFERINGS AND PRAISE TO VAJRASATTVA; EIGHT-LEGGED PRAISE; SONG OF THE SPRING QUEEN

I need not say anything about these verses either. I didn't write them; they come from other practices. I'm sure you can find commentaries on them elsewhere.

OFFERING THE REMAINING TSOK

Earlier, we made offerings to the higher beings. Here, we offer to those who are lower. In Buddhist practice, we make offerings to all universal living beings. The objects of your charity should not be only higher beings. You should give something to everybody: to the buddhas and bodhisattvas, and to animals and other ordinary beings. Everybody is an object of charity.

Furthermore, even though we mean well, our concepts are usually so limited that most of the time we don't really know what true charity is. True charity is giving without ego, being true to your original nature. Remember, we are reflections of each other.

So we offer the leftover tsok in a skull cup as the illusory appearance of great bliss and emptiness united, recognizing that energy as the five divine wisdoms. We offer it to the positive worldly beings, those who help our spiritual growth in the four ways: peaceful, wrathful, developing, and controlling.

CONCLUDING PRAYER OF AUSPICIOUSNESS

These verses are also from elsewhere, so I don't need to comment on them.

CONCLUSION

You can now see the extent of tantra's concern that the unity of your own male and female energies functions within you. The meditation techniques in tantra ensure that these two energies develop within your nervous system and energize your consciousness.

From the Tibetan Buddhist point of view, tantra is the final path. Lord Buddha gave many different teachings on various aspects of method and wisdom, but highest of all was tantra. It shows that men and women are equal when it comes to attaining totality; they can unify the same realizations at the same time and in the same space; they can equally gain everlasting satisfaction.

We have to recognize that both men and women reflect each other. We have equal responsibility to gain the same realizations, reach the same destination, develop the same profound awareness. We also have equal capacity to lead each other: women have the capacity to lead men to the highest destination, and men have the capacity to lead women to the same place. In particular, tantric theory shows clearly that without the help of women, men cannot achieve enlightenment. All the texts say so.

Everybody knows that the Geluk tradition is supposed to be very strict. The Geluk tradition comes from Lama Je Tsongkhapa, who was a monk. He once said that during one of his meditation retreats, at first, many ordinary women would come into his cave, but later, as his meditations progressed, real transformations of Vajrayogini would enter. The implication of this is that because he had given initiations to immature disciples, he experienced the negative result of visions of ordinary women instead of dakinis, but that as time went by, he purified that view.

What all this shows is that although Lama Tsongkhapa's tradition is very strict—and because of our mad elephant mind, we do need it to be strict—when we reach a certain point, when we give up and let go, everything comes to us naturally. I think this is what Lama Tsongkhapa is saying. When he had completely purified himself of all negative imprints, the divine wisdom female was always there.

Milarepa and many other great meditators and saints also had some connection with females. Nagarjuna, for example, had a close relationship with Tara, as did many others. Those female aspects led them to many realizations. Similarly, we all need the help of female practitioners, directly and indirectly, inwardly and outwardly. It is only because of gross misconceptions that men and women put each other down.

When we talk about totality, we are not talking about something superficial; what women can do, what women can't do. We are talking about the potential for total development. In this, there is total equality between men and women. And the dakas and dakinis of tantra are also equally realized, having reached the same level of consciousness and attained the same realizations in order to help each other.

Tantra not only explains in detail the inner qualities of mind that must be realized but also certain female physical characterisitics that are important in the practice of tantra and how these female organs are energized. You can research all this later; I'd only bore you if I went into detail now.

It is important to recognize that when men and women gather together for tsok, it is more than physical. We gather for the infinite progression of human consciousness that eventually leads to total satisfaction. That motivation should be remembered in everyday life, and if it is, men and women will constantly be learning and getting support from each other.

Many great saints among the Tibetan lineage gurus were women, and we take refuge in them. When I first went to Europe, where there are many churches, I watched to see what the people were doing. I noticed the strong connection that Westerners seemed to have with the Virgin Mary. In European churches their devotion is so strong that they seem to offer more candles to her than they do to Jesus. My guess is that when they pray to the Virgin Mary, they feel an organic, heart-to-heart communication with her because of her form. This is simply human experience.

The devotion of Tibetan Buddhists to Tara results from a similar attraction. Not only serious practitioners but even businessmen feel it. They do Tara pujas for success in business. There is definitely something special about her.

The success of Buddhism coming to Tibet was due in large part to women. Tibet's first Dharma king, Songtsen Gampo, was converted to Buddhism by his Nepalese and Chinese wives, whom we regard as emanations of Tara. The king felt that without them, Buddhadharma could not have become perfectly established in Tibet.

This does not apply only in Tibet. Anywhere in the world, even in the political sphere, men cannot succeed without the support of women. There is a lot of evidence for this—you can see for yourselves.

Men and women can live harmoniously and help each other, not just in the temporal sense, but in the attainment of total satisfaction. You have to know this.

The main point is that your impurities are your own projection, your own symptoms. *You* are the one who created your self-image of "I am a bad person." Therefore, you are capable of overcoming this projection by practicing purification.

Now, this is my last talk here, and what can I say?[26] Certainly I would like to thank you all for sharing your pleasures with me; I have enjoyed my stay here very much. As you can see, I'm very healthy, so you should not worry. I'm happy and enjoying life. I would like to thank those people who have put so much energy into developing the facilities here at Vajrapani for the benefit of myself and others, and especially those who have worked so hard taking care of me like a baby. From my heart, thank you so much. I think that's all I can say.

Perhaps I can answer some questions. Are there any difficulties? Sometimes I produce more confusion than clarity, so please ask.

Q: Sometimes Buddhism says that good and evil are the same, and sometimes that good is better than evil. Which is it?
A: That's a good question. From the absolute, or ultimate, point of view, good and evil are the same, absolutely the same: when you experience totality, there is neither goodness nor evil in your consciousness. But relatively speaking, because your conventional mind interprets things as good and evil, they exist. It depends upon which level of mind you're speaking from. But I'd like to make another point here. If you have concrete conceptions of good and evil, you're in trouble. Lord Buddha taught that there is no concrete object of evil, no concrete object of good; both are nondual, both are non–self-existent. They are made real only through the operation of dualistic conceptions.

From the practical point of view, knowing this can help you deal with everyday situations. When good things happen to you, it's not necessarily fantastically wonderful; when bad things happen, it's not a big disaster. So you can see how the good/bad dichotomy demonstrates the reality of our superficial mind. Good and bad are like a dream, nothing to get emotional about. Am I communicating with you or not? Practically, this knowledge is very important. Next time that you feel, "Oh, this is fantastic, excellent, genuine," when your mind projects so many superlative qualities on another person or some object, slow down, check it out more deeply. Try to realize that overreacting to a beautiful object comes from a neurotic view of reality. This perspective keeps you psychologically balanced and your reality stable. If you exaggerate the good qualities of something, your mind is always up and down, soaring and plummeting, causing you so much disappointment. Be realistic, take the middle way: don't expect too much, don't reject too much. Enjoy your relationships in a reasonable way.

Q: Tantra is said to be the quickest path to enlightenment, but I've also heard it's the most dangerous. How do you know when you're ready to risk taking an initiation?
A: You and I, all of us, we're always speculating: "If I do this, maybe something good will happen; if I do that, maybe something bad will happen." Of course, it's true that we never know what's going to happen next; we don't know what's going to happen tomorrow. There are no guarantees. But as

humans, we are always optimistic, speculating that something good is just around the corner.

Let's say that we're planning a trip to the beach to go swimming. We're expecting pleasure: sun, sand, sea—a peaceful day out. We also know that there could be danger—a hurricane, perhaps. That's also speculation. Nevertheless, we still go to the beach, expecting the best.

We go through a similar thought process when we consider taking an initiation. On the negative side, we know there's a great risk that we won't be able to keep the vows we take. But we also know that the benefits are limitless and that the energy we receive has great power. I remember His Holiness Song Rinpoche once saying that since you're going to hell anyway, you might as well take the initiation. He was always very direct. It is extremely important to practice tantra, so even if you're going to break the vows, it's better to take an initiation than not. Even if you're reborn in some miserable place, since the tantric imprints are on your consciousness, you'll eventually be reborn where you can practice it once again. Other lamas have said the same thing.

Furthermore, I don't consider the risky part, the breaking of vows, as a painful experience but rather as some kind of realization. Usually, we never test ourselves, we never put ourselves into testing situations. We just float about in the comfort zone. Until you are really psychologically free, you have to follow rules, or guidelines. But once you have attained liberation, you're free; you don't need those rules anymore. Having psychological rails makes it clear to you when you have crossed the boundary between constructive and destructive behavior. If you reach a point of difficulty you can ask yourself, why? Is it because of your nose, your hands, your body? Or is it because of your mind? In this way, you can see that it's your mind that forces you off the rails.

Having boundaries also helps you estimate the amount of negative energy that forced you to break your vows. This is useful because it allows you to deduce how much positive energy you need to generate to neutralize that negativity. Tantra teaches that you can purify any negativity you can imagine. If you do twenty-one Vajrasattva mantras every day of your life, your mind will be extremely clean-clear. There is no negativity that the Vajrasattva mantra cannot purify. The science of this is very simple. When you break a vow, you generate a certain amount of negative energy; to counteract it, you need to generate an equal amount of positive energy in your mind.

Therefore, when you break a vow, encourage yourself: "I was responsible for that. I can purify it, too." This is the way to liberate yourself. Overcoming your own difficulties with your own skill makes you free. The main thing to remember is that negativities are transitory, conventional, interdependent phenomena. Instead of thinking unrealistically, "It's all my fault. I'm completely negative; I'll never be free," you can think, "I'm capable of creating negativities; I must be capable of purifying them."

Q: When you were talking about the inner offerings, you said that our indiscriminate consumption of food and drink shocks our nervous system. Could you please say more about that?

A: Physical sufferings, like cancer, are a result of our own mismanagement—unconsciousness of what our body needs and what we put into it. We are unrealistic. We don't understand our own organic nervous system: we have a low opinion of it, treat it very disrespectfully, and expect unreasonable things from it. We eat all sorts of things, many of which cannot be digested properly. I believe that all this damage to our nervous system causes cancer.

We have to develop a reasonable understanding of the organic nature of our physical being and treat it with respect. We should know what's appropriate according to time and space and should take the middle way, neither overloading our little body nor living an ascetic extreme.

Simply put, physical disorders come from a disorderly mind. We don't allow our body the time and space it needs to function properly, to digest and assimilate nutrients in a healthy way. We don't breathe properly, either. When we're miserable we hold our breath too long. We don't exhale fully, and our bodies get pumped up with retained air so that our nervous system can't function and our mind shakes uncontrollably. The result of all this is an unhealthy body. Remember the four foundations of mindfulness that the Buddha taught? One of those is mindfulness of the body. We are not mindful of our bodies, so we get sick.

I can probably go so far as to say that the more sophisticated the food produced by modern society, the sicker we get. Of course, there's cancer in India and Nepal, for example, but I think there's more of it in the West. I once saw one health expert, a doctor, report that there are diseases found in the industrial West that are rarely found in the third world, where life is more simple and natural. So I think it's obvious that we're expecting too much of our delicate nervous systems, telling them, "I want to eat this; you have no choice. Take it! Digest!" We can't survive like that. Our bodies are natural, organic phenomena—it's important to develop good eating habits. Food is medicine; it is much better for our health than the plastic, chemical drugs we usually think of as medicine.

APPENDIX 1

The Yoga Method of the
Glorious Supreme Heruka Vajrasattva

Taking refuge

Sang-gyä chö-dang ge-dün-la
Tak-tu dak-ni kyab-su chi
Tek-pa sum-po tam-chä-dang
Näl-jor sang-ngak kan-dro-ma
Pa-wo pa-mo wang-lha-mo
Jang-chup-sem-pa dak-nyi che
Kyä-par-du-yang lop-pön-la
Tak-tu kyab-su chi-war gyi.

Generating bodhichitta

Sem-chän kün-gyi dön-gyi chir
Dak-ni he-ru-kar gyur-nä
Sem-chän tam-chä he-ru-käi
Go-pang chok-la gö-par gyi.

[The vase meditation: The nine-round breathing exercise]

Visualization of [Heruka] Vajrasattva

Rang-gi chi-wor PAM-lä pä-ma-dang AH-lä da-wäi dän-gyi teng-du HUM-lä dor-je kar-po tse nga-pa te-wa-la HUM-gyi tsän-pa.

De-lä wo-zer trö. Dön-nyi jä. Dü yong-su gyur-pa-lä Dor-je Sem-pa kar-po.

The Yoga Method of the Glorious Supreme Heruka Vajrasattva[27]

TAKING REFUGE

(Recite three times:)
Forever, I take refuge in Buddha, Dharma, and Sangha, and in the Sangha of the three vehicles, the dakas and dakinis of secret mantra yoga, the heroes and heroines, the gods and goddesses, the bodhisattvas, and in particular, my guru.

GENERATING BODHICHITTA

(Recite three times:)
I must become Heruka in order to lead all sentient beings to the sublime state of Herukahood.

[The vase meditation: The nine-round breathing exercise]

VISUALIZATION OF [HERUKA]VAJRASATTVA

Out of the void, about six inches above the crown of my head, appears the seed syllable PAM, which transforms into a thousand-petalled lotus. On top of the lotus appears the seed syllable AH, which transforms into a moon disc. In the center of the moon disc stands the seed syllable HUM. Suddenly, the HUM transforms into a white five-pronged vajra that has a HUM at its center. Much radiant light emanates from both the HUM and the vajra, going out into the ten directions and completing the two purposes. The whole universe melts into light. This light then returns to and is absorbed by the HUM in the vajra. The HUM and vajra also melt into light and transform into Heruka Vajrasattva.

Zhäl-chik chak-nyi. Dor-je-dang dril-bu dzin-pa. Dor-je kyil-trung-gi zhuk-pa. Yum Dor-je Nyem-ma kar-mo. Zhäl-chik chak-nyi. Dri-guk-dang tö-pa dzin-pä kyü-pa.

Nyi-ka-ang dar-dang rin-po-chei gyän na-tsok-pä trä-pa. Nyi-käi chi-wor OM drin-par AH tuk-kar HUM. Tuk-käi HUM-lä wö-zer trö-pä rang-dräi ye-she-pa chän drang.

OFFERING TO HERUKA VAJRASATTVA

OM KHANDA ROHI HUM HUM PHAT
OM SVABHAVA SHUDDAH SARVA DHARMA SVABHAVA SHUDDHO HAM

Tong-pa-nyi-du gy-ur. Tong-päi ngang-lä ah-lä tö-pa yang-shing gya-che-wäi nang-du sha nga dü-tsi nga-nam. Zhu-wa-lä jung-wäi ye-she-kyi dü-tsii gya-tso chen-por gyur.

OM AH HUM, HA HO HRI

OM VAJRASATTVA ARGHAM PRATICCHA HUM SVAHA
OM VAJRASATTVA PADYAM PRATICCHA HUM SVAHA
OM VAJRASATTVA PUSHPE PRATICCHA HUM SVAHA
OM VAJRASATTVA DHUPE PRATICCHA HUM SVAHA
OM VAJRASATTVA ALOKE PRATICCHA HUM SVAHA
OM VAJRASATTVA GANDHE PRATICCHA HUM SVAHA
OM VAJRASATTVA NAIVEDYA PRATICCHA HUM SVAHA
OM VAJRASATTVA SHABDA PRATICCHA HUM SVAHA

JAH HUM BAM HOH
Nyi-su me-par gyur.

Vajrasattva is white. He has one face and two arms. He holds a vajra in his right hand and a bell in his left. He is sitting in the full-lotus position with his hands in the embracing mudra. His consort, Dorje Nyema, embraces him, her legs encircling his body. She is white and has one face and two arms. She holds a curved knife in her right hand and a skull cup in her left.

They are both dressed in robes of heavenly silk and adorned by precious jewel ornaments. [They both have seed syllables] OM at the crown chakra, AH at the throat chakra, and HUM at the heart. Brilliant light radiates from the HUM at the heart, invoking the divine supreme wisdom energy of all tathagatas.

OFFERING TO HERUKA VAJRASATTVA

OM KHANDA ROHI HUM HUM PHAT *(Cleanses the offerings)*

OM SVABHAVA SHUDDAH SARVA DHARMA SVABHAVA SHUDDHO HAM *(Purifies them)*

All is void. A seed syllable AH appears out of the void. It turns into a huge white kapala containing the five meats and five nectars. They melt, becoming an ocean of the amrita-energy of divine transcendental wisdom.

(Bless the offerings by saying three times:)
OM AH HUM HA HO HRI

(Offer them with:)
OM VAJRASATTVA ARGHAM PRATICCHA HUM SVAHA
(OM Vajrasattva, accept greeting water HUM SVAHA.)
(*and similarly with* PADYAM [foot-washing water], PUSHPE [flowers], DHUPE [incense], ALOKE [light], GANDHE [perfume], NAIVEDYA [food], and SHABDA [sound/music] *in place of* ARGHAM.)

JAH HUM BAM HO
Become nondual.

EMPOWERMENT BY THE BUDDHAS OF THE FIVE FAMILIES

Lar-yang tuk-käi HUM-lä wö-zer trö. Wang-gi lha-nam chän-drang.

OM PANCHA KULA SAPARIVARA ARGHAM....SHABDA PRATICCHA HUM SVAHA

"De-zhin-shek-pa tam-chä-kyi ngon-par wang-kur-du söl." Zhe söl-wa tap-pä de-nam-kyi ye-she-kyi dü-tsi gang-wäi bum-pa tok-nä OM SARVA TATHAGATA ABHISHEKATA SAMAYA SHRIYE HUM zhe wang kur.

Ku ye-she-kyi du tsi gang Mi-kyö-pä u gyän-ching.

Tuk-kar da-wäi teng-du HUM-gyi tar yi-ge gya-päi ngak-kyi kor-war gyur.

OFFERINGS TO HERUKA VAJRASATTVA

OM VAJRASATTVA ARGHAM...SHABDA PRATICCHA HUM SVAHA
OM VAJRASATTVA OM AH HUM

PRAISE

Nyi-me ye-she dro-wäi päl
Chok-tu mi-gyur de-wa che
Dik-tung ma-lü drung-jin-päi
Dor-je sem-chok-la chak-tsäl.

MANDALA OFFERING

[Optional: long mandala]
OM VAJRA-BHUMI AH HUM! Wang-chen ser-gyi sa-zhi / OM VAJRA-REKHE AH HUM! Chi chak-ri kor-yuk-gi kor-wäi ü-su rii gyäl-po ri-rap / Shar lü-pak-po /

Empowerment by the buddhas of the five families

Again, brilliant light radiates from the HUM at the divine heart, invoking all initiating deities of the five families.

(Make offerings to them with:)
OM PANCHA KULA SAPARIVARA ARGHAM...SHABDA PRATICCHA HUM SVAHA

"All tathagatas, please bestow on me the [Heruka Vajrasattva] initiation." Upon this request, all the tathagatas hold up their initiation vases, which are full of the amrita energy of divine transcendental wisdom, and the amrita starts to flow. As the mantra OM SARVA TATHAGATA ABHISHEKATA SAMAYA SHRIYE HUM is said, the initiation is conferred.

The divine body of perfect absolute wisdom, Heruka Vajrasattva, is completely filled by the amrita energy of blissful transcendental wisdom. Some amrita overflows and turns into Akshobhya, who adorns his crown.

The seed syllable HUM stands at the center of a moon disc at the divine heart, encircled by the one hundred syllable mantra [standing counterclockwise around the edge of the moon disc].

Offerings to Heruka Vajrasattva

OM VAJRASATTVA ARGHAM...SHABDA PRATICCHA HUM SVAHA
OM VAJRASATTVA OM AH HUM

Praise

Nondual divine wisdom, magnificent inner jewel ornament of all mother sentient beings; supreme, unchanging, everlasting great bliss; indestructible, magnificent wisdom mind that releases all sentient beings from all negativities of body, speech, and mind, especially broken vows and pledges: to you I prostrate.

Mandala offering

[Optional: long mandala]
OM Adamantine ground AH HUM! Mighty golden ground/OM Adamantine circumference AH HUM! Outside it is encircled by the circumferential wall,

Lho dzam-büi ling / Nup ba-lang-chö / Jang dra-mi-nyän / Lü-dang lü-pak / Nga-yap-dang nga-yap zhän / Yo-dän-dang lam-chok dro / Dra-mi-nyän-dang dra-mi-nyän-gyi da / Rin-po-chei ri-wo / Pak sam-gyi shing / Dö-jöi ba / Ma-mö-pa-yi lo-tok // Kor-lo rin-po-che / Nor-bu rin-po-che / Tsün-mo rin-po-che / Lön-po rin-po-che / Lang-po rin-po-che / Ta-chok rin-po-che / Mak-pön rin-po-che / Ter-chen pöi bum-pa / Gek-ma / Treng-wa-ma / Lu-ma / Gar-ma / Me-tok-ma / Duk-pö-ma / Nang-säl-ma / Dri-chap-ma / Nyi-ma / Da-wa / Rin-po-chei duk / Chok-lä nam-par gyäl-wäi gyäl-tsän / Ü-su lha-dang mi-yi päl-jor pün-sum-tsok-pa, ma-tsang-wa me-pa, tsang-zhing yi-du wong-wa / Di-dak drin-chen tsa-wa-dang gyü-par chä-päi päl-dän la-ma dam-pa-nam-dang / Kyä-par-du yang La-ma Dor-je Sem-pai lha-tsok-la zhing-kam ül-war gyi-wo / Tuk-je dro-wäi dön-du zhe-su söl // Zhe-nä dak-sok dro-wa mar-gyur nam-käi ta-dang nyam-päi sem-chän tam-chä-la tuk-tse-wa chen-pöi go-nä jin-gyi lap-tu söl!

[Optional: short mandala]
Sa-zhi pö-kyi juk-shing me-tok tram
Ri-rap ling-zhi nyi-dä gyän-pa di
Sang-gyä zhing-du mik-te ül-war gyi
Dro-kün nam-dak zhing-la chö-par-shok!

SECRET MANDALA

De-tong lhän-chik kye-päi ye-she-kyi
Zung-nam pung-kam kye-che-lä jung-wäi
Ri-ling rin-chen ter-bum nyi-dar chä
Kyab-gön tuk-jei ter-la ül-war gyi

INNER MANDALA

Dak-gi chak-dang mong-sum kye-päi yül
Dra-nyen bar-sum lü-dang long-chö chä

in the center of which are Sumeru, King of Mountains/the eastern conti-
nent, Videha/the southern, Jambudvipa/the western, Godaniya/the north-
ern, Kuru/[the eastern minor continents] Deha and Videha/[the southern]
Camara and Apara-camara/[the western] Shatha and Uttara-mantrin/[and
the northern] Kuru and Kauvara/[In the four continents are:] the precious
mountain/the wish-granting tree/the wish-fulfilling cow/the unplowed har-
vest//[on the first level of Mount Sumeru:] the Precious Wheel/the Precious
Jewel/the Precious Queen/the Precious Minister/the Precious Elephant/the
Precious Horse/the Precious General/the Pot of Great Treasure/[on the second level: the eight goddesses,] Lady of Grace/Lady of Garlands/Lady of
Song/Lady of Dance/Lady of Flowers/Lady of Incense/Lady of Lamps/Lady
of Perfume/[on the third level:] the sun/the moon/the precious parasol/the
banner of victory in all quarters/In the center, the most perfect riches of gods
and human beings, with nothing missing, pure and delightful/To my glorious, holy, and most kind root and lineage gurus/and in particular to Guru
Vajrasattva's deity host, I shall offer these as a buddha field//Please accept
them with compassion for the sake of migrating beings. Having accepted
them, to me and all migrating mother sentient beings as far as the limits of
space, out of your great compassion, please grant your inspiration!

[Optional: short mandala]
This ground, anointed with perfume, strewn with flowers,
Adorned with Mount Meru, four continents, sun, and moon,
I offer in visualization as field of buddhas.
May all sentient beings thus enjoy this pure land.

SECRET MANDALA

The right view of shunyata is one with the wisdom of great bliss. This wisdom transforms into Mount Meru, the sun, the moon, and all other phenomena in the universe. I offer everything magnificent to you, ocean of great
kindness, the one who is liberated and who liberates all others as well.

INNER MANDALA

Please bless me and all other sentient beings to be released immediately
from the three poisons, for I am offering without the slightest hesitation or

Pang-pa me-par bül-gyi lek-zhe-nä
Duk-sum rang-sar dröl-war jin-gyi lop

IDAM GURU RATNA MANDALAKAM NIRYATAYAMI

PURIFICATION

Chom-dän-dä Dor-je Sem-pa dak-zhän sem-chän tam-chä-kyi dik-drip-dang
dam tsik nyam-chak tam-chä jang-zhing dak-par dzä-du söl
 Zhe söl-wa tap-pä tuk-käi ngak-treng HUM-dang chä-pa-lä wö-zer trö
 Sem-chän tam-chä-kyi dik-drip jang sang-gyä sä-chä-la nye-päi chö-pa pül
 De-nam-kyi ku-sung-tuk-kyi yön-tän tam-chä wö-kyi nam-par dü-nä
ngak-treng HUM-dang chä-pa-la tim-pä de-lä dü-tsii gyün kar-po bap-pa
yap-yum-gyi jor-tsam-nä bap
 Rang-gi tsang-buk-nä zhuk-te lü tam-chä ye-she-kyi dü-tsii gyün-gyi gang
 Go-sum-gyi dik-drip tam-chä sang-kyi dak-par gyur

MANTRA RECITATION

OM VAJRA HERUKA SAMAYAM ANUPALAYA. HERUKA TENOPATISHTHA. DRIDHO
ME BHAVA, SUTOSHYO ME BHAVA, SUPOSHYO ME BHAVA, ANURAKTO ME BHAVA.
SARVA SIDDHIM ME PRAYACCHA. SARVA KARMA SUCHA ME CHITTAM SHREYAM
KURU, HUM! HA HA HA HA HOH! BHAGAVAN VAJRA HERUKA MA ME MUNCHA.
HERUKA BHAVA MAHA SAMAYA SATTVA AH HUM PHAT!

OFFERINGS AND PRAISE

OM VAJRASATTVA ARGHAM...SHABDA PRATICCHA HUM SVAHA
OM VAJRASATTVA OM AH HUM

Nyi-me ye-she dro-wäi päl
Chok-tu mi-gyur de-wa che
Dik-tung ma-lü drung-jin-päi
Dor-je sem-chok chak-tsäl tö

attachment all objects of my greed, hatred, and ignorance; friends, enemies, and strangers; and my body and all possessions. Please accept all this.

IDAM GURU RATNA MANDALAKAM NIRYATAYAMI

PURIFICATION

"Bhagawan Vajrasattva, please purify all negativities and broken and damaged pledges of myself and other sentient beings."

Because of this request, brilliant light radiates from the mantra rosary and the HUM at the divine heart. It purifies all negativities and obscurations of all sentient beings and becomes an offering for all buddhas and bodhisattvas. The essence of the perfect qualities of their holy body, speech, and mind returns in the form of light, which dissolves into the HUM and the mantra rosary.

[From the HUM and the mantra rosary] a stream of blissful white amrita energy begins to flow down through the chakras of the divine couple. It flows out through the chakra of union and enters my crown chakra. This stream of amrita of transcendental wisdom fills my whole body, destroying all the negativities and obscurations of my body, speech, and mind. These are completely purified.

MANTRA RECITATION

OM VAJRA HERUKA SAMAYAM ANUPALAYA. HERUKA TENOPATISHTHA. DRIDHO ME BHAVA, SUTOSHYO ME BHAVA, SUPOSHYO ME BHAVA, ANURAKTO ME BHAVA. SARVA SIDDHIM ME PRAYACCHA. SARVA KARMA SUCHA ME CHITTAM SHREYAM KURU, HUM! HA HA HA HA HOH! BHAGAVAN VAJRA HERUKA MA ME MUNCHA. HERUKA BHAVA MAHA SAMAYA SATTVA AH HUM PHAT!

OFFERINGS AND PRAISE

OM VAJRASATTVA ARGHAM...SHABDA PRATICCHA HUM SVAHA
OM VAJRASATTVA OM AH HUM

Nondual divine wisdom, magnificent inner jewel ornament of all mother sentient beings; supreme, unchanging, everlasting great bliss; indestructible, magnificent wisdom mind that releases all sentient beings from all negativities of body, speech, and mind, especially broken vows and pledges: to you I prostrate.

Refuge in Heruka Vajrasattva

Dak-ni mi-she mong-pa-yi
Dam-tsik-lä-ni gäl-zhing nyam
La-ma gön-pö kyap-dzö-chik!
Tso-wo dor-je dzin-pa-te
Tuk-je chen-pöi dak-nyi-chän
Dor-wäi tso-la dak kyap-chi

Absorption

Dor-je Sem-päi zhäl-nä: "Rik-kyi bu (or bu-mo) kyö-kyi dik-drip-dang dam-tsik nyam-chak tam-chä jang-zhing dak-gö" Zhe sung-nä rang-la tim-pä rang-gi go-sum-dang Dor-je Sem-päi ku-sung-tuk yer mi che-par gyur

Dedication

Ge-wa di-yi nyur-du dak
Dor-je Sem-pa drup-gyur-nä
Dro-wa chik-kyang ma-lü-pa
Kye-kyi sa-la gö-par-shok!

Refuge in Heruka Vajrasattva

Through ignorance and delusion, I have broken and damaged my pledges. Holy guru, who has the power to liberate me, my inner master, holder of the vajra, whose essence is great compassion, lord of all migratory beings, to you I go for refuge.

Absorption

Vajrasattva says, "Oh son (or daughter) of good family, your negativities and obscurations and damaged and broken pledges are cleansed and purified." Then he dissolves into me. My three doors (of body, speech, and mind) become inseparably one with Vajrasattva's holy body, speech, and mind.

Dedication

Because of this merit, may I quickly become Heruka Vajrasattva and lead each and every sentient being into his divine enlightened realm.

Colophon

Because of encouragement from many intelligent Westerners that there was a need for a text for the sadhana of Vajrasattva that eliminates hindrances and produces profit on the stages of the path and is a preliminary to meditation on the two stages [of highest yoga tantra], one called Muni Jñana [Thubten Yeshe] has written this as an emergency delusion-cutter, so he asks forgiveness.

APPENDIX 2

The Heruka Vajrasattva Tsok Offering

A Banquet of the Greatly Blissful Circle of Pure Offerings: An Antidote to the Vajra Hells

A Banquet of the Greatly Blissful Circle of Pure Offerings: An Antidote to the Vajra Hells

Introduction[28]

THE TANTRIC TEACHINGS of Shakyamuni Buddha state that meditation on Vajrasattva is a preliminary practice for the generation and completion stage meditations of highest yoga tantra. Furthermore, Vajrasattva meditation is necessary during the stages of the path themselves, in order to complete both collections of merit and wisdom, to remove the various blockages and interferences that arise at different points along the path, and to help you familiarize yourself with the successive realizations as they are gained.

In order to practice Vajrasattva, your mind must first be made suitable. This is accomplished by receiving the permissions *(jenang)* of body, speech, mind, qualities, and divine action, which are similar to the four great initiations. After doing this, and abiding in either the extensive or the abridged yoga of this deity, you can begin the *Banquet of the Greatly Blissful Circle of Pure Offerings: An Antidote to the Vajra Hells*, and, as has been said, [you can truly say,] "I am a fortunate, blissful one." These permissions, which are of the highest yoga tantra aspect of Vajrasattva, have been transmitted through the ear-whispered lineage of the Geluk tradition of Tibetan Buddhism, and the warmth of the blessings of this lineage continues undiminished down to the present day. Therefore, this practice of Vajrasattva is available for you to practice, and you can do so secure in the knowledge that it is in no way mistaken.

What follows is a tsok offering ceremony specifically designed for performance in conjunction with the highest yoga tantra aspect of Vajrasattva. The Tibetan term *tsok,* which is often left untranslated, literally means "collection," or "assembly," and in the following practice it is often rendered as "pure offerings." However, the actual tsok is one's meditation on transcendental, blissful wisdom. The entire purpose of offering the tsok ingredients is to generate the experience of this blissful wisdom within oneself and to overcome the ordinary appearance and conception of sensory objects. Thus, it is extremely important that from the very beginning of this practice you prevent ordinary appearances and conceptions from arising. Because the offering of tsok is a profound method for transcending mundane thought, the entire practice should go beyond your ordinary experience of subject and object.[29]

Meditation on the mandala of Guru Vajrasattva: The field for the collection of merit

HUM!
De-tong nyi-su me-päi nam-röl-lä
Jung-wäi Dor-je Sem-päi zhäl-yä-kang
Ten-dang ten-päi kyil-kor yong-dzok dün
Kün-zang chö-trin nam-käi kyön-kün kang

Nyi-me de-wa chen-pöi ka-ying-la
Ngo-tsar dor-nam lha-dang lha-möi tr-ül
Zhi-gyä wang-drak trül-päi gar-kän-gyi
Tap-she yong-su dzok-päi kur zheng-gyur

Blessing the offerings

OM KHANDA ROHI HUM HUM PHAT

OM SVABHAVA SHUDDHA SARVA DHARMA SVABHAVA SHUDDHO HAM

Tong-pa nyi-du gyur tong-päi ngang-lä AH-lä tö-pa yang-zhing gya-che-wäi nang-du sha nga dü-tsi nga-nam zhu-wa-lä jung-wäi ye-she-kyi dü-tsii gya-tso chen-por gyur

OM AH HUM HA HO HRI *(Say three times)*

PRELIMINARIES

Place on the altar clean and beautiful looking offerings as well as *bala* and *madana*.[30] After completing either the abbreviated or elaborate meditation on the generation of oneself in the form of Vajrasattva,[31] visualize as follows:

MEDITATION ON THE MANDALA OF GURU VAJRASATTVA: THE FIELD FOR THE COLLECTION OF MERIT

HUM!
In the space before me,
From the enjoyment of indivisible great bliss and emptiness,
Appear the complete supporting and supported mandalas of Vajrasattva.
Clouds of Samantabhadra's offerings fill all of space.

In the sphere of great nondualistic bliss
All beings miraculously appear as gods and goddesses
Embodying thoroughly developed method and wisdom
As skillful dancers manifesting peace, expansion, power, and wrath.

BLESSING THE OFFERINGS

(The offering ingredients should then be blessed in the following manner by reciting:)
OM KHANDA ROHI HUM HUM PHAT
(All those who create obstacles are dispelled, and by reciting:)
OM SVABHAVA SHUDDHA SARVA DHARMA SVABHAVA SHUDDHO HAM
(They are purified of ordinary appearances. Then visualize:)

All becomes empty and from the sphere of emptiness
Appears the letter AH which transforms
Into a very large and spacious skull cup
Containing the five meats and five nectars.
Melting, they all transform into a great ocean of wisdom nectar.

OM AH HUM HA HO HRI *(Say three times)*

PRESENTING THE OFFERINGS AND RECITING THE MANTRA

Ta-mäl wang-pöi yül-lä rap-dä-shing
Yo-gäi dam-tsik dak-nang de-wa-che
Ngö-drup kün-gyi zhir-gyur dü-tsii chok
Tok-me de-wa chen-pö nye-par dzö

1. HUM! Ka-ying ja-tsön Dor-je Sem-päi ku
La-ma yi-dam kan-dro chö-kyong-gi
Ngo-wor ma-tok nyi-dzin trül-nang dak
Dam-dzä dö-yön na-ngäi tsok-chö-la
La-ma Dor-je Sem-pa nye-chir bül
Lhän-kye de-chen kye-war jin-gyi-lop

OM VAJRA HERUKA SAMAYAM ANUPALAYA. HERUKA TENOPATISHTHA. DRIDHO
ME BHAVA, SUTOSHYO ME BHAVA, SUPOSHYO ME BHAVA, ANURAKTO ME BHAVA.
SARVA SIDDHIM ME PRAYACCHA. SARVA KARMA SUCHA ME CHITTAM SHREYAM
KURU, HUM! HA HA HA HA HOH! BHAGAVAN VAJRA HERUKA MA ME MUNCHA.
HERUKA BHAVA MAHA SAMAYA SATTVA AH HUM PHAT!

2. HUM! Ka-ying ja-tsön Dor-je Sem-päi ku
Dö-yön de-la chak-päi nam-she ngä
Däl-jor dön-me ja-wäi trül-nang dak
Dam-dzä dö-yön na-ngäi tsok-chö-la
La-ma Dor-je Sem-pa nye-chir bül

Presenting the offerings and reciting the mantra

This pure offering is the yogi's commitment (samaya)
And, as the pure vision of their great bliss,
Transcends being an object of ordinary senses.
It is the basis of all attainments and the supreme nectar.
Therefore, O Guru, with your nonsuperstitious
Simultaneously born great bliss, please enjoy it!

1. HUM! O miraculous rainbow cloud
Appearing in the space of dharmakaya,
Holy body of Vajrasattva—
Having purified the hallucinated vision
And dualistic conception that fails to recognize
That the guru, in essence, is the deity,
The dakini, and the Dharma protector—
In order to please you, Guru Vajrasattva,
I am presenting these sacred ingredients
As pure offerings to be enjoyed by your five senses.
Please bless me to generate simultaneously born great bliss.[32]

OM VAJRA HERUKA SAMAYAM ANUPALAYA. HERUKA TENOPATISIITIIA. DRIDHO
ME BHAVA, SUTOSHYO ME BHAVA, SUPOSHYO ME BHAVA, ANURAKTO ME BHAVA.
SARVA SIDDHIM ME PRAYACCHA. SARVA KARMA SUCHA ME CHITTAM SHREYAM
KURU, HUM! HA HA HA HA HOH! BHAGAVAN VAJRA HERUKA MA ME MUNCHA.
HERUKA BHAVA MAHA SAMAYA SATTVA AH HUM PHAT![33]

2. HUM! O miraculous rainbow cloud
Appearing in the space of dharmakaya,
Holy body of Vajrasattva—
Having purified the hallucinated vision
Of the five sense consciousnesses' clinging
To the pleasure of desirable objects,
Thereby depriving this perfect human birth of all meaning—
In order to please you, Guru Vajrasattva,
I am presenting these sacred ingredients
As pure offerings to be enjoyed by your five senses.
Please bless me to abandon clinging

Tse-dii nang-zhen dok-par jin-gyi-lop
OM VAJRA HERUKA SAMAYAM....

3. HUM! Ka-ying ja-tsön Dor-je Sem-päi ku
Tsül-min yi-je nam-tok lä-nyön-gyi
Drip-yok nyi-dzin dön-gyi trül-nang dak
Dam-dzä dö-yön na-ngäi tsok-chö-la
La-ma Dor-je Sem-pa nye-chir bül
Nge-jung nam-dak kye-war jin-gyi-lop
OM VAJRA HERUKA SAMAYAM....

4. HUM! Ka-ying ja-tsön Dor-je Sem-päi ku
Rang-nyi che-dzin duk-ngäl kün-gyi go
Nyi-dzin dü-kyi gong-pöi trül-nang dak
Dam-dzä dö-yön na-ngäi tsok-chö-la
La-ma Dor-je Sem-pa nye-chir bül
Nam-dak jang-sem kye-war jin-gyi-lop
OM VAJRA HERUKA SAMAYAM....

5. HUM! Ka-ying ja-tsön Dor-je Sem-päi ku
Tok-pä par-zhak ming-kyang tak-yö-la
Nyi-dzin dri-ma ngän-päi trül-nang dak
Dam-dzä dö-yön na-ngäi tsok-chö-la
La-ma Dor-je Sem-pa nye-chir bül

To the ordinary concepts and appearances of this life.
OM VAJRA HERUKA SAMAYAM....

3. HUM! O miraculous rainbow cloud
Appearing in the space of dharmakaya,
Holy body of Vajrasattva—
Having purified the hallucinated vision:
The demon dualistic conception and veiling obscurations
Of improper attention, superstition, karma, and delusions—
In order to please you, Guru Vajrasattva,
I am presenting these sacred ingredients
As pure offerings to be enjoyed by your five senses.
Please bless me to generate immaculate renunciation.
OM VAJRA HERUKA SAMAYAM....

4. HUM! O miraculous rainbow cloud
Appearing in the space of dharmakaya,
Holy body of Vajrasattva—
Having purified the hallucinated vision
Of holding oneself more dear than others:
The door to all suffering and the dualistic conception
That is the chief of all evils—
In order to please you, Guru Vajrasattva,
I am presenting these sacred ingredients
As pure offerings to be enjoyed by your five senses.
Please bless me to generate immaculate bodhichitta.
OM VAJRA HERUKA SAMAYAM....

5. HUM! O miraculous rainbow cloud
Appearing in the space of dharmakaya,
Holy body of Vajrasattva—
Having purified the hallucinated vision:
The stench of dualistic conception holding
What is merely imputed by superstition as true—
In order to please you, Guru Vajrasattva,
I am presenting these sacred ingredients

Chak-gya chen-po tok-par jin-gyi-lop
OM VAJRA HERUKA SAMAYAM....

6. HUM! Ka-ying ja-tsön Dor-je Sem-päi ku
Ta-mäl nang-zhen kün-tok tra-rak-kyi
Nyi-dzin lung-shuk drak-pöi trül-nang dak
Dam-dzä ye-she nga-yi ts-ok-chö-la
La-ma Dor-je Sem-pa nye-chir bül
Nge-dön wang-zhi top-par jin-gyi-lop
OM VAJRA HERUKA SAMAYAM....

7. HUM! Ka-ying ja-tsön Dor-je Sem-päi ku
Nye-tung drak-char wang-me bap-pa-lä
Dor-je nyäl-wa nyong-wäi trül-nang dak
Dam-dzä yeshe nga-yi tsok-chö-la
La-ma Dor-je Sem-pa nye-chir bül
Dak-pa rap-jam ba-zhik char-war shok
OM VAJRA HERUKA SAMAYAM....

OFFERING TO THE VAJRA MASTER

Dor-je dzin-pa gong-su söl
Pa-wo pa-mo tsok-kor de
Zung-dang dzin-päi trö-pa dräl
Dü-tsii de-la tak-tu röl
A LA LA HO!

As pure offerings to be enjoyed by your five senses.
Please bless me to realize the great seal of emptiness.
OM VAJRA HERUKA SAMAYAM....

6. HUM! O miraculous rainbow cloud
Appearing in the space of dharmakaya,
Holy body of Vajrasattva—
Having purified the hallucinated vision
Of ordinary appearance and conception:
The eighty superstitions both gross and subtle,
The violent, uncontrollable wind of the dualistic mind—
In order to please you, Guru Vajrasattva,
I am presenting these sacred ingredients
As pure offerings to be enjoyed by your five senses.
Please bless me to receive the four actual empowerments.
OM VAJRA HERUKA SAMAYAM....

7. HUM! O miraculous rainbow cloud
Appearing in the space of dharmakaya,
Holy body of Vajrasattva—
Having purified the hallucinated vision
Of experiencing the vajra hells
Resulting from the uncontrollable downpour
Of negative actions and broken samaya—
In order to please you, Guru Vajrasattva,
I am presenting these sacred ingredients
As pure offerings to be enjoyed by your five senses.
May infinite purity alone arise!
OM VAJRA HERUKA SAMAYAM....

OFFERING TO THE VAJRA MASTER

(The offering of tsok to the vajra master should now be made while reciting:)
O holder of the vajra, please pay attention to me!
This pure offering presented by the assembled circle of dakas and dakinis,
This nectar free of all divisions of subject and object,
Transcendentally blissful, please enjoy it eternally!
A LA LA HO!

E-MA! De-chen ye-she, kyäi!
Tsok-chen tum-mo bar-wäi drö
Ma-sam jö-dä ga-de-la
Kün-kyang aho sukha che
AHO MAHA SUKHA HO!

OUTER AND INNER OFFERINGS TO VAJRASATTVA

OM GURU VAJRASATTVA SAPARIVARA ARGHAM...SHABDA PRATICCHA HUM
SVAHA
OM GURU VAJRASATTVA SAPARIVARA OM AH HUM

VERSES OF PRAISE

Gang-gi tsän-tsam jö-pä kyang
Lä-ngän dik-tung ma-lü-pa
Kä-chik nyi-la drung-jin-päi
Dor-je Sem-pa-la chak tsäl

EIGHT-LEGGED PRAISE

OM Chom-dän pa-wöi wang-chuk-la chak-tsäl HUM HUM PHAT!
OM Käl-pa chen-pöi me-dang nyam-päi wö HUM HUM PHAT!
OM Räl-päi chö-pän mi-zä-pa-dang dän HUM HUM PHAT!
OM Che-wa nam-par tsik-pa jik-päi zhäl HUM HUM PHAT!
OM Tong-trak chak-ni bar-wäi wö-zer-chän HUM HUM PHAT!
OM Dra-ta zhak-seng dung-dang katwang dzin HUM HUM PHAT!
OM Tak-gi pak-päi na-za dzin-pa-chän HUM HUM PHAT!
OM Ku-chen dü-ka gek-tar-dzä-la dü HUM HUM PHAT!

(The vajra master then replies:)
O hail, great blissful wisdom!
The great collected offering,
The seed that causes the tumo heat to explode,
This joyful, blissful experience beyond concepts, beyond words—
Welcome, great eternal bliss!
AHO MAHA SUKHA HO!

OUTER AND INNER OFFERINGS TO VAJRASATTVA

(The outer and inner offerings are then presented while reciting:)
OM GURU VAJRASATTVA SAPARIVARA ARGHAM...SHABDA PRATICCHA HUM
SVAHA
OM GURU VAJRASATTVA SAPARIVARA OM AH HUM

VERSES OF PRAISE

(Praise is offered by reciting the following:)
Merely thinking of just your name
Eradicates all obstacles
And immediately purifies all negative karma.
Thus to you, unsurpassed Vajrasattva,
I pay homage and make prostration.

EIGHT-LEGGED PRAISE

(Next recite the following in praise of Heruka and Vajravarahi:)
OM I prostrate to the Bhagawan, lord of the brave ones HUM HUM PHAT!
OM To you whose brilliance equals the fire that ends a great eon HUM HUM
   PHAT!
OM To you who have an inexhaustible crowning top-knot HUM HUM PHAT!
OM To you with bared fangs and a wrathful face HUM HUM PHAT!
OM To you whose thousand arms blaze with light HUM HUM PHAT!
OM To you who hold an axe, uplifted noose, a spear, and skull-staff HUM
   HUM PHAT!
OM To you who wears a tiger-skin cloth HUM HUM PHAT!
OM I bow to you whose great smoke-coloured body ends all obstructions
   HUM HUM PHAT!

OM Chom-dän-dä-ma dor-je pak-mo-la chak-tsäl HUM HUM PHAT!

OM Pak-ma rik-mäi wang-chuk kam-sum-gyi HUM HUM PHAT!

OM Jung-pöi jik-pa tam-chä dor-je chen-pö jom HUM HUM PHAT!

OM Dor-je dän-zhuk zhän-gyi mi-tup wang-je chän HUM HUM PHAT!

OM Tum-mo tro-möi zuk-kyi tsang-pa kem-par dzä HUM HUM PHAT!

OM Dü-nam trak-ching kem-pä zhän-gyi chok-lä gyäl HUM HUM PHAT!

OM Muk-je reng-je mong-je kün-lä nam-par gyäl HUM HUM PHAT!

OM Dor-je pak-mo jor-je dö-wang-ma-la dü HUM HUM PHAT!

SONG OF THE SPRING QUEEN

1. HUM! De-zhin shek-pa tam-chä-dang
Pa-wo dang-ni näl-jor-ma
Kan-dro dang-ni kan-dro-ma
Kün-la dak-ni söl-wa-dep
De-wa chok-la gye-päi He-ru-ka
De-wä rap-nyö ma-la nyen-jä-nä
Cho-ga zhin-du long-chö-pa-yi ni
Lhän-kye de-wäi jor-wa-la zhuk-so
A-LA-LA! LA-LA HO! A! I! AH! ARA-LI HO!
Dri-me ka-dröi tsok-nam-kyi
Tse-wä zik-la lä-kün dzö

2. HUM! De-zhin shek-pa...söl-wa-dep
De-wa chen-pö yi-ni rap-kyö-pä
Lü-ni kün-tu yo-wäi gar-gyi-ni
Chak-gyäi pä-mar röl-päi de-wa che
Näl-jor-ma tsok-nam-la chö-par dzö
A-LA-LA! LA-LA HO! A! I! AH! ARA-LI HO!
Dri-me ka-dröi tsok-nam-kyi
Tse-wä zik-la lä-kün dzö

OM I prostrate to the Bhagawati, Vajravarahi HUM HUM PHAT!

OM To the queen of the female arya practitioners, invincible in the three realms HUM HUM PHAT!

OM To you who destroy all fears of evil spirits with your great diamond-like means HUM HUM PHAT!

OM To you whose eyes empower those who sit upon the diamond throne not to be conquered by anyone HUM HUM PHAT!

OM To you whose wrathful body on inner fire can desiccate Brahma HUM HUM PHAT!

OM To you who terrify and dry up all demons and thus can vanquish all other forces HUM HUM PHAT!

OM To you who triumph over all that can make one ill-tempered, excited, or stupefied HUM HUM PHAT!

OM I bow down to Vajravahari, the consort who overpowers lust HUM HUM PHAT!

SONG OF THE SPRING QUEEN

(Here, the "Song of the Spring Queen" may be sung to request realizations:)

1. HUM! We make our requests to you,
The tathagatas who are thus gone,
As well as to the viras, yoginis, dakas, and dakinis.
Heruka, who enjoys great bliss,
Intoxicated with bliss brings satisfaction to the consort
And in accordance with the precepts of practice
Enters into the union of innate bliss.
A-LA-LA! LA-LA HO! A! I! AH! ARA-LI HO!
You, the multitudes of immaculate dakinis,
Look upon us with love; bestow all the powerful attainments.

2. HUM! We make our requests…dakinis.
Through the stirring of the mind of great bliss
Through the moving dance of the body
There arises the great bliss played within the lotus of the consort.
This bliss we offer to the multitudes of yoginis.
A-LA-LA! LA-LA HO! A! I! AH! ARA-LI HO!
You, the multitudes of immaculate dakinis,
Look upon us with love; bestow all the powerful attainments.

3. HUM! De-zhin shek-pa…söl-wa-dep
Yi-wong zhi-wäi nyam-kyi gar-dzä-ma
Rap-gye gön-po kyö-dang ka-dröi tsok
Dak-gi dün-du zhuk-te jin-lop-la
Lhän-kye de-chen dak-la tsäl-du söl
A-LA-LA! LA-LA HO! A! I! AH! ARA-LI HO!
Dri-me ka-dröi tsok-nam-kyi
Tse-wä zik-la lä-kün dzö

4. HUM! De-zhin shek-pa…söl-wa-dep
De-chen tar-päi tsän-nyi dän-pa kyö
De-chen pang-päi ka-tup du-ma-yi
Tse-chik dröl-war mi-zhe de-chen yang
Chu-kye chok-gi ü-na nä-pa yin
A-LA-LA! LA-LA HO! A! I! AH! ARA-LI HO!
Dri-me ka-dröi tsok-nam-kyi
Tse-wä zik-la lä-kün dzö

5. HUM! De-zhin shek-pa…söl-wa-dep
Dam-gyi ü-su kye-päi pä-ma zhin
Chak-lä kye-kyang chak-päi kyön ma-gö
Näl-jor-ma chok pä-mäi de-wa-yi
Si-päi ching-wa nyur-du dröl-war dzö
A-LA-LA! LA-LA HO! A! I! AH! ARA-LI HO!
Dri-me ka-dröi tsok-nam-kyi
Tse-wä zik-la lä-kün dzö

6. HUM! De-zhin shek-pa…söl-wa-dep
Drang-tsii jung-nä-nam-kyi drang-tsii chü
Bung-wäi tsok-kyi kün-nä tung-wa tar
Tsän-nyi druk-dän tso-kye gyä-pa-yi
Chu-ching-pa-yi ro-yi tsim-par dzö
A-LA-LA! LA-LA HO! A! I! AH! ARA-LI HO!
Dri-me ka-dröi tsok-nam-kyi
Tse-wä zik-la lä-kün dzö

3. HUM! We make our requests…dakinis.
Yoginis dance with enchanting, soothing movements
The protector so exceedingly to please,
And the multitudes of dakinis
Come before us and bless us.
Bestow upon us innate great bliss.
A-LA-LA! LA-LA HO! A! I! AH! ARA-LI HO!
You, the multitudes of immaculate dakinis,
Look upon us with love; bestow all the powerful attainments.

4. HUM! We make our requests…dakinis.
The great bliss that is possessed of liberating qualities—
The great bliss without which freedom cannot be gained in one life
Though one endures many asceticisms—
That great bliss abides within the center of the supreme lotus.
A-LA-LA! LA-LA HO! A! I! AH! ARA-LI HO!
You, the multitudes of immaculate dakinis,
Look upon us with love; bestow all the powerful attainments.

5. HUM! We make our requests…dakinis.
As with a lotus born out of mud,
Great bliss, though born of desire is unstained by its faults.
O supreme yoginis, by the bliss of your lotus
May the bonds of samsara be quickly untied.
A-LA-LA! LA-LA HO! A! I! AH! ARA-LI HO!
You, the multitudes of immaculate dakinis,
Look upon us with love; bestow all the powerful attainments.

6. HUM! We make our requests…dakinis.
Like a swarm of bees drawing forth the nectar of flowers
May we likewise be sated
By the captivating nectar of the mature lotus
Possessed of six qualities.
A-LA-LA! LA-LA HO! A! I! AH! ARA-LI HO!
You, the multitudes of immaculate dakinis,
Look upon us with love; bestow all the powerful attainments.

OFFERING THE REMAINING TSOK

OM AH HUM *(Say three times)*

De-tong yer-me gyu-mäi ka-pa-lar
Ye-she nga-yi dü-tsii tsok-lhak-nam
Zhing-kyong drek-pa de-gyä tsok-la bül
Dam-chö drup-päi lä-zhii trin-lä dzö

CONCLUDING PRAYER OF AUSPICIOUSNESS

Pün-tsok ge-lek je-wäi trün-päi ku
Ta-yä dro-wäi re-wa kong-wäi sung
Dro-wäi sam-pa ji-zhin zik-päi tuk
Rang-sem la-mar jäl-wäi tra-shi shok

Jung-gyüi chi-war bar-do kye-wa sum
Jong-je ku-sum lam-du kyer-wäi tü
Rang-sem nyuk-sem tra-mo jäl-wa-lä
Ku-tuk zung-juk char-wäi tra-shi shok

Trö-dräl ka-ying tong-pa chen-pöi yum
Nang-si de-wa chen-pöi ye-she-la
Kyü-päi ya-tsän kor-dä ngö-po kün
De-tong chen-por dom-dzä tra-shi shok

Offering the remaining tsok

(Finally, the way to offer the remainder of the tsok is as follows:)
OM AH HUM *(Say three times)*

To the assembly of the eight classes of wrathful governing protectors
I present all the remaining pure offerings—
The nectar of the five wisdoms contained in this skull cup—
An illusory appearance of indivisible bliss and emptiness.
Do your duty, the four rites for Dharma practitioners.

Concluding prayer of auspiciousness

May all be auspicious for me to see my mind as the lama:
Who understands perfectly all beings' thoughts,
Whose speech fulfills countless beings' wishes,
And whose pure body arises from an infinite collection of merit.

May all be auspicious for realizing the unity of dharmakaya and rupakaya
By discovering my own subtle, continually residing consciousness
Through the power of taking the three bodies as the path:
The antidote to coming death, bardo, and rebirth.

May all be auspicious for everything within samsara and nirvana
To be synthesized with great emptiness and great bliss
Through the unusual embrace of the mother: the sphere of space
Beyond all puzzling divisions, and the father:
The great blissful wisdom, the appearance of all existent phenomena.

Colophon and Dedication[34]

On the special day of the daka and dakinis—the twenty-fifth day of the
eleventh month of the Iron Bird year (January 19, 1982)—Venerable Lama
Thubten Yeshe wrote this tsok offering of Heruka Vajrasattva for a puja
performed at Bodhgaya under the bodhi tree by an international gathering
of sangha and lay students who together made hundreds and thousands of
offerings. This puja was offered by the Italian gelong Thubten Dönyö, a
disciple having unsurpassed understanding of the sutra and tantra path to

enlightenment and indestructible devotion to Shakyamuni Buddha's teachings, and who is adorned outwardly with saffron robes and inwardly with the three sets of vows.

This tsok offering was written with the prayer that all the sangha of the ten directions enjoy harmonious relationships with one another, guard the precepts of pure moral conduct, and accomplish the practice of the three higher trainings, thereby becoming skillful guides providing great help to all beings. It is dedicated to the speedy return of our great guru of unmatched and inexpressible kindness, Kyabje Trijang Dorje Chang. For the benefit of all sentient beings, our mothers, may we remain inseparable from this great guru during our entire path to enlightenment.

Furthermore, it has been noted that in many countries today—Tibet, for example—those whose lives are *not* opposed to the three ordinations of the pratimoksha, bodhichitta, and tantric vows are not considered to be human beings! Yet even in such extremely degenerate times there are still many fortunate practitioners, and it is very important that these yogis and yoginis have a method, such as this Vajrasattva practice, powerful enough for achieving the exalted realization of simultaneously born great bliss and emptiness. This profound method is easy and simple to practice, accumulates a great store of meritorious potential, and is capable of destroying all the negativities resulting from breaking one's pledged commitments. In fact, it is such a powerful method that many lamas of the Geluk tradition have stated that even transgressions of root tantric vows can be purified by reciting the Vajrasattva mantra. Therefore, one should understand that there is no negativity so strong that it cannot be purified through the practice of Vajrasattva.

For all these reasons, then, this tsok offering has been composed by Vajrasattva yogi and follower of Guru Shakyamuni Buddha's teachings, the bhikshu Muni Jñana.[35]

POSTSCRIPT

The following poem in jest came uncontrollably and without premeditation to the mind of the author while he was composing this work:[36]

> All of samsara appears
> As a foe to one who fears
> He might be gored and torn
> By the proverbial rabbit's horn

Of tantric ordinations:
The golden ground foundation.

In the common path untrained,
In tantra unordained,
He has no initiation;
What a situation!
How strange! What a joke!
He's a sky-flower yogi!

This tsok offering can be made to other highest yoga tantra deities by substituting that deity's name for Vajrasattva's and by blessing the offerings in accordance with the yoga method of that deity and reciting that deity's mantra.

The above was translated with the kind assistance of Lama Thubten Zopa Rinpoche and Ven. Konchog Yeshe, and edited by Jonathan Landaw. The "Song of the Spring Queen" was adapted from a translation by Ven. Jampa Gendun and Andy White, and the praises to Heruka and Vajravarahi were adapted from a translation by Alexander Berzin.[37]

APPENDIX 3

Tibetan Texts

1

ༀ། །དཔལ་མཆོག་དང་པོ་ཡེ་ཤེས་

དཔའ་རྣལ་འབྱོར་

བཤུགས་

སོ༎

༣

༄༅། །སྐྱབས་འགྲོ་སེམས་བསྐྱེད་ནི། སངས་རྒྱས་ཆོས་
དང་དགེ་འདུན་ལ། །ཇི་ག་ཏུ་བདག་ནི་སྐྱབས་སུ་མཆི། །
ཐེག་པ་གསུམ་པོ་ཐམས་ཅད་དང་། །རྣལ་འབྱོར་གསང་
སྔགས་མ་ཁྱབ་འགྲོམ། །དཔའ་བོ་དཔའ་མོ་དབང་ལྷུ་
མོ། །བྱང་ཆུབ་སེམས་དཔའ་བདག་ཉིད་ཀྱེ། །ཁྱེད་
པར་ཡང་དགྱོབ་དཔོན་ལ། །ཇི་ག་ཏུ་སྐྱབས་སུ་མཆི་
བར་བགྱི། །སེམས་ཅན་ཀུན་གྱི་དོན་གྱི་ཕྱིར། །
བདག་ནི་དེ་རུ་གར་གྱུར་ནས། །སེམས་ཅན་ཐམས་
ཅད་དེ་ར་ག་ནི། །བོ་འཆང་ཆམ་ཆེག་ལ་འགོ་ང་པར་བགྱི།
ལས་གསུམ། །རྗེ་སེམས་དཔའི་བསྐྱོམ་བཟླས་ནི། རང་གི་སྙིང་
པོ་ཕོ་ལས་པདྨ་དང་། །ཡ་ལས་ཟླ་བའི་གདན་གྱི།
སྟེང་དུ་ཧཱུྃ་ལས་རྡོ་རྗེ་དཀར་པོ་ཧཱུྃ་ལྤ་ལྡོབ་ལ་ཐུ་གོས།
མཚོན་པ། །དེ་ལས་འོད་ཟེར་འཕྲོས། །རོ་ག་ཉེས་
བྱས་འདས་ལོས་སུ་གྱུར་པ་ལས་རྗེ་རྗེ་སེམས་དཔའ་
དགར་པོ་ཞལ་གཅིག་ཕྱག་གཉིས་རྗེ་རྡོར་དུ་ལག་འཛིན་
པ། རྗེ་རྗེ་སྐྱིལ་ཀྲུང་གིས་བཞུགས་པ། ཡུམ་རྗེ་
རྗེ་སྙེམས་མ་དགར་མོ་ཞལ་གཅིག་ཕྱག་གཉིས་གྱི་གྲུག

ༀ

དང་ཕྱེད་པ་འཛིན་པས་འཁྱུང་བ། གཉིས་ཀ་དང་དང་
དངན་པོ་ཆེའི་རྒྱན་སྤྲུ་ཚོགས་པས་སྤྲས་པ། གཉིས་
ཀའི་སྐྱི་ཐོར་ཚོགོ། མགྲིན་པར་ཨཱཿ ཐུགས་ཀར་ཧཱུྃ
ཐུགས་ཀའི་ཧཱུྃ་ལས་ནི་དངར་འཕྲོས་པས་རང་འདྲའི་ཡེ
ཤེས་པ་སྤྱན་དྲངས། །ཨོཾ་བཛྲ་རཱ་ཛི་ཧཱུྃ་ཐཱ་ཕཊ། སྤྲ་
བྲཀྵསྤྲ་སྤྲངས། སྦྱོང་བ་ཉིད་དུ་གྱུར། སྦྱོང་བའི་དང་
ལས་ཨཱ༔ལས་ཐོད་པ་ཡངས་ཤིང་རྒྱ་ཆེའི་ནང་དུ་ༀ་ལཱུ
བདུད་རྩེ་སྣ་རྣམས་ཞུ་བ་ལས་བྱུང་བའི་ཡེ་ཤེས་ཀྱི་བདུད་
རྩེ་རྒྱ་མཚོ་ཆེན་པོར་གྱུར། ཨོཾ་ཨཱཿ ཧཱུྃ་ཧ་ཧོ་ཧྲཱིཿ ལན
གསུམ་གྱིས་མཆོད་ཅིང་རྣམས་སྒྲུ། རང་འདྲའི་ཡེ་ཤེས་པ་སྤྲུན
དངས། ཨོཾ་བཛྲ་ༀ་དྷ་ཨརྒྷཾ་པྲ་ཏཱི་ཙྪ་སྭཱ་ཧཱ། ཞེས་པ་ནས།
ཤཔྟ་པྲ་ཏཱི་ཙྪ་སྭཱ་ཧཱ། ཧ༔ཧཱུྃ་པོ་ཧཱུྃ༔ གཉིས་སུ་མེད
པར་གྱུར། སྒྱུར་ཡང་ཐུགས་ཀའི་ཧཱུྃ་ལས་ཐོ་ཟེར
འཕྲོས། དབང་གི་ལྷ་རྣམས་སྤྱན་དངས། ཨོཾ་བཛྲ
ཀ་ལ་ས་རྀ་ལྟོར་ཨ་རྐྱེནས། །འདྲུའི་ཀྱི་མཚོ།
དེ་བཞིན་ཤེགས་པ་ཐམས་ཅད་ཀྱིས་མཆོན་པར་དང་
བསྐུར་དུ་གསོལ། ཞེས་གསོལ་བ་བཏབ་པས། དེ

༩

རྣམས་ཀྱིས་ཡེ་ཤེས་ཀྱི་བདུད་རྩིས་གང་བའི་བུམ་ཐོགས་ནས
ནས༔ ཨོཾ་ས་ཧཱུ་བྲྀ་གཏ་ཨ་བྲྀ་ཏྲྀ་གཏ་སམ་ཡ་ཤྲཱི་ཡེ་ཧཱུཾ
ཞེས་དར་བསྐུལ། སྐུ་ཡེ་ཤེས་ཀྱི་བདུད་རྩིས་གང་བ
མེ་བསྒྲིངས་པས་དངུ་བཀྲུན་ཅིང་། ཐུགས་ནཱ་ར་སྐྲ་བའི་སྦྱིང་
དངུ་གི་མཐར་ཨེ་བོ་བཀྲུ་བའི་སྲུ་གས་ཀྱིས་བསྲོ་བར་གྱུར༔
ཨོཾ་བཛྲ་ས་ཏུ་ཨ་ཀྲཱུ་ནས༔ འབྲུ་འི་བར་གྱིས་ཅེ་སྐྱོང་དང་༔ ཨོཾ
བཛྲ་ས་ཏུ་ཨ་ཨུཿཧཱུཾ་ གིས་ནར་མཚོ་ད་འགུལ། གཉིས་མེད་ཡེ
ཤེས་འགྲོ་བའི་དཔལ། ཁཅེ་གི་ཏུ་མེ་འགྱུར་བདེ་བ་ཆེས།།
སྲིག་ལྡང་མ་ལུས་དུ་འབྱིན་པའི། ༐ཛྲ་སེམས་མ་མ་ཚོ༵
ལ་ཕྱག་འཚལ། ཨཏྱ་ལུས་ནས བདེ་སྟོང་ལྷུན་ཆེ་བ
སྐྱེས་པའི་ཡེ་ཤེས་ཀྱི། ཁ་ནུང་རྣམས་ཕུ་བ་ཁམས་སྐྱེ
མཆོད་ལས་འབྱུང་བའི། རེ་གྱིར་རྒྀན་ཆེན་གཏེར་ཐུམ་ཏེ
སྦྱར་བཞས། སྐུ་ཕུས་མ་གཱི་ན་ཐུགས་རྗེའི་གཏེར་ལ་དཔྱལ
བར་བགྱི། བདག་གི་ཆགས་སྲུང་ཀྲྀ་ངས་གསུམ་སྐྲ༵
བའི་ཕུལ། དགུ་གི་ཏེ་ན་བར་གསུམ་ལུས་དང་ཡོངས
སྐྱེད་བཙ། ཁ་ངས་ཡ་མེ་ད་བ་འ་བུལ་གྱི་ལེ་ངས
བཞེས་ནས། ཀྲྀས་གསུམ་རང་སར་གྲོ་ལ་བར་བྱིན་གྱིས

༥

རྫོགས། ཁྱེ་དེ་ནུར་ར་ཏུ་མཧྲལ་ཀོ་ཉི་ཏྲུ་ཡུ་མི། ཁཚེ་
ལྣེར་འདས་རྡོ་རྗེ་སེ་མས་དཔའ་འདག་གཞན་སེ་མས་ཅན་
ཐམས་ཅད་ཀྱི་སྲིག་སྒྲིབ་དང་མཆོག་ཉམས་ཚག་ཐམས་
ཅད་བྱང་ཞིང་དག་པར་མཛད་དུ་གསོལ། ཞེས་གསོལ་
བཏབ་པ་ནས། ཕྱགས་ཀྱིན་སྐུ་གསས་ཕྱེ་དྲུང་བཅས་
པ་ལས་འོད་ཟེར་འཕྲོ། སེ་མས་ཅན་ཐམས་ཅད་ཀྱི་
སྲིག་སྒྲིབ་སྦྱངས། སངས་རྒྱས་སྲས་བཅས་པ་མཆེན་
པའི་མཆེད་པའི་ཁྱལ། དེ་རྣམས་ཀྱི་སྐུ་གསུང་ཐུགས་
ཀྱི་ཡོན་ཏན་ཐམས་ཅད་འདི་དག་ཏུ་རྣམ་པར་བསྲུས་ནས་སྣུ་
ཕྱེ་ཕུང་བཅས་པ་ལ་ཐིམ་པས། དེ་ལས་འདུ་རྗེ་
རྒྱན་དཀར་པོ་བབས་པ་ཡབ་ཡུམ་གྱི་སྤྱི་བར་མཆམས་ནས་
བབས། རང་གི་ཆེངས་སྤག་ནས་ཞུགས་ཏེ་ལུས་ཐམས་
ཅད་ཀྱི་ཡེ་ཤེས་ཀྱི་དུ་རྗེའི་རྒྱན་གྱིས་གང་། སྣོག་གསུམ་
གྱི་སྲིག་སྒྲིབ་ཐམས་ཅད་རབས་ཀྱིས་དག་པར་གྱུར།
ཨོ་བཛྲ་ཅི་དྲ་གསམ་ཡ། མ་ནུ་པུ་ལ་ཡ། ཅེ་དུ་ག།
དྲེ་ནོ་པ་ཏི་ཌྲ་ཏེ་རྡོ་མི་སྱུ་ས། སུ་ཏོ་ཀྱི་མི་སྱུ་ས། སུ་
པོ་ཁྱི་མི་སྱུ་ས། ཨ་ནུ་ར་ཀྟོ་མི་སྱུ་ས། སཪྦ་སི་དྲི་སྱུ་ཙ

༧

ཡ་རཱུ། །ས་པ་ཀ་མ་སུ་ཏ་མེ། །ཏེ་ཊེ་ཥྲི་ཡཿ ག་ར་ཧཱུྃ། ཧཱུ་ཧཱུ་ཧཱུ་ཧོཿ ཕྲ་ཝ་ཐན། བརྫེ་ཏེ་ར་ག་ནུ་མེ་མ་རཱུ། དེ་རུ་ག་ཙཱུ་ཥ། མ་ནྡུས་མ་ལ་ས་དུ་ཨ་ཿ་ཧྥི་ཝ་ན། ཏེ་ར་གཏེག་སོག་ས་བཟོཿ །ཨོཾ་བཏུ་ས་དུ་ཨ་རྒྱ་ཞེ་སོག་ས་དང་། བཙེ་ས་མ་རོ་ཡོ་འེ་ས་སོག་ས་ཀྱི་ས་སྟོད། །བདག་ནི་མེ་ཞེས་རྫས་པ་ཡི་ས། །ཧྃ་མཚོག་ལ་ས་ནི་འག་ལ་ཞིང་མ་ཊ་མྃ། སྲུ་མ་གི་ན་རེས་སྐྲུ་ས་མ་ཛོ་ཅིག །གཏོ་བོ་ཊེ་ཊ་འཇོཿ པ་སྟེ། །ཐུག་ས་ཊེ་ཆེན་པོ་འི་བདག་ཉི་ད་ཧན། །འགྲོ་བ་འི་གཏོ་ལ་བདག་སྐྲ་བས་མ་ཆེ། །ཊེ་ཊེ་ས་མ་ས་དཔ་འི་ཞ་ལ་ནས་རེ་ག་ས་ཀྱི་ཥཱུ་ཟོ་ཏ་ཀྱི་ཀྲ་སྐྲུ་བ་དང་དག་མ་ཚོག་འཛྃ་ཙག་ས་ཐམ་ས་ཧ་ད་བྱུ་ཞིང་དག་གི་ཞེས་ག་སུ་ས་ནས་ར་ད་ལ་ཐིམ་པ་ས་ར་ད་གི་སྐུ་ག་སུ་མ་དང་ཧྲེ་ཊེ་ས་མ་ས་དཔ་འི་སྐྲ་གསུང་ཐུག་ས་ཕྲིན་ལས་སྟོད་པ་ར་གྱུར།། །

དེས་པ་འཇི་ནུ་པ་ཕྱོག་ས་ཀྱི་ཀྲི་ལྟུན་ད་མ་ཞི་ག་ནས་ལ་མ་རེ་མི་གྱི་གཏག་ས་སེ་ལ་སོ། འདོན་དང་། རེ་ག་ཛིས་བསྐྲ་མ་པ་འི་སྟོན་འགྲོ་ཊེ་ས་མ་ས་ཀྱི་བསྐྲེན་བསྐྲབ་འཇ། །འདོན་ཞིག་དགོས་ཊེ་ས་བསྐུ་ལ་མ་བྱུ་ང་བ་འི་རྐྱེ་ནུ་ས། སུ་ནི་ཊོ་ཉི་འི་མི་ར་ཅ་གྱི་ས། ཊོ་རུ་ཆེ་དུ་སྐྲོ་ར་ཕྱེ་ས་པ་ས་ནས། །བཟོད་པ་གསོལ། །འཛམ་སྐྱི་ར་སྐུ་ལ...

ཉ

ཡིངས་ཐེག་པ་ཆེན་པོའི་སྒྲུན་སྟོན་གནངས་སྤྱར་བསྒྲུན་ཞུས་ཏེ་དོན་གཉེར་ཅན་
དགལ་འགྲོམས་སྤེལ་བགྱིས་པའོ།།   །ལཿམངྒ་ལོཾ།། །།

༄༅། །རྡོ་རྗེ་རྣལ་འབྱོར་བའི་བག་ཆེན་པོ་ཚོགས་ཀྱི

འཁོར་ལོ་བདེ་ཆེན་དགའ་སྟོན

ཞེས་བྱ་བ་བཞུན

ས�609‍།།

༡

༄༅། །བཞི་མ་ལྱན་དངས་ཀྱི་རྒྱུད་ལས་རྡོ་རྗེ་སེམས་བསྐྱེམ་·····
བརྣས་ཏེ།   ལམ་བསྒྲིད་རྟོགས་ཀྱི་རིམ་པ་བསྒྲིམ་པའི་སྐྱོན་འགྲོ་དང་།
བར་དུ་ལམ་ཐབས་ཤེས་ཀྱི་གོ་མིལས་པ་ཡོངས་སུ་རྟོགས་པའི་གོ་གནས་སེ་ལ་ཕོག་འོའི་
ཀྱི་ཐབས་མ་ཁས་སྐུ་དུ་བྱུར་བར་གསུངས།   དེ་ཡར་ཕོག་མར་རྒྱུ་སྐྱོ་ང་དང་
སྐྱབ་པའི་རྗེ་ནུ་མ་དག་ལས་ལྱ་འི་ཡི་སྐྱ་གུ་སུ་ཕུགས་ཡོན་ཐ་ན་འཕིན་ལམས་ཀྱི
རྗེས་གནང་དང་བཞིའི་མེལས་པ་དང་འཕེལ་བའི་ཉི་རྣམས་ཙན་ཕོབ་པ་སྟོེ་ནུད་སོ་ངས་
ནལ་འཕྲོ་པས་སྐྱ་འི་རྣ་འི་ལ་རྒྱས་བསྣམ་ལ་གནས་ནས་རྗེ་རྒྱལ་བའི་·····
གཅེན་པོ་ཆོགས་ཀྱི་ནོར་ལའི་དག་ནེ་སྐྲོལས་ལ་ཧ་གྲུ་ཆུང་བའི་སྲལ་བབ་བ་དགའི
བདེ་བ་ཆེན་པོ་ལ་འཆི་ལས་པ་ལྱ་རེ།།   ཧྲ་མིད་ལྱག་ལ་ཀྱི་རྡོ་སེམས་རྗེས
གནང་བའི་རྒྱུད་པ་ནི་དག་ལྱ་ན་སྐྱ་ནི་བརྒྱུད་ནས་ཡུང་བའི་མན་ངག་ཐབ་མོ་གཞན་
ལ་མེད་པའི་ཉྱད་ཆོས་སུ་བ་བ་ཧྲ་མ་བདི་འི་གསུང་རྒྱུན་ལས་ཡུང་ལིང་།
ད་སྤྱིར་ལྱ་ན་སྐྱབས་ཀྱི་རྒྱུད་འི་རྡོ་མ་ལ་བདག་མས་ཤེ་རང་གི་ཕྱིན
ཉི་རྒྱུ་ལྱེ་དང་ར་རྟོས་པའི་འཕག་སྐྱིན་ཏ་ཏའི་ཆོས་ཀྱི་མ་ཆོས་འདི་ལ་ནོར་·····
དང་   དེ་རྗེ་གནེ་ལ་བདུ་དུ་འཕ་འི་ཞི་ཤེན།   ཀེ་ལྱ་རྱགས་ན་བཙོ་·····
ངུ་ལ་བར་གྱུར་ཏུ་རེ།   གསོ་ཞི་ལྱ་དུ་རྡོ་འི་འི་དག་རྒྱ་བཙན་བཅོ་འི
རེ་ལས་གོགས་ཀྱི་ཕྱི་ཏ་ཆྱི་ར་བ་ནགས་ནས།   ཆོགས་ཀྱི་ནི་དུ་ནམ
རྡེ་སེ་མས་དཔའི་དཀྱི་ལ་སྐྱིམ་བ་ནི།   ཧུྃཿ   བདེ་སྟོང་བ་འིམ·····

༣

ཀུ་མེད་པའི་རྣམ་རོལ་ལས།   །སྐྱུང་བའི་རྡོ་རྗེ་སེམས།...

དཔའི་གཞལ་ཡས་ཁང་།   །ཧྲིན་དང་བརྟེན་པའི་......

དཀྱིལ་འཁོར་ཡོངས་རྫོགས་མཐུན།   །ཀུན་བཟང་......

མཆོད་སྤྲིན་ནམ་མཁའི་ཕྱིན་ཀུན་བཀང་།   །གཉིས་......

མེད་བདེ་བ་ཆེན་པོའི་ཁབ་ད་བྱེརས་ལ།   །དོ་མ་ཆེན་

འཕྲོ་ནམས་སྤྲ་ད་སྐྱོ་བའི་ཐུབ་ལ།   །ཞི་རྒྱས་དབང་

དག་སྒྱུལ་པོའི་གནས་གནས་ཀྱི།   །ཕབས་ཞེས་ཡོངས།

སུ་རྟོགས་པའི་སྐྱུར་བཞེངས་གྱུར།   །ཆོགས་ཀྲས་ཏྲེ་

སྣས་བྱ་རྒྱ་ནི།   །ཨོ་བཐུ་རོ་ཚེ་ས་བབས་ས།   སྐུ་གྲུ་ཐུ་ས

སྐུ་ས།   །སྟོང་བའི་དང་ལས་ལ་ལས་ཕྲེད་པ་ཡས།......

ཞིང་རྒྱུ་ཆེ་བའི་ནང་ད་ཀ་སྐྲུ་བ་དུ་རྗེ་སྐུ་རྣམས་ལྷབ་ལས།

སྐྱུང་བའི་ཡེ་ཤེས་ཀྱི་བད་རྗེ་ནི་རྒྱུ་མ་ཆོ་ཆེན་པོ་གྱུར།

ཨ ཨཱུྃ ་ཧཱུྃ ་ཏྲྃ ་ཧྲཱིཿ   ཞེས་གསུམ།   །ཐམ་ལ་དབང་

པོའི་ཡུལ་ལས་རབ་འདས་བཞིན།   །ཡོ་བེ་དི་མ

ཚོག་དག་སྤྲ་བདེ་ཆེ།   །དངོས་གྲུབ་ཀུན་གྱི་གཞི།

གྱུར་བདུ་རྗེའི་མ་ཆེ་ན།   །ཧྲིག་མེད་བདེ་བ་ཆེན་པོའི།

མ་ཉེས་པར་མཛོད།   །ཧཱུྃ ཿ མ་བནྡ་གྲོལ་རས་འཧབ

༩

ཚོན་རྟེ་རྗེ་ཤེ་མས་དཔའི་སྲོ།   །ཁྲག་ཡིད་མ་མ་མཁན་
འབྲི་ཚིས་སྐྱོང་གི   །རོ་བོར་མ་རྗེ་གས་བཙིས་འཐེན་
འབྲུལ་སྲུང་ངག   །ཁམ་རྟ་ས་བདོ་ལིན་སུ་སླུ་ངེ་ཚོ་ནུ།
མ་ཚོད་ལ།   །ཁྲུ་མ་རྗེ་རྗེ་ཤེ་མས་དཔའ་མ་ཉེ་ས་བྱིར་
ཁྲུལ།   །ཁྲེན་སྐྱེ་ས་བཌེ་ཆེ་ན་སྐྱེ་པ་བྱེན་གྱེ་ས་རྲོལ།
ཨོ་བ་ཏྲི་ར་གས་མ་ལ།   །མ་སུ་བ་ལ་ལ།   །ཅེ་ར་ག །
ཅེ་བོ་བ་ཏི་ཏུ།   །རི་རྗེ་མ་སྲ་ཁ།   །སུ་བ་ཙུ་མ་སྲ་ཁ།
སུ་བ་ཙུ་མ་སྲ་ཁ།   །ཡ་ནུ་རྒྱེ་མ་སྲ་ཁ།   །ས་ཙ་
ནྲེ་བྱུ་བ་ཡ་ཏུ།   །ས་ན་ག་མྲ་སུ་རུ་མེ་རྗེ་རྒུ་ཡོ།ཿ
ག་ནུ་ཏུ།   །ཅ་ཅ་ཅ་ཆོཿ སྲ་བ་ཁ་བ།   །བ་ཨེ་ར་ག །
མ་མེ་མ་ཏུ།   །ཅེ་ར་ག་བྱུ་ཁ།   །མ་རྟུ་ས་མ་ལ་ས་དུ།
ཡུཿ རྟུ་ཡ་བ།   །ཞེ་ས་བཏོ།   །རྟུཿ མ་བན་དབྱེ་ས
འཐའ་ཚོ་ན་རྗེ་རྗེ་ཤེ་མས་དཔའི་སྲོ།   །རྟོ་ཡིན་འདེ
ལ་ཚ་གས་བའི་རྣ་མ་ཤེས་སླུ་ལ།   །དཔ་འབྱུར་དོན
ཨེ་ད་བྱ་བའི་འབྲུལ་སྲུང་ངག   །ཁམ་རྟ་ས་བདོ་ཡོན
སུ་སླུ་རྗེ་ཚོ་གས་མ་ཚོད་ལ།   །ཁྲུ་མ་རྗེ་རྗེ་ཤེ་མས་དཔའ་
མ་ཉེ་ས་ཕྱེ་ར་བྱུ།   །ཁི་འདེ་རི་སྲུང་ཞེ་ལྲོ་ག་པར

༥

ཅིན་ཕྱས་རྫོགས། །ཨོཾ་བཛྲ་ཀྲི་ཏ་ག་རས་མ་ལ་ ཞེས་སོགས་
བརྗོད། ཧཱུྃ༔ མཁའ་དབྱིངས་ཕྱིརས་འཇའ་ཚོན་རྗེ་རྗེ་སེ་མས་
པའི་སྐུ། །ཚུལ་མིན་ཡིད་ཕྱེད་རྣམ་རྟོག་ལས་ཉི་ན་གྱི། །
སྐྱིབ་ག་ཡོག་གཏིས་རྟོན་དོག་ནི་གྱི་འབུལ་སྲུང་ངའ། །
དམ་རྫས་བདོད་ཡོན་སྣ་ལྔའི་ཚོགས་མཆོད་ལ། །ཁྱ
མ་རྗེ་སེ་མས་དབང་མཉེས་ཕྱིར་འབུལ། །ཉེས་
ཕྱུང་རྣམ་དག་སྐྱེ་བ་ཕྱི་གྱིས་རྫོགས། །ཨོཾ་བཛྲ་ཏི་ར་
གར་ས་མ་ལ་ ཞེས་སོགས་བརྗོད། ཧཱུྃ༔ མཁའ་ད་ཕྱིརས་
འཇའ་ཚོན་རྗེ་རྗེ་སེ་མས་དབའི་སྐུ། །དང་ཉི་ད་གཉེས་
བརྫིན་སྲུག་བ་སྐྲལ་ཀུན་གྱི་སྟེ། །གཉིས་འཛིན་བདུད་
ཀྱི་བགེ་པོའི་འབུལ་སྲུང་ངའ། །དམ་རྫས་བདོད་
ཡོན་སྣ་ལྔའི་ཚོགས་མཆོད་ལ། །ཁྲུམ་རྗེ་རྗེ་སེ་མས་
དབའ་མཉེས་ཕྱིར་འབུལ། །རྣམ་དག་འྱུང་སེ་མས་
སྐྱེ་བ་ཕྱི་གྱིས་རྫོགས། །ཨོཾ་བཛྲ་ཏི་ར་ག་ས་མ་ལ་
ཞེས་བརྗོད། ཧཱུྃ༔ མཁའ་དབྱིརས་འཇའ་ཚོན་རྗེ་རྗེ་སེ་མས་
དཔའི་སྐུ། །རྟོག་ལས་པར་བཞག་མེ་ཀྱུ་འབྱབགས་
ཕོད་ལ། །གཉིས་འཛིན་རྗེ་ནི་རྗེ་མ་དང་བའི་འབུལ་སྲུང

༦

རྣ། །དམ་ཚིག་འདོད་ཡོན་སྣ་ལྔའི་ཚོགས་མཆོད་ལ། །
བླ་མ་རྡོ་རྗེ་སེམས་དཔའ་མཉེས་ཕྱིར་འབུལ། །ཁྲུག །
རྒྱ་ཆེན་པོ་རྟོགས་པར་བྱེད་གྱིས་རློབས། །ཨོཾ་བཛྲ་ཨཱི་
གཱ་ས་མ་ཡ་ཞེས་སོགས་བརྗོད། ཧཱུྃཿ མ་བཞད་ཕྱིར་ཨེས །
འདའ་འཚེ་རྡོ་རྗེ་སེམས་དཔའི་སྐུ། །ཐབ་མ་ལ་སྤྲང་
ཞེན་གནོ་ཏྟོག་ཕྱར་བགས་ཀྱི། །བཅུས་ཤོ་རྗེ་ཞིན་རྙེང་ཕྱུ།
དྲག་པོའི་འཕྲུལ་སྐུ་དང་། །དམ་ཚིག་ཡེ་ཤེས་ལྷ །
ཡི་ཚུ་གུ་མཆོད་ལ། །བླ་མ་རྡོ་རྗེ་སེམས་དཔའ་མཉེས་ཕྱིར
དེས་འདོད་དའ་ཞི་ཕོ་བར་བྱེད་གྱིས་རློབས། །ཨོཾ
བཛྷཏི་ར་གཱ་ས་མ་ཡ་ ཞེས་སོགས་བརྗོད། ཧཱུྃཿ མ་བཞ
ཕྱིར་འཛའ་འཚེ་རྗེ་རྡོ་རྗེ་སེམས་དཔའི་སྐུ། །ཉེས །
ལྷ་རྡུ་གྲ་ཆར་དབར་མེ་ད་བཞལ་པ་ལས། །རྗེ་རྗེ་དགྱུལ །
བོ་ཆྱིང་བའི་འཕྲུལ་ལ་སྐུ་དང་། །དམ་ཚིགས་ཡེ་ཤེས་ལྷ །
ཡི་ཚོགས་མ་མཆོད་ལ། །བླ་མ་རྡོ་རྗེ་སེམས་དཔའ་དབའ
མཉེས་ཕྱིར་འབུལ། །དག་བ་རབ་འབྱམས་འབའ་ཞིག །
འཆར་བར་འབོག །ཨོཾ་བཛྷཏི་ར་གཱ་ས་མ་ཡ་ ཞེས་སོགས
བརྗོད། དེས་རྗེ་རྗེ་སྤྲུབ་པའི་འབྱལ་ཚིགས་འབུལ་བའི་ རྗེ་རྗེ⸺

ॱ

འདི་ནི་པ་དཔེ་ངེས་སུ་གསལ་མོལ།། ।དཔལ་འབོ་དཔའ་མོ་
ཚོགས་འཁོར་བའི་ཌི།། །ཀ་རྭུད་དར་འཕྲིན་པའི་སྐྱེས་པ་
བས།ༀ །འདུད་རྗེ་ནི་བདག་ཏུ་གག་ཏུ་རོལ།། །ཁ་ལ་
ལ་ཌི།ༀ །སྒྲིབ་པོ་ཤིན་གྱིས།། །ཨེ་མ་བདེ་ཆེན་ཡེ་ཤེས་
ཀྱི།ༀ །ཚིག་ས་ཆེན་གདུག་མོ་འབར་བའི་འོད།། །སྨྲ་
བས་མ་བརྗོད་དངས་དག་འབའ་ལ།། །ཀུན་ཏུ་ཨ་རྟོ་
རྒྱུན་ཆེ།ༀ །ཨ་ཙི་ཨ་དུ་སུ་བཞི།ༀ །ༀ་བཱ་ན་བཛྲ་
ག་ཊ་ས་པའི་སྒྲུ་ར་ཨ་ཛྲཱ་ ནས་ །འབྲུ་ངི་བས་ཀྱེ་ཀྱེ་སྐྱེ་དངས།།
གདངི་མཚོ་ན་ཚམ་བརྗོད་པས་གཏུང་ །ལས་དང་རྫོག།
སྒྱུ་མ་སྒྱུལ་བ།ༀ །སྐུ་ནི་ཚིག་ཉིད་ལ་དུ་འཕྲིན་པའི། །
རྗེ་རྗེ་ནོ་མས་དཔལ་ལ་ཕྱག་འཚལ།། །ཞེས་བསྔོ།།
ད་ནས་སྐྲ་བ༥ུ་དི་ཀྱིས་བསྒྲིག་པ།།   ༀ་བཙ་མ་སྒྱུན་དཔའ་བའི་
དབང་ཕྱུག་ལ་ཕྱུག་འཚ་ལོ་ཧཱུྃ་ཧཱུྃ་ཕཊ།། །ༀ་བསྒྱལ་བ
ཆེན་པོ་ནི་མི་དང་བདུམ་པའི་ཌི་ནི་ཧཱུྃ་ཧཱུྃ་ཕཊ།། །ༀ
དཔལ་པའི་ཚོ་བས་མོ་ཟད་པ་དང་སྒྲུ་ཧཱུྃ་ཧཱུྃ་ཕཊ།། །ༀ
མཆེ་བ་རྣམ་པ་ར་གཙིགས་པ་འཇིགས་པའི་འཝལ་ཧཱུྃ་ཧཱུྃ་ཕཊ།།
ༀ་སྒྱིང་ཕྱག་ཕྱུག་ཞེ་འབར་བའི་འོད་ཟེར་ཅན་ཧཱུྃ་ཧཱུྃ་ཕཊ།། །

༦

རྦ༔ ཌཌཌ ཌཌ ཌཌ ཌ ཌ ཌཌ ཌཌ ཌ ཌ ༎

ཌ ཌ ཌ ཌ ཌ ཌ ཌ ཌ ཌ ཌ ཌ ཌ ༎ ཌ

ཌ ཌ ཌ ཌ ཌ ཌ ཌ ཌ ཌ ཌ ཌ ༎ ༁ ཧཱུྃ

ཌ ཌ ཌ ཌ ཌ ཌ ཌ ༎ ཧཱུྃཿ ཌ ཌ ཌ ཌ

ཌ ཌ ཌ ཌ ཌ ཌ ཌ ཌ ཌ ༎ ཌ ཌ ཌ

ཌ ཌ ཌ ཌ ཌ ཌ ༎ ཌ ཌ ཌ ཌ ཌ ཌ

ཌ ཌ ཌ ཌ ཌ ཌ ཌ ༎ ཌ ཌ ཌ ཌ ཌ

ཌ ཌ ཌ ཌ ཌ ༎ ཌ ཌ ཌ ཌ ཌ ཌ ཌ ཌ

ཌ ཌ ཌ ཌ ཌ ཌ ཌ ཌ ཌ ༎ ༁ཨོཾ

ཌ ཌ ཌ ཌ ཌ ཌ ཌ ཌ ༎ ཧཱུྃཿ ཌ ཌ

ཌ ཌ ཌ ཌ ཌ ཌ ཌ ཌ ཌ ཌ ༎ ཌ ཌ ཌ

ཌ ཌ ཌ ཌ ཌ ཌ ཌ ཌ ༎ ཌ ཌ ཌ ཌ

ཌ ཌ ཌ ཌ ཌ ༎ ཌ ཌ ཌ ཌ ཌ ཌ ཌ ཌ

ཌ ཌ ཌ ཌ ཌ ༎ ཌ ཌ ཌ ཌ ཌ ཌ ཌ ཌ

ཌ ཌ ཌ ཌ ཌ ༎ ཌ ཌ ཌ ཌ ཌ ཌ ཌ ཌ

ཌ ཌ ཌ ༎ ཌ ཌ ཌ ཌ ཌ ཌ ཌ ཌ ཌ ཌ ༎ ཌ ཌ

ཕ

འགྲོ་དང་ཞི་མཁའ་བའི་འགྲོ་མ། ཀུན་ལ་བདག་ཉི་གས་ལ་
བ་ལྡེབས། ཁདེ་བ་ཆེ་ལ་དགྱེས་པ་ཡི་དེ་རུ་ཀ །
 བས་རབ་ཏུ་སྤྱིས་མ་ལ་བསྟེ་ཞུས་ནས། ཚེ་ཁ
བ་ཞིན་ཏུ་ཡིད་ས་སྟོང་པ་ཡིས་ཞོ། ཁྱེན་སྐྱེས་བདེ་བའི་
སྐྱུད་པ་ལ་ཞུས་སོ། ཁ་ལ་ལ། ལ་ལ་ཛི
ཡ་ཨི་ཨྂཿ ཡ་ར་ལི་ཛིཿ རྗེ་ཨེད་མ་ཁབ་འགྲོ་བི་ཚོག་སྒྱུ་
རྣམས་ཀྱིས། ཁབ་ཇེ་བས་གཉིས་གས་ལ་ལ་བ་རྒུན་
མཆོད། ཧྱྂ། རེ་བཞིན་ག་ཞེ་གས་པ་ཐབས་
ཏུ་དང་ ཁསལ་འོ་དང་ཞི་རྣ་ལ་འབྱུར་མ། །
གཞན་འགྲོ་དང་ཞི་མཁའ་བ་འགྲོ་མ། ཀུན་ལ་བདག་ཞི
གསལ་བ་འདེབས། ཁབ་དེ་བ་ཆེན་པོས་ཡིན་ཞེ་ར་བ
བསྐྱེད་ནས། ཁྲུས་ནི་ཀུ་ཉྩ་ག་ལོ་བའི་བར་ཙུས
ཞེ། ཁྲུས་རྒྱ་ཚེ་བ་རྣར་རེ་ལ་པོ་འ་བདེ་བཆེ། ཟླ
འབྱུར་མཚོག་ས་རྣམས་ལ་མཆོད་པར་མཛོད། ཁཡ
ལ་ལ། ལ་ལ་ཛི ཡ་ཨི་ཨྂ ཡ་ར་ལི་ཛིཿ
རྗེ་ཨེད་མ་ཁབ་འགྲོ་བི་ཚོག་ས་རྣམས་ཀྱིས། ཁབ་ཇེ
བས་ག་ཉིས་ག་ས་ལ་ལ་ས་ཀུན་མཆོད། ཧྱྂ། རེ

১০

བཞིན་ག་ཞིགས་པ་ཐམས་ཅད་དང་། །དཔའ་བོ་དང་ནི་
རྣལ་འབྱོར་མ། །མཁའ་འགྲོ་དང་ནི་མཁའ་འགྲོ་མ། །
གནས་ལ་བདག་ནི་གསོལ་བ་འདེབས། །ཡིད་འོང་ནི་
བདེའི་ཉམས་ཀྱི་གར་མཛོད་མ། །རབ་འབྱིམས་མགོན་པོ་
ཉིད་དང་མཁའ་འགྲོའི་ཚོགས། །བདག་གི་མདུན་དུ་
བཞུགས་ཏེ་ཉིན་རྟོ་ནས་ལ། །སྤྱན་སྔས་བདེ་ཆེན་བདག
ལ་སྩལ་དུ་གསོལ། །ཡལ་ལ། ཝལ་ཏྃཿ ཨ
ཨི་ཨཱུཿ ཨ་ར་ལི་ཏྃཿ རྗེ་མེད་མཁའ་འགྲོའི་ཚོགས
རྣམས་ཀྱི། །བཅུ་བས་ག་ཞིགས་ལ་ལས་གན······
མཛོད། །ཧཱུྃ་ཿ དེ་བཞིན་ག་ཞིགས་པ་ཐམས······
ཅད་དང་། །དཔའ་བོ་དང་ནི་རྣལ་འབྱོར་མ། །མཁའ
འགྲོ་དང་ནི་མཁའ་འགྲོ་མ། །གནས་ལ་བདག་ནི་གསོལ
བ་འདེབས། །བདེ་ཆེན་ཐར་པའི་མཚན་ཉིད་ལྡུན་བ······
ཉིད་ཿ །བདེ་ཆེན་སྐྱབས་བའི་དག་ན་ཐུབ་དུ་མ་ཡོས། །
ཚོག་ཅིག་གི་ཕྲོ་བར་མི་བཞིན་བདེ་ཆེན་རྒྱ། །ཀྲུ་སྐྱིབ
མ་ཆོག་གི་དངས་ན་གནས་པ་ཡིན། །ཡལ་ལ།
ལ་ལ་ཏྃཿ ཨ་ཨི་ཨཱུཿ ཨ་ར་ལི་ཏྃཿ རྗེ་མེད་མཁའ······

༷༷

འགྲོའི་ཚོགས་རྣམས་ཀྱིས། །བརྗེ་བས་བཟེགས་ལ་

ལས་གུན་མཛོད། །ཕྱྂ། །དེ་བཞིན་གཤེགས་པ་

ཐམས་ཅད་དང་། །དཔའ་བོ་དང་ནི་རྣལ་འབྱོར་མ། །

མཁའ་འགྲོ་དང་ནི་མཁའ་འགྲོ་མ། །ཀུན་ལ་བདག་ནི་

གསོལ་བ་འདེབས། །འདམ་སྐྱེ་དྲུས་སུ་སྐྱེས་པའི་

པདྨ་བཞིན། །ཆགས་ལས་སྐྱེས་ཀྱང་ཆགས་པའི་

སྐྱོན་མ་གོས། །རྣལ་འབྱོར་མ་མཆོག་པདྨའི་བདེ་

ཡིས། །སྲིད་པའི་མཚེ་བ་སྐྱུར་དུ་འགྲོལ་བར་མཛོད། །

ཨ་ལ་ལ། །ལ་ལ་ཧོཿ ཨ་ཨི་ཨུཿ ཨ་ར་ལི་ཧོཿ

རྗེ་མིད་མཁའ་འགྲོའི་ཚོགས་རྣམས་ཀྱིས། །བརྗེ་

བས་གཟིགས་ལ་ལས་གུན་མཛོད། །ཕྱྂ། །དེ་

བཞིན་གཤེགས་པ་ཐམས་ཅད་དང་། །དཔའ་བོ་དང་

ནི་རྣལ་འབྱོར་མ། །མཁའ་འགྲོ་དང་ནི་མཁའ་འགྲོ་

མ། །ཀུན་ལ་བདག་ནི་གསོལ་བ་འདེབས། །སྒྲུ་

སྐྱེའི་ཕྱུང་གནས་རྣམས་ཀྱི་སྐྱུང་ཕྱེའི་བཅུད། །ཧུ་

འདི་ཚོགས་ཀྱིས་ཀུན་ནས་འཕྱུང་བ་ལྟར། །མཚན་ཉིད་

དག་ལྡན་མ་ཚོ་སྐྱེ་ཀྲུལ་པ་ཡིས། །འཚུ་བཅིས་

༡༣

པ་ཡིར་ཡིས་ཚིམ་པར་མཛོད། །ཨ་ལ་ལ། ཝ་ལ་
ཏི༔ ཨ་ཨི་ཨུ༔ ཨཱ་ར་ལི་ཏི༔ རེ་མེ་ཀ་ཝ་འཁྲོའི་
ཚོགས་རྣམས་ཀྱིས། །བརྗེ་བས་ག་ཟིགས་ལ་ལས་
ཀུན་མཛོད། དེ་ནས་ཚོགས་སླུག་འཐུལ་བནི། ཨོཾ་ཨཱཿཧཱུྃཿ
ལན་གསུམ་མཛོད། བདེ་སྟོང་དབྱེར་མེད་སྒྱུ་མའི་གར།
ལར༔ །ཡེ་ཤེས་ལྔ་ལི་བདུད་རྩི་རོ་ཚོགས་སླུ་ག་རྨ།
ཟེར་སྐྱིང་དེ་གས་པ་སྤྲི་བཀྱུད་ཚོགས་ལ་འབུལ། །ངམ་
ཚོས་སྤྲུ་བའི་ཡས་བཞིའི་འཕྲིན་ལས་མཛོད།།
ཕུན་ཚོགས་ངི་ལེ་གས་ཏུ་བའི་རྒྱུན་པ་ཝི་ས། །
མཐའ་ཡས་འགྲོ་བའི་རེ་སྐྱོང་བའི་གསང་། །འགྲོ་
བའི་ནས་ལ་པ་ཇི་བཞིན་གཟིགས་པའི་ཐུགས། །རང་
ཤེམས་སྣང་མཐའ་མཐལ་བའི་བགྲོ་ཤེས་ལོག །རྒྱུ
རྒྱུའི་འཆི་བར་བར་རི་སྐྱི་བ་གསུམ། །སྐྱིང་དེ་སྐུ་གསུམ་
ལམ་དུ་འགྲི་ར་བའི་མཐུས། །རང་སེམས་ག་ཚུ་བ།
ཤེམས་པོ་མི་མ་ཧ་ལ་བ་ལས། །སྐུ་ཐུགས་ཟུང་
འཇུག་འཁ་ར་བའི་བགྲ་ཤེས་ལོག །སྐྲིན་བ་ལ་མ་འབན་
འཕྲེས་སྟོང་པ་ཆེན་པོའི་སྐུ། །སྐུ་སྐྱེ་ད་བདེ་བ

༡༣

ཆེན་པོའི་ཡེ་ཤེས་ལ། །འཁྱུང་པའི་ཡ་མཚན་དབོར་
ངས་དངོས་པོ་ཀུན། །འདི་སྙིང་ཆེན་པོ་སྟོ་མ་
མཇིང་བགྲུ་ཞིང་འོད། །ཤེལ་བའི་ཞི་

བོ་དྲུ་ལ་སོགས་པའི་འཛིན་གྱི་ཡུལ་ཀྲུ་མར་པོ་སྟོམ་བ་གསུམ་འགྱི་བསམ་
དང་རལ་འདྲ་མ་སོ་ན། །འགྲིམ་མིའི་གལ་ཏུ་མི་ཀྲུ་བ་འི་སླ་བས་སྤྱིགས་མ་
ལས་ཀུང་ཆེམ་སྤྱིགས་མར་འགྱུར་བས། ཀླལ་པ་དང་ཤུར་བའི་སྤྱགས་ཀྱི་
རྒྱ་འབྱུར་བ། ནམས་ཀྱི་སྤྱི་ཡུ་འཛིངས་བ་ལ་ཞིན་ཏུ་དཔར་བའི་རྡོ་རེ་མེ་ཁྱི་
ཆུམས་མེ་ལ་འཛིག་བའི་སྤྲུ་འཛིག་བ་དེ་བ་ཆེན་བའི་ཡེ་ཤེས་ཀྱི་རང་ཁུ་ཐོན་
བ་ལ་མེ་དང་མི་རུང་བའི་གནས་སུ་མཕོ་བསྟི་ལྤུར་བརོ་ནམས་ཀྱི་ཚིགས་རྣས་བོ་
བསོག་བ་དང་། འམ་ཚིག་ཆུམས་ཚགས་ལ་སྟོང་བ། ལྤག་པར་རེ་བི་
འགི་ལྤུན་པའི་ཀྲུ་མ་བ། གཤེ་བོ་ཡེ་གཱ་བདྱ་འདུམས་བཙུན་ནས་སྟུ་གས་ཀྱི་རྩ་ལྤུང་
ཡང་གཤར་གཤུལ་པས་ནལ་ནས་ཀྲུ་བདེས་མ་དགའ་བའི་སྤྱིག་ལ་མེ་དཔར་ཡིན།
ཆེས་པའི་གནས་ནས་སུ་ཤར་བི། །བགྲི་ན་གསུམ་ལྤུན་ཀྱི་རྩ་བའི་ས་བ་
ཤེས་བ་ནི་ཀྱི་ཉེ་ག་བཞིང་རྡེ་རྙ་རྩ་དམ་པའི་གནས་ཏེ་དཔ་ཡུལ་ས་འགྱི་མ་ཀྲི
བདགས་ཏྲ་ཉེ་ས་ལྤུང་ལྡིམ་འབྱུད་བའི་རྙ་རྒྱ་ནས་རྒྱུན། རེ་ནས་འདིས་པའི
རྙས་དང་ཌབ། མེ་ད་ཀྱི། །ཕེས་ལྤུང་ཆར་བཞིན་བབས་ལ་འདེ་ནས་མཆེ། །
དབ་མེ་རྡོ་རྗེ་དཔྱལ་བ་སོ་བི་གྱི་སྟོ་ནས། །ཞིན་གྱུ་རྒྱ་ལ་བི་ཟྤགས་རྗེ

༡༩

ༀ་ན་ཏུ་སྱུ་ར༔ ༔རྗེ་རྗེ་ཐེག་པའི་ཐབས་མཁས་མ་ཚོགས་ཧྲཱུ་ཞབ༔ ༔ཁྱུང་ཁྲི་ཚེག༔
ཚལ་བ་རྗེ་ཞེན་ས་ཀུང༔ ༔ཁྱེ་མ་ལུ་དུ་ལས་ནས་ཕྲིན་ དང་ཨེ་མ་ཨོ༔ །ཞེས་
གསུམ་པར་སྦྱར་རོ༔ ༔འདི་ནི་ནས་མ་ཚོགས་རྗེ་རྗེག་ནས་དང་རང་གི་སྐྱོབས་ཨ་
མ་རྒྱག་ལ་རུང་འཕེལ་ལྱ་ཀྱི་མ་མ་བོ་བི་སྣྲུ་དུ་ལུགས་བཞི༔ ༔ཕྲུབ་པའི་ནེ་སྙན་ས་ལ་
ཡོད་ཚེས་ཀྱི་ནས་པ་ཏེ་ན་པོ་སྟེ་ནས་གསུམ་ལ་སྤྲུ་ནང་སྐྱེ་གི་ན་མ་ར་བོ་བ་ཤེ་ཏ་
ཡོ་ར་གི་སྤྲུ་བབ་སྤུན་ནེ་ན་པོ་ཀྱི་ལྱུག་ལས་མ་ཡི་སྣོ་ན་ད་པ་ལ་རྗེ་རྒ་ན་
ཧུང་རྒྱུལ་བ་ནེ་དྲུ་ད་མ་སྱི་ར་ཐེག་པ་ཚེ་ན་པའི་ངོ་འདུ་ནང་མ་ཐ་ནད་མ་ཚོ་
སྱེ་ན་སྤྲུ་ལྱུང་རྒྱུ༔ ཚ་ར་དང་༔ ༔ཚེག་ས་ཀྱི་ཕ་བོ་ལ་སྙན་ཞ་སྒྱི་ཧྲོ་ག་སྣོ་
ཚེག་ཏ་ནེ་བརྒྱུ་རྗོ་ནང་བཚང་ལ་བོ་ན་ཀྱི་ཉེ་ལས༔ ༔ཕྲི་བོ་ ༢༥ ༥༣
སྤྲུ་ན ༡ ཚེས་ ༣ ༔ བོ་ད་རྒྱལ་བོ་ ༡༢༠༨ སྤྲུ་བ ༠༡ ཚེས་ ༡༠
མ་ནང་འབྲོ་དུ་དུ་འེ་དུས་ཚེ་ན་ཏེ་ན་ཕྱོག་ས་བཅུ་བོ་ན་དུ་ན་རྣམ་ཕྲ་ནས་མ་ཐུན༔
ཁྲི་མས་ག་ཚོར་ས་ལ་མ་བསྒྲ་པ་ས་གསུམ་སྒྱི་ཅ་མས་ལ་ཝ་ན་མ་ཐ་རྒྱུན་ཏེ་ཡེ་མས༔
ཚ་བགྲི་ནོ་ནྲུ་ཚེ་ན་བོ་ལ་ནེ་ར་ལུ་བ་ནེ་སྨོ་ན་ཚེ་ག་ད་ར་ས་ར་སྤྲུ་ག་ད་ནེ་ཚེས༔
གསུམ་བ་རོ་ནོ་བ་འི་དག༔ ༔ཁ་ཐ་ནྲུ་རྗེ་རྗེ་ཡེ་མས་ར་ན་པ་ཞེ་ན་སྤྲུ་ར་ལ་ན་ཀྱུ་འི་ག༔
སྣོ་ལྱུ་རྗེ་ནྲུ་ནེ་མ་ཚ་ནྲུ་ཞི་ས་ག་ཞེས་བཙི་བ་བོ༔   །
༔ ༔གསེ་བ་ཀྱི་ག་ཞི་སྤྲུ་ག་ས་སྨོ་ན་ར་བོ་ར་ས༔ །འཧྲུ་གི་རོ་ག་ས་
ན་སྤྲུ་སྒྱི་ར་པ་ར་ཁམ་ས༔ ༔ཕྲུ་མ་ཁྲི་ མ་ད་ར་པ་ར་གི་ལྱུ་ར་མ་སྨི་ག༔   །

༡༥

ནམ་མཁའི་མཛོད་ལྱོལ་གོར་འཕྲུལ་ལམ་མཆེར། །ཞེས་གྱང་སྨྲས་སོ།། །

ར་ ཚིགས་ཚེས་དེ་ནིན་གྲུ་ཀྱི་ཡི་དམ་གནེན་ལཔར་སྤྱུ་དྲེ་ཚིགས་བཅེན་སྐྲིགས་
པར་མེལ་ཏེ། །དབེར་ནྱ་མེ་གྲུ་སྟོལ་ལམ་རྤྱུར་ན་ར་སྐྲོལ་ལམ་འབིེ་ལ་པྱིར་
ལ་གཎས་ནས་ཚོགས་གིུ་ནིར་དུ་ནྲུ་མ་སྟོལ་ལམ་འི་དུ་ཐལ་བོར་སྐྲིམས་པའི་སྐྱ་ནས། །
ཆུ་བའི་འཕགས་མ་སྟོལ་ལམ་འི་གཎལ་ལས་བར། །ཞེས་དང་། མ་བར་
དཔྱིངས་འདར་ཚོན་འཕགས་མ་སྟོལ་ལམ་འི་སྨྲ། །ཞེས་དང་། སྟྲོ་ཁ་མ་
ཉེ་གཉི་གཔལ་བ་དུ་རྗེ་ནོ་ནེར་དར་བཔར་ར་ནཝིཔ་ འི་དཀིགས་རྣམ་སྐྲིད་
བཞིན་བར་ཐ་ལ་སྤུར་ཞེན་གྱི་པལ་པུ་ཉེ་སྤྲྱུ་ཐ་མ་བཅུ་ད་ར་གཔར་འལམ་སྟེ
སྟོལ་ལམ་འི་སྤྲུ་གས་ཉེ་གཚག་ཆེ་བ་ནས།། གཎར་འདེ་འཇེ་གས་
གཎུམ་པོ་གཎལ་ལ་འདང་དེ་བཞིན་དུ་ར་ར་གི་ བ་དགའ་སྐྲ་རྒྱམ་བསྲུམ་ལ་གནས་
ནས་མ་ཚོད་པ་ གྱི་ཧྲུམ་ས་སྟེ་ལྱོ་སྐྲ་དང་ པཡ་ར་ར་གི་འ་ཆོ་
ལྱུ་འུ་ནོ། །ལུ་བཞིན་མི་གས་རྣམ་ས་སྟོ་བའ་ར་ཉེ་དེ་དེ་འཇེ་བི་ཐྲི་
དབར་བཞི་ལེན་པ་འི་མི་གས་པ་ལུ་ར་ཐ་སྟྱི་ཚ་བོར་ད། ཉེ་སྟྲོ་ཚེ་
ཚི་གས་ལོ་གས་རྒྱལ་བསྲུམ་ཚེ་རེ་གས་འུ་ནོ།། །

ར་ དབེན་ཀྱུ་ནྲུ་ཐྱུམ་པ་འཇེམ་སྟྲོ་ཞེ་གས་པ་ཆེ་བ་ནེ་བའི་གོ་འདུན་གྱི་ཚིགས་
འདུན་ཚེན་ཚོས་ཚོགས་ནས་ལམ་པོ་ནྲུ་དྲེ་ཞེས་རེ་གས་ཐྲ་གར་དུ་སྤུར་ར་འཝས་ཚེ་
ཐྱེ་གོ་བའི་དོ་གི་མེ་རྟྱུབ་ཚོས་སྟྲྱི་གི་སྟོལ་བ་གཎེ་བ་གི་ཆུས་ཁི་ནོ་དུ་ལམ་

༡༤

བཟང་ངོ་། །ལྥ་ཀ་ཤེས་རབ་མཐའ་ཡི། །

དགོངོ། །བག་ཆགས། །ཐུ་རྒྱུད་ནབ་མ་རྣམས་ཀྱི་བྱིན- - - -

རླབས་དང་། །ཡིད་ལ་རྗེ་རྗེ་སེ་ལས་དཔའི་དངོས་གྲུབ་ཆེ། །

གནས་གསུམ་མཁའ་འགྲོ་ཆོས་སྐྱོང་འཕྲིན་ལས་ཀྱིས། །འགྲོ

ཀུན་གདུལ་བདེས་ཆེ་ཡ་ལས་བག་ཤིས་ཤོག །

APPENDIX 4

Translation and Explanation of the Hundred-Syllable Mantra

Translation and Explanation of the Hundred-Syllable Mantra

OM VAJRA HERUKA SAMAYAM ANUPALAYA. HERUKA TENOPATISHTHA. DRIDHO ME BHAVA, SUTOSHYO ME BHAVA, SUPOSHYO ME BHAVA, ANURAKTO ME BHAVA. SARVA SIDDHIM ME PRAYACCHA. SARVA KARMA SUCHA ME CHITTAM SHREYAM KURU HUM! HA HA HA HA HOH! BHAGAVAN VAJRA HERUKA MA ME MUNCHA. HERUKA BHAVA MAHA SAMAYA SATTVA AH HUM PHAT!

OM is the seed syllable that symbolizes the divine vajra body, that is, the holy body of an enlightened being. The vajra body is union-oneness with divine vajra speech and mind. At present, your body, speech, and mind function separately, but when you attain the enlightened state of Heruka Vajrasattva your divine body, speech, and mind will function simultaneously.

VAJRA HERUKA. The pure energy of the indestructible divine wisdom thought of the greatest, blissful, innermost heart, which encompasses all phenomena.

SAMAYAM. When during an initiation you give your sacred word of honor to keep your vows and pledges purely, a subtle energy is generated within your mind and inner nervous system. This energy automatically releases you from negativity. This is what samaya means. It is the exact opposite of the half-hearted promises people usually make; promises that are so easily broken. Where your samaya is involved, you should not rationalize, even for the sake of your life.

ANUPALAYA. The power of divine loving kindness, which can bring you to eternal happiness.

HERUKA TENOPATISHTHA. Magnificent Heruka, be close within my heart.

DRIDHO. Indestructible, eternal, never-changing.

ME BHAVA. Grant me the divine, indestructible wisdom of the realization of the absolute true nature of myself and all other universal phenomena.

SUTOSHYO ME BHAVA. Vajrasattva, through being close to me, grant me the greatest, joyful divine wisdom, which brings great bliss.

SUPOSHYO ME BHAVA. May this blissful energy develop perfectly within my heart.

ANURAKTO ME BHAVA. May I be influenced by the divine attachment reflection of compassionate wisdom, which is utterly beyond duality.

SARVA SIDDHIM ME PRAYACCHA. Grant me completely all magnificent realizations.

SARVA KARMA SUCHA ME. Grant me all divine wisdom actions of Vajrasattva.

CHITTAM SHREYAM KURU. May your magnificent divine wisdom function in my heart.

HUM. The seed-syllable that symbolizes the nature of the divine vajra heart, the greatest divine blissful wisdom.

HA HA HA HA HOH. These five syllables symbolize the five wisdoms of the five dhyani buddhas.

BHAGAVAN. The enlightened one.

VAJRA HERUKA. The greatest, indestructible blissful wisdom.

MA ME MUNCHA. Do not abandon me.

HERUKA BHAVA. Be indestructibly held in my heart, by my keeping indestructible samaya, just as you hold the indestructible vajra.

MAHA. Greatest.

SAMAYA. As above.

SATTVA. The divine wisdom thought.

AH. The seed-syllable symbolizing divine vajra speech.

HUM. As above.

PHAT! Destroy all negative distractions!

APPENDIX 5
Blessing the Shi-dak Torma

OM VAJRA AMRITA KUNDALI HANA HANA HUM PHAT!
OM SVABHAVA SHUDDHA SARVA DHARMA SVABHAVA SHUDDHO HAM!

Tong-pa nyid-du gyur.
Tong-päi ngang-lä DRUNG-lä rin-po-che nö-yang shing-gya che-wä nang-du
OM-ö du-zhu wa-lä jung-wä tor-ma zag-pa me-pä ye-she kyi dü-tsi gya-tso
chen-por gyur

OM AH HUM *(say three times)*
NAMA SARVA TATHAGATA AVALOKITE OM SAMBARA SAMBARA HUM
  (say three times)

Chom-dän de-zhin shek-pa gyäl-wa rin-chen mang-la chak tsäl-lo
De-zhin shek-pa zug-tse dam-pa-la chak tsäl-lo
De-zhin shek-pa ku-jam lä-la chak tsäl-lo
De-zhin shek-pa jig-pa tham-chä dang-dräl wa-la chak tsäl-lo

Pün-tsok dö-yön nga-dän pa
Dü-tsi gya-tso tor-ma di
Sa-yi lha-mo te-ma sok
Tong-sum shi-dak tham-chä dang
Tse-ring chä-nga ten-kyong gi
Gang-chen nä-pa tham-chä dang
Kye-par yu-jor de-nyi kyi
Lha-lü shi-dak nam-la bül
Zhe-nä dak-chak yön-chö nam
Lä-dang ja-wa chi-chi kyang
Kor-long tra-dok ma-tse pa
Tün-kyen yi-shin drub-par tzö
Dak-gi sam-pä tob-dang ni

Blessing the Shi-dak Torma[38]

OM VAJRA AMRITA KUNDALI HANA HANA HUM PHAT!
OM SVABHAVA SHUDDHA SARVA DHARMA SVABHAVA SHUDDHO HAM!

All becomes empty.
From within emptiness, from DRUNG, comes a broad, vast jewelled vessel,
inside of which, from OM melting into light, there arises a torma of a great
ocean of undefiled nectar of wisdom.

OM AH HUM *(Say three times)*
NAMA SARVA TATHAGATA AVALOKITE OM SAMBARA SAMBARA HUM
   (Say three times)

I prostrate to the bhagawan, the tathagata Many Jewelled One (Bahuratna)
I prostrate to the tathagata Supreme Beautiful Form (Varasurupa)
I prostrate to the tathagata Infinite-Bodied One (Paryantakaya)
I prostrate to the tathagata Free from All Fear (Sarvabhayashri)

This torma, an ocean of nectar
Endowed with the five perfect sensual objects,
I offer to Tema, goddess of the earth,
And all land owners of the three thousand worlds;
To the five sister goddesses of long life,
And all protectors of stability who reside in Tibet.
And especially to the devas, nagas,
And land owners dwelling in this very region.
Having accepted, I request you to gather, as we wish,
All harmonious conditions for whatever actions
We and the sponsors perform
Without showing anger or jealousy.
By the power of my thoughts,

De-zhin shek-pä jin-tob dang
Chö-kyi ying-gi tob-nam kyi
Dön-nam gang-dak sam-pa yi
De-dak tham-chä chi-rik pa
Tok-pa me-par jung-gyur chik

By the power of the blessings of the tathagatas,
And by the power of the sphere of reality,
May any purpose we desire,
All whatsoever, be realized without obstruction!

Notes

1. Lama Yeshe Wisdom Archive numbers 000154, –166, –392, and –596.
2. See Pabongka Rinpoche, *Liberation in the Palm of Your Hand* (Boston: Wisdom, 1991), pp. 216–23 (the four opponent powers) and pp. 430–70 (karma).
3. This is in 1974, when there were only two very basic toilets: Sam and Sara!
4. See Lama Yeshe's *Bliss of Inner Fire,* which contains his teachings on tumo from the Six Yogas of Naropa.
5. In 1981–82 Lama Yeshe prepared his first batch of chulen pills according to traditional procedures, using extremely valuable natural ingredients detailed in a booklet published by Wisdom at the time. The pills were then blessed through the recitation of one million Heruka Vajrasattva mantras. In the summer of 1982, using these pills under the leadership of the late great yogi Geshe Jampa Wangdu, fifty Dharma students from all over the world made successful retreats at Tushita Retreat Centre, Dharamsala, India, showing that this practice is no longer for Tibetans alone. These fasting retreats are still conducted at some FPMT centers, using pills made by the Tibetan Medical and Astrological Institute, Dharamsala.
6. See Lama Yeshe's *Introduction to Tantra,* pp. 129 ff.
7. See appendix 4 for a translation and explanation of this mantra. As mentioned in the preface, Sanskrit in this book has been rendered approximately as should be pronounced and without diacritical marks. Most lamas "Tibetanize" Sanskrit, and students usually pronounce mantras the way their teachers transmit them. It is said that faith in a mantra is more important than how it is pronounced.
8. See Lama Zopa Rinpoche's *Direct and Unmistaken Method,* available from the Lama Yeshe Wisdom Archive, for complete instructions on taking precepts.
9. Some people also place a fourth torma in the offering bowl that represents the food offering, as shown in the altar drawing. Otherwise, this bowl would contain some other food or water. Whatever it contains should be offered daily. Lama Zopa Rinpoche emphasizes that other food can replace traditional tormas, as mentioned by Lama Yeshe. There are many variations in these ritual matters, and you should consult your lama to see what you should do.
10. A short way of blessing the torma is as follows: First recite HA HO HRI three times with your hands in the correct mudra, left above the right, open, facing forward, thumbs pointing right. With this recitation, all faults of color, smell, taste, and potentiality are purified, and the torma becomes blissful nectar. Then recite OM AH HUM three times. The nectar increases vastly and is blessed. Visualize that it becomes inexhaustible. After that, make the outer offering: OM VAJRASATTVA

ARGHAM...SHABDA PRATICCHA HUM SVAHA. Finally, recite the praise *Nyi-me ye-she...* from the sadhana, substituting *...ch'ak-ts'äl-tö* (homage and praise) for *...la-ch'ak-ts'äl* in the last line. For a longer blessing ritual, you can perform the inner offering from, for example, the Vajrayogini sadhana, or the blessing of the Heruka Vajrasattva tsok as explained in part 4 of this book.

11. Geshe Tsulga, of Sera-je Monastic University (and resident teacher at the FPMT's Kurukulla Center in Boston), explains that you can offer this torma every day, visualizing that you are offering a "fresh" bit of it each time; or, you can place a biscuit or other food offering beside this torma and offer that as the principal torma each day. The best time to offer this torma is during the last session of the day. After the mantra recitation, before the offering and praise, bless the torma as above; then visualize that letters HUM on the tongues of Heruka Vajrasattva and Yum Nyema Karmo transform into hollow tubes of rainbow light the width of a wheat grain in diameter. With recitation of the mantra OM VAJRASATTVA SAPARIVARA IDAM BALINTA KAKA KAHI KAHI, these radiate out to the torma and extract its essence, great bliss. Then return to the sadhana.

12. The special protector is Four-Armed Mahakala. Ideally you should offer this torma three times: once at the beginning of retreat, next around the middle, and finally, when your retreat has finished. The Mahakala *kang-sö* (fulfillment and restoration) ritual can be performed when you make this offering.

13. Lama Zopa Rinpoche says that this third torma offering can be done just once, at the beginning of the retreat. However, it can also be done every day, or three times during the retreat, along with the Mahakala kang-sö, as above. See appendix 5 for a ritual for blessing the shi-dak torma.

14. See *Liberation in the Palm of Your Hand,* p. 146, for more benefits of offering water.

15. The same applies to the Heruka Vajrasattva tsok puja. Geshe Tsulga says that in retreat, it would be good to do the Heruka Vajrasattva tsok daily, as long as it doesn't prevent you from reaching your goal of one hundred thousand mantras. You should definitely do it on the tenth and the twenty-fifth of each Tibetan month, the usual tsok days.

16. Geshe Tsulga explains that for a perfect accumulation and to receive the blessings of Heruka Vajrasattva swiftly, powerfully, and continually, you should recite the *ye-she pä-nga.* After you have finished one hundred thousand Vajrasattva mantras, recite another ten thousand (i.e., ten percent of the total), substituting the syllables HA ANDZE SVAHA for the PHAT at the end of the usual mantra. Thus, it now finishes *...SAMAYA SATTVA AH HUM HA ANDZE SVAHA.* The Dorje Khadro fire puja can be done after this.

17. Geshe Tsulga says that you need to count one hundred thousand mantras and do a fire puja to be qualified to do certain activities, such as those mentioned in a manual compiled by the Tibetan lama Ngulchu Dharmabhadra. Self-initiation is one example of these. Of course, you can do a fire puja no matter how many mantras you have counted, but if it's under one hundred thousand, you won't be

qualified to do the special activities. Each deity has its own collection of activities (*lä-tsok*).

18. Tib: *tsa-me-nga;* literally, "five no choice." It means you have no choice but to be reborn in hell when the life in which you created that action has finished.

19. See p. 144, where Lama explains why he sometimes *doesn't* do this.

20. The principal object of refuge can also be Vajradhara, as Lama explains in the main commentary.

21. See note 18, above. While in common terms these five are "inexpiable" sins, the powerful methods of tantra do allow you to purify them.

22. See also "The meditation seat," pp. 75 ff., and p. 142, where Lama explains how to make a portable meditation seat.

23. Lama Yeshe organized the first Enlightened Experience Celebration (EEC), a large international gathering of his Western students, at Bodhgaya, India, in 1982. This six-month series of teachings, initiations, and retreats was attended by more than two hundred students, almost one hundred of whom were monks and nuns. Since Lama passed away, Lama Zopa Rinpoche has organized two more EECs, with the fourth scheduled for 2004 in Mongolia

24. See, for example, Lama Yeshe, *Cittamani Tara* commentary (transcript), Kopan, January/February 1979, lectures 5–7.

25. See Lama Yeshe's *Introduction to Tantra*, chapter 10.

26. Sadly, this was indeed Lama's last talk at Vajrapani Institute. Despite his assurances, a few months later, in Nepal, his health began to deteriorate rapidly, and he passed away in Los Angeles at dawn on March 3, 1984, the first day of the Tibetan new year. A few days later, Lama was cremated at Vajrapani, where a beautiful stupa has been erected in his memory.

27. The translation of the sadhana presented here combines Lama Yeshe's original translation, which was interspersed with commentary, and Martin Willson's version, found in the transcript *Heruka Vajrasattva: Sadhana and Ritual Feast* (Boston: Wisdom Publications, 1984), a literal translation of Lama's Tibetan text.

28. This interpretive translation was made by Jon Landaw, working together with Lama Yeshe, Lama Zopa Rinpoche, and Ven. Konchog Yeshe. Some suggested corrections were made later by Thubten Chödak and Piero Cerri. Martin Willson's literal translation of the introduction (see note 27) follows:

> In the tantras of the Lord, it is taught that meditation and mantra recitation of Vajrasattva is an excellent skillful means as a preliminary to practicing the developing and completing stages of the path, and for producing profit and eliminating hindrances to perfect practice of method and wisdom at the intermediate stages of the path.
>
> Initially, to make your continuum a fit vessel, you should receive from the gurus the permission (*jenang*) of the body, speech, mind, qualities, and activities of this deity, having blessing connected with conviction toward the four empowerments. The practitioner who has done this and is abiding in

the long or short yoga of this deity [i.e., you must have generated yourself as the deity, either by the full sadhana or by a shorter method such as that given in the section "Preliminaries" (see note 29, below)] has the chance to begin *The Banquet [of Great Bliss]: The Ritual Feast That Counters the Vajra Hells;* as has been said: "Fortunate am I in great bliss."

The transmission of this permission of Vajrasattva in the highest yoga tantra tradition is that it comes from the speech of the lord of the siddhas Dharmavajra as a special teaching not found except in the profound oral instructions of the ear[-whispered] lineage of Gadän. Until now the warmth of the transmission of the blessings is undiminished; the practice is there for oneself to do, now it has reached [one]. Do not hold through a flock of magpie-like, deluded wrong prayers that this teaching is erroneous and its practitioners are devils *(mara)*. If you do, you will surely go to hell.

29. This last paragraph is not in the text but is from an explanation of tsok given to Jon Landaw by Lama Yeshe while they were working on the translation. We felt it was helpful to include it here.

30. *Bala* and *madana:* Sanskrit terms for the sacramental offerings of meat and alcohol respectively. Although meat and alcohol might be how these substances appear to ordinary perception, they should not be thought of as such, but should instead be seen in their true nature of simultaneously born bliss and void and always referred to as "bala" and "madana."

31. The Heruka Vajrasattva sadhana given in appendix 1 is an elaborate meditation for generating yourself as the deity. The following abbreviated method was suggested by Lama Zopa Rinpoche:

a) Take refuge and generate bodhichitta.

b) Meditate on the four immeasurables.

c) Do the special generation of bodhichitta, for example: "In particular, for the sake of all mother sentient beings, quickly, quickly I must somehow obtain the precious state of complete and perfect buddhahood. Therefore, I shall practice the yoga of the profound path of Guru Vajrasattva."

d) Recite the *Hundreds of Deities from the Land of Joy (Gan-dän lha-gyä-ma),* followed by the *Mik-tse-ma.*

e) Do a glance meditation on the lamrim, for example, the *Foundation of All Good Qualities (Yön tän zhir gyur ma)* by Lama Tsongkhapa or the lamrim prayer from the *Guru Puja.*

f) Then, the Lama Tsongkhapa visualized in front of you absorbs into your heart, and you become one with him. If you have received an empowerment of highest yoga tantra, experience nondual bliss and void. Then, that which you label "I" manifests as Vajrasattva.

32. Lama Zopa Rinpoche suggests (letter to students, March 27, 1984) that as you offer the tsok with each verse, think that it generates great bliss in the mind of Guru Vajrasattva, who is the embodiment of all gurus, Buddha, Dharma, and Sangha.

33. As you recite the mantra, you can practice the män-de, yän-de, and pung-de purifications as explained in the commentary. Lama Zopa adds:

> Visualize strong nectar and light rays flowing from Guru Vajrasattva, completely purifying all sentient beings' obscurations and negative karma, including any particular problem being experienced by some being for whom you'd like to pray. All realizations of the entire path, especially those mentioned in the immediately preceding verse, are generated in your own and all other sentient beings' minds.

34. Martin Willson made his translation from a Tibetan text printed at the She-rig Par-khang (from which the Tibetan text in appendix 3 was copied). It seems that Lama Yeshe later added a little material to the version that Jon Landaw translated. The end matter from Martin Willson's translation is as follows:

> a) Conclusion. If in Tibet and many other countries of the world [the times] are not totally incompatible with the rules of the three vowed disciplines, [still] they are more degenerate by far even than the degenerations in cases of destinies not included in the human. Therefore, fortunate mantric practitioners should see that undertaking the practice of Vajrasattva, who is very brave in overcoming their sins and offences, is a basis indispensable for attaining the realization of the wisdom-knowledge of the great bliss of unification. And since, in general, it powerfully gathers the accumulation of merits and makes good damaged and broken pledges, and since it has especially been taught by Geluk lamas that reciting one hundred thousand one hundred syllable mantras will purify even tantric downfalls, you should take it as something you can depend on that this yoga annihilates impure evil.
>
> As my root guru endowed with the three kindnesses, the Heruka of definitive meaning, Trijang Dorje Chang, has said in his holy teaching, *Self-entry to the Body Mandala of Ganta[pada Shri Chakrasamvara]: A Stream of Water Washing Off the Dirt of Misdeeds and Offences:*
>
> > When we think that through long-familiar delusion
> > And recklessness, faults and offences pour down like rain,
> > We fear being helplessly driven to vajra hell.
> > Yet most swift is the Conqueror's compassion—
> > Relying on a short but most profound rite,
> > The skilled in Vajrayana can
> > Uproot offences and misdeeds—how marvellous!

b) Colophon. At Vajrasana (Bodhgaya), a disciple of mine with remarkable undersanding of the path uniting sutra and tantra, who, having found firm, confident faith in the teachings of the Sage (Shakyamuni Buddha), manifests in saffron, possessing the three [vowed disciplines], the Italian *gelong* Thubten Dönyö, with the wish of special intention, offered under the Bodhgaya bodhi tree in the company of an international Mahayana sangha [members of the International Mahayana Institute] a hundred five-fold offering-clouds, a thousand ritual feasts, and 18,000 rupees for general purposes.

Because of this need, on the third day of February 1982, the tenth day of the twelfth month of the Tibetan year 2108, the day of the great gathering of dakinis, praying that the Sangha of the ten directions may be harmonious and pure in morality, reach the end of the practice of the three trainings of the direct path, and perform extensive benefit for sentient beings, and wishing to say in words what I recall seeing, I, a prattling practitioner of Vajrasattva, the Buddhist monk called Muni Jñana, have written this by hand.

This too is said:

From fear that the golden ground be shattered
By a rabbit's horn of tantric vows,
All existence rises as one's foe.
Strange, if minds not ripened by empowerment
And the common path transformed by magic
Into yogins, like sky-lotuses!

c) Adaptation for use with other deities. This ritual feast may also be adapted for offering a ritual feast to other deities of highest yoga tantra. To adapt it to the highest yoga tantra aspect of Tara, for example, [do the following]: abiding in the yoga of Tara (i.e., visualizing yourself as Tara), visualize as the field for the accumulation [of merit] the mandala of Guru Tara. At this point (first verse of the visualization of the mandala of Vajrasattva), say, "*Jung-wäi pak-ma Dröl-mäi zhäl-yä-kang* (Appears before me the palace of Arya Tara....)" In the offering verses (verses 1 through 7) say "*Ka-ying Ja-tsön pak-ma Dröl-mäi ku* (Rainbow in space that is Arya Tara's body!" [and adapt the fifth line similarly].

[After each verse,] keeping the visualization that from the twenty-one Taras nectar and light rays dissolve into you, think that all offences and misdeeds, the results of clinging to ordinary appearance, are purified, while you recite Tara's mantra twenty-one times.

Similarly for Guhyasamaja, Heruka, Yamantaka, or others, perform the corresponding long or short self-generation, and abiding in this, consecrate the offerings by either the general procedure or (that deity's) special procedure. Keeping the above visualization, or doing a visualization like that for taking the four empowerments in concentration, recite the heart and near-heart mantras twenty-one times or more, long or short as is practicable.

35. Thub(ten) Yeshe in Sanskrit: Muni(shasana) Jñana.

36. See above for a more literal translation. Jon Landaw worked on this version with Lama Yeshe and says that taking the liberty of putting it into English verse necessitated a little license with the vocabulary. He also mentions that "the hardest point to render was in stanza one. The phrase 'rabbit's horn of tantric ordination' means that the person, who is so fearful of breaking his samaya that he sees everything as his enemy, never really received the empowerment in the first place. Thus, for him the initiation was like a rabbit's horn.... I tried to re-emphasize [this point] in line three of the second stanza."

37. At the very end of the end matter, the Tibetan text has a final verse of auspiciousness that does not appear to have been translated by either Jon Landaw or Martin Willson. In phonetics, this reads:

> Tsa-gyu la-ma nam-kyi jin-lap dang
> Yi-dam Dor-je Sem-päi ngö-drup che
> Nä-sum khan-dro chö-kyong trin-lä kyi
> Dro-kün tän-de tsim-pä tra-shi-shok

An edited version of a translation of this verse provided by Thubten Chödak and Piero Cerri reads:

> Through the blessings of all the root and lineage lamas,
> The great accomplishments of the mind-bound deity Vajrasattva, and
> The divine actions of the dakinis and protectors of the three places,
> May auspiciousness allow all beings to be satisfied by ultimate peace!

38. Thanks to David Molk for providing this text and translation.

Glossary

(Skt = Sanskrit; Tib = Tibetan)

Abhidharma (Skt; Tib: chö-ngön-pa). One of the three baskets *(tripitaka)* of the Buddhist canon, the others being Vinaya and the Sutra; the systematized philosophical and psychological analysis of existence that is the basis of the Buddhist system of tenets and mind training.

Akshobhya (Skt; Tib: Mikyöpa, "Imperturbable"). One of the five dhyani buddhas, or heads of the five buddha families, who represent the fully purified *skandhas,* or aggregates, of form, feeling, recognition, compositional factors, and consciousness. Akshobhya is blue in color, represents the fully purified aggregate of consciousness, and is lord of the vajra family.

Ajatashatru (Skt). Early Indian king who imprisoned and killed his father, Bimbisara. Realizing the enormity of this sin and guided by the Buddha, he purified this negativity and became an arhat.

Angulimala (Skt). A character in a classic Dharma story of choosing the wrong guru and committing horrendous actions. In this case, he killed 999 people and made a rosary out of their thumbs. He was prevented by the Buddha from killing his thousandth victim, which, according to the wrong guru, would have led him to liberation. He was able to purify and become an arhat.

arhat (Skt). Literally, "foe destroyer." A person who has destroyed his or her delusions and attained liberation from cyclic existence.

Avalokiteshvara (Skt; Tib: Chenrezik). The buddha of compassion. A male meditational deity embodying fully enlightened compassion.

bodhichitta (Skt). The altruistic determination to reach enlightenment for the sole purpose of enlightening all sentient beings.

bodhisattva (Skt). Someone whose spiritual practice is directed toward the achievement of enlightenment. One who possesses the compassionate motivation of bodhichitta.

buddha (Skt). A fully enlightened being. One who has removed all obscurations veiling the mind and has developed all good qualities to perfection. The first of the Three Jewels of refuge. See also *enlightenment.*

central channel. See *sushumna.*

chakra (Skt). Energy wheel. A focal point of energy along the central channel *(sushumna)* upon which one's concentration is directed, especially during the completion stage of highest yoga tantra. The main chakras are the crown, throat, heart, navel, and secret.

channels (Skt: nadi). A constituent of the vajra body through which energy winds and drops flow. The central, right, and left are the major channels; the channels total 72,000 in all.

chulen (Tib). Literally, "taking the essence." Chulen pills are made of essential ingredients; taking but a few each day, accomplished meditators can remain secluded in retreat for months or years without having to depend upon normal food. See also note 5.

compassion (Skt: karuna). The wish for all beings to be separated from their mental and physical suffering. A prerequisite for the development of bodhichitta. Compassion is symbolized by the meditational deity Avalokiteshvara.

completion stage (Tib: dzok-rim). The second of the two stages of highest yoga tantra, during which control is gained over the vajra body through such practices as inner Āre.

daka (Skt; Tib: khan-dro). Literally, a "sky-goer." A male being who helps arouse blissful energy in a qualified tantric practitioner.

dakini (Skt; Tib: khan-dro-ma). Literally, a "female sky-goer." A female being who helps arouse blissful energy in a qualiĀed tantric practitioner.

damaru (Skt). A small hand drum used in tantric practice.

delusion (Skt: klesha; Tib: nyön-mong). An obscuration covering the essentially pure nature of the mind, being thereby responsible for suffering and dissatisfaction; the main delusion is ignorance, out of which grow desirous attachment, hatred, jealousy, and all the other delusions.

Dharma (Skt). Spiritual teachings, particularly those of the Buddha. Literally, that which holds one back from suffering. The second of the Three Jewels of refuge.

dharmakaya (Skt). The "truth body." The mind of a fully enlightened being, which, free of all coverings, remains meditatively absorbed in the direct perception of emptiness while simultaneously cognizing all phenomena. One of the three bodies of a buddha (see also *nirmanakaya* and *sambhogakaya*).

divine pride. The strong conviction that one has achieved the state of a particular meditational deity. Cf. *generation stage*.

dorje (Tib; Skt: vajra). The magical weapon of the Vedic god Indra, made of metal and very sharp and hard; adamantine. A thunderbolt. A tantric implement symbolizing method (compassion or bliss), held in the right hand (the male side), usually in conjunction with a bell, which symbolizes wisdom and is held in the left hand (the female side).

Dorje Khadro (Tib; Skt: Vajradaka). A deity who functions to purify negativities through his specific fire puja *(jin-sek)*. See also *ngöndro*.

drops. A constituent of the vajra body used in the generation of great bliss. Of the two types, at conception, the red drops are received from one's mother and the white drops from one's father.

dualistic view. The ignorant view characteristic of the unenlightened mind in which all things are falsely conceived to have concrete self-existence. To such a view, the appearance of an object is mixed with the false image of its being independent or self-existent, thereby leading to further dualistic views concerning subject and object, self and other, this and that, etc.

dzok-rim (Tib). See *completion stage*.

ego-grasping. The ignorant compulsion to regard one's self, or I, as permanent, self-existent, and independent of all other phenomena.

empowerment. See *initiation*.

emptiness. See *shunyata*.

enlightenment (Skt: bodhi). Full awakening; buddhahood. The ultimate goal of Buddhist practice, attained when all limitations have been removed from the mind and all one's positive potential has been realized. It is a state characterized by unlimited compassion, skill, and wisdom.

four classes of tantra. The division of tantra into kriya (action), carya (performance), yoga, and anuttara yoga (highest yoga).

Geluk (Tib). The Virtuous Order. The order of Tibetan Buddhism founded by Lama Tsongkhapa and his disciples in the early fifteenth century.

generation stage (Tib: kye-rim). The first of the two stages of *highest yoga tantra*, during which one cultivates the clear appearance and divine pride of one's chosen meditational deity.

graduated path (Tib: lamrim). A presentation of Shakyamuni Buddha's teachings in a form suitable for the step-by-step training of a disciple. The lamrim was first formulated by the great Indian teacher Atisha (Dipankara Shrijñana, 982–1055) when he came to Tibet in 1042.

Guhyasamaja (Skt; Tib: Sangwa Dupa). Male meditational deity from the father class of highest yoga tantra; a manifestation of the buddha Akshobhya.

guru (Skt; Tib: lama). A spiritual guide or teacher. One who shows a disciple the path to liberation and enlightenment. In tantra, one's teacher is seen as inseparable from the meditational deity and the Three Jewels of refuge. See also *root guru.*

guru yoga (Skt). The fundamental tantric practice, whereby one's guru is seen as identical with the buddhas, one's personal meditational deity, and the essential nature of one's own mind.

Heruka Chakrasamvara (Skt; Tib: Korlo Demchog). Male meditational deity from the mother tantra class of highest yoga tantra; the principal deity connected with the Heruka Vajrasattva practice; Lama Yeshe's yidam.

highest yoga tantra (Skt: anuttara yoga tantra). The fourth and supreme division of tantric practice, consisting of the generation and completion stages. Through this practice, one can attain full enlightenment within one lifetime.

Hinayana (Skt). Literally, the "Small Vehicle." It is one of the two general divisions of Buddhism. Hinayana practitioners' motivation for following the Dharma path is principally their intense wish for personal liberation from conditioned existence, or *samsara*. Cf. *Mahayana.*

initiation Transmission received from a tantric master allowing a disciple to engage in the practices of a particular meditational deity. It is also referred to as an empowerment.

inner fire (Tib: tumo). The energy residing at the navel chakra, aroused during the completion stage of highest yoga tantra and used to bring the energy winds into the central channel. It is also called inner or psychic heat.

inner offering (Tib: nang-chö). A tantric offering whose basis of transformation is one's five aggregates visualized as the five meats and the five nectars. While the relevant inner offering mantra of the particular deity is recited (e.g., in Heruka-associated practices it is OM KHANDA ROHI HUM HUM PHAT), the basis is purified, transformed, and magnified by mantra, mudra, and concentration. The external support for this meditation is often a blessed inner offering pill *(nang-chö ril-bu)* dissolved in black tea or alcohol.

insight meditation (Pali: vipassana). The principal meditation taught in the Theravada tradition and is based on the Buddha's teachings on the four foundations of mindfulness. It is sometimes called mindfulness meditation. In the Mahayana, *Vipashyana* (Skt) means investigation of and familiarization with the actual way in which things exist and is used to develop the wisdom of emptiness.

jorchö (Tib). The preparatory rites (see Pabongka Rinpoche, *Liberation in the Palm of Your Hand* [Boston: Wisdom, 1991], pp. 131–247).

Kagyu (Tib). The order of Tibetan Buddhism founded in the eleventh century by Marpa, Milarepa, Gampopa, and their followers.

Kalarupa (Skt). Wrathful male meditational deity connected with Yamantaka.

kapala (Skt; Tib: tö-pa). Skull cup, e.g., the one held by Yum Dorje Nyema.

karma (Skt; Tib: lä). Action; the working of cause and effect, whereby positive actions produce happiness and negative actions produce suffering.

kriya (Skt). First of the four classes of tantra; action tantra.

kundalini (Skt). Blissful energy dormant within the physical body, aroused through tantric practice and used to generate penetrative insight into the true nature of reality.

kusha (Skt). Kind of long-stranded grass used under the retreat seat, during tantric initiations, and for making brooms in India. Shakyamuni Buddha made a seat out of kusha grass when he meditated under the bodhi tree at Bodhgaya and attained enlightenment.

kye-rim (Tib). See *generation stage*.

lama (Tib). See *guru*.

lamrim (Tib). See *graduated path*.

liberation. See *nirvana*.

Madhyamaka (Skt). The middle way; a system of analysis founded by Nagarjuna, based on the prajñaparamita sutras of Shakyamuni Buddha, and considered to be the supreme presentation of the wisdom of emptiness.

maha-anuttara (Skt). Also called *anuttara*. See *four classes of tantra* and *highest yoga tantra*. It is divided into generation and completion stages.

Mahakala (Skt). Wrathful male meditational deity connected with Heruka; a Dharma protector favored by Lama Yeshe.

mahamudra (Skt; Tib: chak-chen). The great seal. A profound system of meditation upon the mind and the ultimate nature of reality.

Mahayana (Skt). Literally, the "Great Vehicle." It is one of the two general divisions of Buddhism. Mahayana practitioners' motivation for following the Dharma path is principally their intense wish for all mother sentient beings to be liberated from conditioned existence, or *samsara,* and to attain the full enlightenment of buddhahood. The Mahayana has two divisions: Paramitayana, or Sutrayana, and Vajrayana. Cf. *Hinayana*.

mandala (Skt; Tib: khyil-khor). A circular diagram symbolic of the entire universe. The abode of a meditational deity.

Mañjushri (Skt; Tib: Jampelyang). Male meditational deity embodying fully enlightened wisdom.

mantra (Skt). Literally, protection of the mind. Mantras are Sanskrit syllables recited in conjunction with the practice of a particular meditational deity that embody the qualities of that deity.

mantra rosary. A mantra visualized as a rosary, its syllables representing beads; usually circular, as in the syllables of the one hundred syllable mantra standing around the edge of the moon disc.

Mara (Skt). Personification of the delusions that distract us from Dharma practice; what Buddhists might call the "devil"; what Shakyamuni Buddha overcame under the bodhi tree as he strove for enlightenment.

Marpa (1012–96). Founder of the Kagyu tradition of Tibetan Buddhism. He was a renowned tantric master and translator, and a disciple of Naropa and the guru of Milarepa.

middle way. The view presented in Shakyamuni Buddha's prajñaparamita sutras and elucidated by Nagarjuna that all phenomena are dependent arisings, thereby avoiding the mistaken extremes of self-existence and nonexistence, or eternalism and nihilism. Cf. *Madhyamaka.*

Milarepa (1040–1123). Foremost disciple of Marpa, famous for his intense practice, devotion to his guru, attainment of enlightenment in his lifetime, and his many songs of spiritual realization.

mudra (Skt; Tib: chag-gya). Literally, seal, token. A symbolic hand gesture, endowed with power not unlike a mantra. A tantric consort.

Nagarjuna (Skt). The second century A.D. Indian Buddhist philosopher who propounded the Madhyamaka philosophy of emptiness.

nang-chö (Tib). See *inner offering.*

ngöndro (Tib). Preliminary practice(s) found in all schools of Tibetan Buddhism, usually done 100,000 times each; the four main ones are recitation of the refuge formula, mandala offerings, prostrations, and Vajrasattva mantra recitation. The Geluk tradition adds five more: guru yoga, water bowl offerings, Damtsig Dorje purifying meditation, making *tsa-tsas* (small sacred images, usually made of clay), and the Dorje Khadro burnt offering *(jin-sek).*

nirmanakaya (Skt). The "emanation body"; the form in which the enlightened mind appears in order to benefit ordinary beings. One of the three bodies of a buddha. See also *dharmakaya* and *sambhogakaya.*

nirvana (Skt; Tib: thar-pa). The state of complete liberation from samsara; the goal of a practitioner seeking his or her own freedom from suffering (see *Hinayana*). "Lower nirvana" is used to refer to this state of self-liberation, while "higher nirvana" refers to the supreme attainment of the full enlightenment of buddhahood.

Nyingma (Tib). The "ancient" order of Tibetan Buddhism, which traces its teachings back to the time of Padma Sambhava, the eighth century A.D. Indian tantric master invited to Tibet by King Trisong Detsen to clear away the influences obstructing the establishment of Buddhism. This school includes in its canon works and translations dating from the early period of the dissemination of Buddhism in Tibet.

Padampa Sangye (Tib). Indian yogi and contemporary of Milarepa who propagated the *Zhi-che* (pacification) lineage.

pandit (Skt). Scholar; learned man.

Paramitayana (Skt). The "Perfection Vehicle"; one of the two division of the Mahayana. This is the gradual path to enlightenment traversed by bodhisattvas practicing the six perfections of charity, morality, patience, effort, concentration, and wisdom, through the ten bodhisattva levels *(bhumis)* over countless eons of rebirths in samsara for the benefit of all sentient beings. It is also called *Sutrayana.* See also *Vajrayana.*

prajñaparamita (Skt). The "perfection of wisdom"; the teachings of Shakyamuni Buddha in which the wisdom of emptiness and the path of the bodhisattva are set forth. The basis of Nagarjuna's philosophy.

pratimoksha (Skt). See *vows.*

puja (Skt). Literally, "offering." The word is often used loosely, as in "Let's do a puja," to refer to performing a ritual, such as the *Guru Puja (Offering to the Spiritual Master; Tib: Lama Chöpa),* or reciting a sadhana, such as the Heruka Vajrasattva sadhana in this book.

refuge. The door to the Dharma path. A Buddhist takes refuge in the Three Jewels of Buddha, Dharma, and Sangha, fearing the sufferings of samsara and believing that the Three Jewels have the power to lead him or her out of suffering, to happiness, liberation, or enlightenment.

root guru (Tib: tsa-wäi lama). The teacher who has had the greatest influence upon a particular disciple's entering or following the spiritual path.

sadhana (Skt). Method of accomplishment; the step-by-step instructions for practicing the meditations related to a particular meditational deity.

samadhi (Skt). See *single-pointed concentration*.

samaya (Skt; Tib: dam-tsik). Sacred word of honor; the pledges and commitments made by a disciple at an initiation to keep tantric vows for life or to perform certain practices connected with the deity, such as daily sadhana recitation, or offering the *Guru Puja* on the tenth and the twenty-fifth of each Tibetan month.

sambhogakaya (Skt). The "enjoyment body"; the form in which the enlightened mind appears in order to benefit highly realized bodhisattvas. One of the three bodies of a buddha. See also *dharmakaya* and *nirmanakaya*.

samsara (Skt; Tib: khor-wa). Cyclic existence; the six realms of conditioned existence, three lower—hell, hungry spirit *(Skt: preta)*, and animal—and three upper—human, demigod, and god. It is the beginningless, recurring cycle of death and rebirth under the control of delusion and karma and fraught with suffering. It also refers to the contaminated aggregates of a sentient being.

Sangha (Skt). Spiritual community; the third of the Three Jewels of refuge. Absolute Sangha are those who have directly realized emptiness; relative Sangha are ordained monks and nuns.

secret mantra (Tib: sang-ngak). See *tantra*.

seed syllable. In tantric visualizations, a Sanskrit syllable arising out of emptiness and out of which the meditational deity in turn arises. A single syllable representing a deity's entire mantra.

sentient being. Any unenlightened being; any being whose mind is not completely free from gross and subtle ignorance.

Shakyamuni Buddha (563–483 B.C.). Fourth of the one thousand founding buddhas of this present world age. Born a prince of the Shakya clan in North India, he taught the sutra and tantra paths to liberation and full enlightenment; founder of what came to be known as Buddhism (from the Sanskrit, *buddha*—"fully awake").

shi-dak (Tib). Landlord; place owner. Buddhism teaches that each place has associated with it a sentient being who considers that he owns it. Offerings are made to this being to request the temporary use of that place for, e.g., retreat.

shunyata (Skt). The absence of all false ideas about how things exist; specifically, the lack of the apparent independent, self-existence of phenomena. Usually translated as emptiness or voidness.

single-pointed concentration (Skt: samadhi). A state of deep meditative absorption; single-pointed concentration on the actual nature of things, free from discursive thought and dualistic conceptions.

sushumna (or *avadhuti, Skt; Tib: tsa uma*). The central channel, or *nadi,* which runs from the crown of the head to the secret chakra. It is the major energy channel of the vajra body, visualized as a hollow tube of light in front of the spine (see chapter 3).

sutra (Skt). A discourse of Shakyamuni Buddha; the pretantric division of Buddhist teachings stressing the cultivation of bodhichitta and the practice of the six perfections. See also *Paramitayana.*

tantra (Skt; Tib: gyü). Literally, thread, or continuity. The texts of the secret mantra teachings of Buddhism; often used to refer to these teachings themselves. Cf. *Vajrayana.*

tathagata (Skt; Tib: de-zhin shek-pa). Literally, one who has realized suchness; a buddha.

Theravada (Skt). One of the eighteen schools into which the Hinayana split not long after Shakyamuni Buddha's death; the dominant school today, prevalent in Thailand, Sri Lanka, and Burma, and well represented in the West.

torma (Tib). An offering cake used in tantric rituals. In Tibet, tormas were usually made of tsampa, but other edibles such as biscuits and so forth will suffice.

tsampa (Tib). Roasted barley flour; a Tibetan staple food.

tsok (Tib). Literally, gathering—a gathering of offering substances and a gathering of disciples to make the offering.

Tsongkhapa, Lama Je (1357–1417). Founder of the Geluk tradition of Tibetan

Buddhism and revitalizer of many sutra and tantra lineages and the monastic tradition in Tibet.

tumo (Tib). See *inner fire*.

twelve links of dependent arising (Skt: pratitya samutpada; Tib: ten-drel chu-nyi). Shakyamuni Buddha's explanation of how delusion and karma bind sentient beings and samsara, causing them to born into suffering again and again; depicted pictorially in the Tibetan "wheel of life."

Vajradhara (Skt; Tib: Dorje Chang). Male meditational deity; the form through which Shakyamuni Buddha revealed the teachings of secret mantra.

Vajrapani (Skt; Tib: Chakna Dorje). A male meditational deity embodying the power of all enlightened beings to accomplish their goals.

Vajrasattva (Skt; Tib: Dorje Sempa). Male meditational deity symbolizing the inherent purity of all buddhas. A major tantric purification practice for removing obstacles created by negative karma and the breaking of vows.

Vajravarahi (Skt; Tib: Dorje Pakmo). Female meditational deity; consort of Heruka.

Vajrayana (Skt). The adamantine vehicle; the second of the two Mahayana paths. It is also called Tantrayana or Mantrayana. This is the quickest vehicle of Buddhism, as it allows practitioners to attain enlightenment within one lifetime. See also *tantra*.

Vajrayogini (Skt; Tib: Dorje Näljorma). Female meditational deity from the mother tantra class of highest yoga tantra; sometimes a consort of Heruka.

Vinaya (Skt; Tib: dül-wa). The division of the Buddhist scriptures concerned with monastic discipline—the rules for the behavior of monks and nuns and the conduct of their communal business.

Vipassana (Pali). See *insight meditation*.

vows. Precepts taken on the basis of refuge at all levels of Buddhist practice. Pratimoksha precepts (vows of individual liberation) are the main vows in the Hinayana tradition and are taken by monks, nuns, and lay people; they are the basis of all other vows. Bodhisattva and tantric precepts are the main vows in the Mahayana tradition. See also *Vinaya*.

Yamantaka (also *Vajrabhairava, Skt; Tib: Dorje Jigje*). Male meditational deity from the father tantra class of highest yoga tantra.

yana (Skt). Literally, vehicle; a spiritual path that takes you from where you are to where you want to be. See also *Hinayana, Mahayana,* etc.

yidam (Tib). Literally, "mind-bound." One's own personal, main—or, as Lama Yeshe used to say, favorite—deity for tantric practice. The deity with which you have the strongest connection.

yum (Tib). Literally, "mother"; female consort of a male tantric deity (the father, *yab*), as in Yum Dorje Nyema Karmo, the consort of Heruka Vajrasattva.

Chronology

Intellectuals, beware!

This "word of caution to the intellectual" was written by Lama in 1974, as the preface to a short Chenrezig sadhana he had composed during his and Lama Zopa Rinpoche's first visit to Australia, and augmented in 1976 for use with the Heruka Vajrasattva sadhana.

Parts 1 & 2

A Commentary to the Heruka Vajrasattva Sadhana and Retreat Instructions, April–May 1974, Kopan Monastery, Nepal. Archive number 000048.

Additional Retreat Instructions (from Chenrezig Retreat Instructions), probably 1976, Chenrezig Institute, Australia. Archive number 000730.

Part 3

1. Combination of Vajrasattva Explanation, 6 February 1974, and Vajrasattva Guru Yoga, 28 January 1976, both Kopan Monastery. Archive numbers 000173 and 000051 respectively.
2. Vajrasattva Initiation, June 1977, Chenrezig Institute. Archive number 000805.
3. Vajrasattva Commentary, July 1980, Vajrapani Institute, USA. Archive number 000620.
4. Vajrasattva Explanation during Vajrayogini Commentary, excerpt, 2 April 1983, Tushita Retreat Centre, India. Archive number 000320.
5. Introduction to Vajrasattva Initiation, 20 April 1983, Tushita Retreat Centre. Archive number 000964.
6. Introduction to Vajrasattva Initiation, 17 July 1983, Vajrapani Institute. Archive number 000071.

PART 4

Ritual text composed 19 January 1982, Bodhgaya, India.

Commentary and Oral Transmission of the Heruka Vajrasattva Tsok, 2 February 1982, Bodhgaya. Archive number 000175.

A Brief Explanation of Tsok, 22 April 1983, Tushita Retreat Centre. Archive number 000965.

Commentary on the Heruka Vajrasattva Tsok, 3–31 July 1983, Vajrapani Institute. Archive number 000179.

Suggested Further Reading

Gyatso, Geshe Jampa. *Everlasting Rain: Purification Practice in Tibetan Buddhism.* Edited by Joan Nicell. Boston: Wisdom Publications, 1996.

Gyatso, Tenzin, the Fourteenth Dalai Lama. *Deity Yoga: In Action and Performance Tantra.* Translated and edited by Jeffrey Hopkins. Ithaca: Snow Lion Publications, 1981.

———. *The Union of Bliss and Emptiness: A Commentary on the Lama Choepa Guru Yoga Practice.* Translated by Thupten Jinpa. Ithaca: Snow Lion Publications, 1988.

———. *The World of Tibetan Buddhism: An Overview of Its Philosophy and Practice.* Translated and edited by Geshe Thupten Jinpa. Boston: Wisdom Publications, 1995.

Khyentse Rinpoche, Dilgo. *Guru Yoga: According to the Preliminary Practice of Longchen Nyingtik.* Translated by Matthieu Ricard. Ithaca: Snow Lion Publications, 1999.

Kongtrul, Jamgön. *Creation and Completion: Essential Points of Tantric Meditation.* Translated and introduced by Sarah Harding. Commentary by Thrangu Rinpoche. Boston: Wisdom Publications, 2002.

Mackenzie, Vicki. *Reincarnation: The Boy Lama.* Boston: Wisdom Publications, 1996.

Pabongka Rinpoche. *Liberation in the Palm of Your Hand.* Trans. Michael Richards. Boston: Wisdom Publications, 1991.

Yeshe, Lama Thubten. *Becoming the Compassion Buddha: Tantric Meditation for Everyday Life.* Edited by Robina Courtin. Boston: Wisdom Publications, 2003.

————. *The Bliss of Inner Fire: Heart Practice of the Six Yogas of Naropa.* Edited by Robina Courtin and Ailsa Cameron. Boston: Wisdom Publications, 1998.

————. *Introduction to Tantra: The Transformation of Desire.* Edited by Jonathan Landaw. Boston: Wisdom Publications, 1987, 2001.

Yeshe, Lama, and Lama Zopa Rinpoche. *Wisdom Energy: Basic Buddhist Teachings.* Edited by Jonathan Landaw with Alexander Berzin. Boston: Wisdom Publications, 1976, 2000.

Zopa Rinpoche, Lama Thubten. *The Door to Satisfaction: The Heart Advice of a Tibetan Buddhist Master.* Boston: Wisdom Publications, 2001.

————. *Teachings from the Vajrasattva Retreat.* Edited by Ailsa Cameron and Nicholas Ribush. Weston, MA: The Lama Yeshe Wisdom Archive, 2000.

————. *Transforming Problems into Happiness.* Boston: Wisdom Publications, 2001.

————. *Ultimate Healing: The Power of Compassion.* Edited by Ailsa Cameron. Boston: Wisdom Publications, 2001.

More teachings by Lama Yeshe and Lama Zopa Rinpoche can be obtained from the Lama Yeshe Wisdom Archive and from the FPMT Education Department.

About the Author

 LAMA THUBTEN YESHE (1935–1984) was born in Tibet and educated at the great Sera Monastic University. He fled the Chinese oppression in 1959 and in the late 1960s, with his chief disciple Lama Thubten Zopa Rinpoche, began teaching Buddhism to Westerners at Kopan Monastery in Kathmandu, Nepal. In 1975 they founded the international Buddhist organization, the Foundation for the Preservation of the Mahayana Tradition (FPMT), which now has more than 160 centers, projects, and services worldwide.

DR. NICHOLAS RIBUSH, MB, BS, a graduate of Melbourne University Medical School (1964), has been a student of Lama Yeshe and Lama Zopa Rinpoche and a full time worker for their international organization, the Foundation for the Preservation of the Mahayana Tradition (FPMT), for over forty years. Since 1996 he has been director of the Lama Yeshe Wisdom Archive (lamayeshe. com), which organizes and preserves thousands of teachings and images of Lama Zopa and Lama Yeshe.

To find out more about the FPMT, contact:

FPMT International Office
1632 SE 11th Avenue
Portland, OR 97214-4702 USA
Telephone: 503-808-1588 • Fax: 503-808-159
www.fpmt.org

Also from Wisdom Publications

Introduction to Tantra
The Transformation of Desire
Lama Thubten Yeshe
Edited by Jonathan Landaw, foreword by Philip Glass

"The best introductory work on Tibetan Buddhist tantra available today."
—Janet Gyatso, Harvard University

The Bliss of Inner Fire
Heart Practice of the Six Yogas of Naropa
Lama Thubten Yeshe
Edited by Robina Courtin and Ailsa Cameron
Foreword by Lama Zopa Rinpoche

"An impressive contribution to the growing body of Buddhist literature for an English-reading audience."
—*The Midwest Book Review*

Wisdom Energy
Basic Buddhist Teachings
Lama Thubten Yeshe and Lama Zopa Rinpoche
Edited by Jonathan Landaw

"This is a superb book that presents basic Buddhist teachings with great lucidity and clarity."
—*Resource Magazine*

When the Chocolate Runs Out
A "Little Book of Wisdom"
Lama Thubten Yeshe

"Lively and enlightening."
—*Spirituality and Practice*

Transforming Problems into Happiness
Lama Zopa Rinpoche
Foreword by His Holiness the Dalai Lama

"A masterfully brief statement of Buddhist teachings on the nature of humanity and human suffering... This book should be read as the words of a wise, loving parent."
—*Utne Reader*

Essence of the Heart Sutra
The Dalai Lama's Heart of Wisdom Teachings
His Holiness the Dalai Lama with Thupten Jinpa

"Lovingly and wisely edited by Jinpa, the bulk of the book is consumed with a fairly meaty exploration of the Heart of Wisdom sutra, a classical Mahayana text, and as such will be useful to established practitioners as well as neophytes."
—*Publishers Weekly*

Practicing the Path
A Commentary on the Lamrim Chenmo
Yangsi Rinpoche
Preface by Lama Zopa Rinpoche, foreword by Geshe Lhundub Sopa

"It brings this great classical tradition into the very palms of our hands."
—Jose Ignacio Cabezón, University of California, Santa Barbara

Ultimate Healing
The Power of Compassion
Lama Zopa Rinpoche

"This truly is an awesome book."
—Lillian Too

Peacock in the Poison Grove
Two Buddhist Texts on Training the Mind
Geshe Lhundub Sopa
With Leonard Zwilling and Michael J. Sweet

"It belongs on the shelf—and a readily accessible one at that!—of every scholar and every practitioner of Tibetan Buddhism."
—Roger Jackson, Carleton College

Wheel of Great Compassion
The Practice of the Prayer Wheel in Tibetan Buddhism
Lorne Ladner
Foreword by Lama Zopa Rinpoche

"A delightful introduction to the prayer wheel!"
—*DharmaLife*

Wisdom

About Wisdom Publications

Wisdom Publications is the leading publisher of classic and contemporary Buddhist books and practical works on mindfulness. To learn more about us or to explore our other books, please visit our website at wisdompubs.org or contact us at the address below.

Wisdom Publications
199 Elm Street
Somerville, MA 02144 USA

We are a 501(c)(3) organization, and donations in support of our mission are tax deductible.

Wisdom Publications is affiliated with the Foundation for the Preservation of the Mahayana Tradition (FPMT).